Endorsements

Dr. Greg Van Dussen's newest work combines a pastor's grasp of the powerful spirituality of camp meetings with a historian's understanding of the historical times and needs--then and now. Mining copious primary sources that range across time, space, culture, and gender, he probes the dynamics fueling the Wesleyan and Wesleyan Holiness movement in North America and its transformative power. Readers of Van Dussen's *Circuit Riders on the Road to Glory* will find this a welcome companion piece. And if you think you already know camp meetings, you are in for some surprises.
   —Kathleen Smith Kutolowski, Associate Professor and Chair Emerita, Department of History, SUNY Brockport

Van Dussen's book is a useful reminder of the critical place camp meetings held in the heyday of 19th century American Methodism. If scriptural salvation was the "engine that drove the train" of past Methodism, oftentimes camp meetings were the shape of the train itself! This book is filled with the words and testimonies of countless numbers of past Methodists who enjoyed the power of early camp meetings.
   —Lester Ruth, Duke University Divinity School

In *Power Ahead*, Rev. Van Dussen transports us into the world, foreign to many of us, of camp meetings past and present. His carefully researched descriptions of these remarkable gatherings range widely across history from early Presbyterian Scotland to the present, and demographically to include Native Americans and African Americans. His narrative poignantly recounts this unique phenomenon and reminds us of the fundamental role evangelical Protestantism played, and continues to play, in shaping American and Canadian cultures.
   —Prof. W. Bruce Leslie, SUNY Distinguished Service Professor

Many of us have experienced the blessing of getting away from the busyness of daily life to gather with God's people at places we regard as holy

ground. Greg provides an inspirational account of these sacred places where God has moved throughout the centuries to forgive, heal, save, and transform. This book will inform and inspire its readers to reflect upon God's grace and power available to all who come together to seek and worship him on the holy ground where camp meetings take place.
 —Rev. Dr. David Cooke, Pastor, Findley Lake United Methodist
    Church; Board Member, The Camp at Findley

Readers of this book will find a very thorough examination of the heritage, the message, and the vision of the camp meeting movement both in the United States and Canada. Delving deeply into writings about the camp meeting from the first half of the nineteenth century, the author presents a very full picture of what camp meetings were like and what their impact was. In this way he prepares the way for a treatment of the *raison d'etre* for continuation of this expression of the Christian faith in the twenty-first century.
 —John Oswalt, Asbury Theological Seminary

CAMP MEETINGS

Power for the Road Ahead

D. Gregory Van Dussen

*The Asbury Theological Seminary Series in
World Christian Revitalization Movements in Pietist/Wesleyan Studies*

EMETH PRESS
www.emethpress.com

Camp Meetings: Power for the Road Ahead

Copyright © 2022 by D. Gregory Van Dussen

Printed in the United States of America on acid-free paper

All rights reserved. No part of this book may be reproduced or transmitted in any form or by any means, electronic or mechanical, including photocopying, recording, or by any information storage and retrieval system, without the written permission of the publisher, except where permitted by law. For permission to reproduce any part or form of the text, contact the publisher. www.emethpress.com. P. O. Box 533, Jackson, Georgia 30233

Library of Congress Cataloging-in-Publication Data

Names: Van Dussen, D. Gregory, author.
Title: Camp meetings : power for the road ahead / D. Gregory Van Dussen.
Description: Jackson, Georgia : Emeth Press, [2022] | Summary: "What was it like to travel to an early camp meeting? What drew people there? What did they find at the camp ground upon their arrival? The experience varied with different times, places, cultures, and denominations, yet it spoke to universal human, especially spiritual needs. In their heyday these annual events gathered people from considerable distances to seek the presence and power of God in their lives. Whatever else they accomplished was secondary to this foundational purpose. So important was it, that a preacher or lay participant might attend more than one, if that should become feasible. Reaching neighboring regions and across state and national boundaries, they attracted people in ways that justified the sacrifices such travel entailed"-- Provided by publisher.
Identifiers: LCCN 2022047936 (print) | LCCN 2022047937 (ebook) | ISBN 9781609471866 (paperback) | 9781609471880 (case bound) | ISBN 9781609471873 (kindle edition)
Subjects: LCSH: Camp meetings.
Classification: LCC BX8475 .V36 2022 (print) | LCC BX8475 (ebook) | DDC 269/.24--dc23/eng/20221117
LC record available at https://lccn.loc.gov/2022047936
LC ebook record available at https://lccn.loc.gov/2022047937

Credits

Many thanks to Cythia Wood, President of Berwick Camp in Nova Scotia, for providing photos of the camp, and to Dr. Shirley Mullen, for permission to use photos of Beulah Camp Ground in New Brunswick.

Thanks also to Jim Keiper, Deacon Sue Russell, Rev. Todd Daningburg, Rev David and Diane Kofahl, Dr. Shirley Mullen, Cynthia Wood, and others who have shared their experiences of worship, fellowship, and spiritual growth at several camp meetings, and who offered suggestions for fruitful research. Thanks to Editor Larry Wood and team at Emeth Press, for encouraging this project and seeing it through to completion. Special thanks to Rev. Karen McCaffery for technical assistance in putting this book together. I am also grateful for readers of my earlier books who have encouraged me to press on with this work.

Dedication

To those who have walked the road of life with me,
shining "like the sun in the kingdom of their Father,"
who now, standing among "the great cloud of witnesses,"
shine their light on the road ahead.[1]

"How blessed the truth that Christians never part for the last time."[2]
– Alfred Cookman

---

[1] Matthew 13:43; Hebrews 12:1, NIV.
[2] Henry B. Ridgaway. *The Life of the Rev. Alfred Cookman (etc.)*. New York: Nelson & Phillips; Cincinnati: Hitchcock & Walden, 1874, 394.

Contents

Foreword / xi

Chapter 1. Setting / 1

Chapter 2. Overview / 17

Chapter 3. Roots and Precedents / 35

Chapter 4. Breaking Away from Routine and Distraction / 73

Chapter 5. Finding God in Creation / 81

Chapter 6. Expanded Fellowship / 89

Chapter 7. Point of Commitment / 109

Chapter 8. Growing in Grace toward an Eternal Destiny / 127

Chapter 9. Inspiration for Mission / 141

Chapter 10. Decline, Renewal, and Hope I / 151

Chapter 11. Decline, Renewal, and Hope II / 195

Chapter 12. Message / 213

Chapter 13. Power for the Road Ahead / 223

Foreword

Camp meetings provide spiritual nourishment in the lives of people who attend them. Each year the attendees prepare for a spiritual meeting of the mind, body, and soul. In *Power for the Road Ahead*, Van Dussen provides a rich historical narrative in which he presents, for persons familiar and unfamiliar with the tradition, the purpose and accomplishments of camp meetings. Further, he explains how the camp meeting developed over time. His book draws upon historical references such as books, journals and descriptive accounts of those who participated in them. Each chapter of his book includes vivid accounts of the tradition that spans across decades. Van Dussen's comprehensive volume provides information for the researcher who is interested in delving deeper into the history of camp meetings.

An outsider to the tradition can understand camp meetings through the organization of his book content, and an insider can gain a broader, more in-depth perspective of the camp meeting tradition. As Van Dussen sets the stage to describe the historical context, he encourages the reader to "imagine a time." This approach allows the reader the flexibility needed to visualize and begin to truly understand the phenomenon known as camp meeting.

Van Dussen's book eloquently describes the sermons, devotions, praying and song, all of which are key elements that comprise the camp meeting tradition. He includes the diverse perspectives of the indigenous people of North America, African Americans, German and Anglo-Americans, and through an examination of various denominations – from Scottish Presbyterian Sacramental meetings, to the Methodist family of churches, which gave camp meetings their distinctive, lasting shape.

Imagine a time when people lived in isolation from one another and when farming was a main way of life for most people. After the crops had been harvested, they could finally take "time off" to travel to camp meeting. There were no forms of technology that connected people daily, there were no telephones, no internet. People desired to travel to a camp meeting in the woods so that they could review their commitment to study the word of God. This "vacation" time was much needed. They would return home with a renewed faith, commitment, and a clearer understanding of the word of God. They were strengthened both mentally and physically through the daily sermons, prayer, and spiritual worship. This spiritual renewal was essential in managing the challenges of everyday life.

As I read *Power for the Road Ahead*, I reminisced about my own experiences and thought about the numbers of people that I witnessed whose lives were positively impacted and reinforced or whose spirits were nourished by the powerful sermons provided by the host pastors on the grounds. Being a witness to the testimonies of camp participants is a heartfelt experience as they explain how their lives were transformed in positive ways after having gone through some difficult times. The excitement gleaned through witnessing the transformation of camp participants whose bodies are overpowered by the Holy Spirit is very difficult to describe in words.

Dr. Van Dussen sees participation in camp meeting as providing resources which many in today's 21st century society associate with having a life coach or psychologist. For people who grew up attending camp meeting, there is something very special about communing in nature under the open sky with time to contemplate, meditate, to visit with family and friends, to reflect upon the good and the bad days and, for most, realizing that the good days outweigh the bad. There is something very special about being able to come together to sing and praise and give gratitude for their many blessings.

Dr. Van Dussen's book will serve as an inspirational compilation of resources for scholars and camp enthusiasts and participants. He skillfully provides a cohesive account of camp meetings, pulling historical narrative from resources, past and present, and identifying challenges and implications for future camps. Camp meetings continue to serve as an essential means for replenishing one's bodily temple with faith, belief, and hope, while also preparing us with power for the road forward.

—Dr. Minuette Floyd, University of South Carolina

"His presence makes our paradise,
And where he is, is heaven."
> −Thomas Rankin, citing John Milton, *Paradise Lost*, in P.P. Sandford. *Memoirs of Mr. Wesley's Missionaries to America*. New-York: G. Lane & P.P. Sandford, 1843, 218.

Therefore, let us examine ourselves; and if we have departed in any degree from the doctrine taught by the apostles, or from their zeal, spirit, and manner of enforcing them, or from genuine simplicity of manner or dress, let us return to the good old way with full purpose of heart, that the Lord may continue to bless and prosper us until the great work to which we are called is accomplished.
> −Bishop William McKendree, Sermon, December 1, 1823, in Robert Paine. *Life and Times of William M'Kendree (etc.)*. Nashville: Publishing House of the Methodist Episcopal Church, South, 1874, ii, 472.

"Whatever we lose, let us never lose that simplicity which is attended with life, light, and love, and with power from on high."
> −Thomas Rankin, Journal, 1773, in P.P. Sandford. *Memoirs of Mr. Wesley's Missionaries to America*. New-York: G.Lane & P.P. Sandford, 1843, 223.

"The experience of our fathers instructs us; their example stimulates us; and the truths they delivered guide us safely on in our perilous course...."
> −Nathan Bangs. *The Life of the Rev. Freeborn Garrettson (etc.)*. New-York: T. Mason & G. Lane, 1839, 45.

"Your sports, and all your glittering toys,
Compar'd with our celestial joys,
Like momentary dreams appear,
Come, go with us, your souls are dear."
> −Orange Scott, ed. *The New and Improved Camp Meeting Hymn Book*. Published by the Compiler, 1830, 55.

1

Setting

"See! The winter is past; the rains are over and gone.
Flowers appear on the earth; the season of singing has come." [1]

"Come all who would to glory go,
And leave the world of sin and woe,
Forsake your sins without delay,
Believe and you shall win the day.[2]

What was it like to travel to an early camp meeting? What drew people there? What did they find at the camp ground upon their arrival? The experience varied with different times, places, cultures, and denominations, yet it spoke to universal human, especially spiritual needs. Some aspects of those first camp meetings may be familiar to many, even today, while others seem outlandish and foreign. Camp meetings changed a great deal across the nineteenth-century and beyond, sometimes morphing into holiday resorts or educational communities; church camps or conference centers. Their importance in the life of most churches has diminished to the point where many will be surprised to learn that active camp grounds exist to this day. In their heyday these annual events gathered people from considerable distances to seek the presence and power of God in their lives. Whatever else they accomplished was secondary to this foundational purpose. So important was it, that a preacher or lay participant might attend more than one, if that should become feasible. Reaching neighboring regions and across state and national boundaries, they attracted people in ways that justified the sacrifices such travel entailed.

---

[1] Song of Songs 2:11&12, NIV
[2] Anon., in Joseph Hillman, ed. *The Revivalist (Etc.)*. New York: Nelson & Phillips; et al., 1872, 113.

James Finley

One early example attracted a young man who would become one of the best known Methodist preachers in what was then the great northwest – Ohio. James Finley, who would in time take part in countless camp meetings, described his visit to Cane Ridge, Kentucky in 1801, when curiosity drove him to see for himself what was happening there. Upon his arrival, Finley encountered "a vast sea" of worshipers, behaving in surprising ways that he tried to observe while remaining a spectator. He had no idea how important such gatherings would become for his own future ministry and for the expansion of the Methodist movement. There was much he would have to process before he would find himself radically transformed by the experience.

Finley had a connection to the Cane Ridge Presbyterian congregation, where his father had once been pastor. He and some friends traveled toward the meeting, staying with a family who oriented them as best they could to what they could expect. Eventually,

> We arrived upon the ground, and here a scene presented itself to my mind not only novel and unaccountable, but awful ["that strikes with awe; that fills with profound reverence," or what we might describe as awesome.] beyond description. A vast crowd, supposed by some to have amounted to twenty-five thousand, was collected together. The noise was like the roar of Niagara. The vast sea of human beings seemed to be agitated as if

by a storm. I counted seven ministers, all preaching at one time, some on stumps, others in wagons, and one – the Rev. William Burke [a Methodist], now of Cincinnati – was standing on a tree which had, in falling, lodged against another. Some of the people were singing, others praying, some crying for mercy in the most piteous accents, while others were shouting most vociferously. While witnessing these scenes, a peculiarly-strange sensation, such as I had never felt before, came over me. My heart beat tumultuously, my knees trembled, my lip quivered, and I felt as though I must fall to the ground. A strange supernatural power seemed to pervade the entire mass of mind there collected. I became so weak and powerless that I found it necessary to sit down. Soon after I left and went into the woods, and there I strove to rally and man up my courage. I tried to philosophize in regard to these wonderful exhibitions, resolving them into mere sympathetic excitement – a kind of religious enthusiasm, inspired by songs and eloquent harangues. My pride was wounded, for I had supposed that my mental and physical strength and vigor could most successfully resist these influences.

After some time I returned to the scene of excitement, the waves of which, if possible, had risen still higher. The same awfulness of feeling came over me. I stepped up on to a log, where I could have a better view of the surging sea of humanity. The scene that then presented itself to my mind was indescribable. At one time I saw at least five hundred swept down in a moment, as if a battery of a thousand guns had been opened upon them, and then immediately followed shrieks and shouts that rent the very heavens. My hair rose up on my head, my whole frame trembled, the blood ran cold in my veins, and I fled for the woods a second time, and wished I had staid at home. While I remained here my feelings became intense and insupportable. A sense of suffocation and blindness seemed to come over me, and I thought I was going to die. ... Notwithstanding all this, my heart was so proud and hard that I would not have fallen to the ground for the whole state of Kentucky.

He ran from this strange encounter, but could not hide. On the way home, he stayed overnight with a knowing host, who prayed and sang with him until "suddenly my load was gone, my guilt removed, and presently the direct witness from heaven shone full upon my soul. Then flowed such copious streams of love into the hitherto waste and desolate places of my soul, that I thought I should die with excess of joy." Everything was different now as nature seemed to rejoice with him in a radically new day. Finley said, "O what a day it was to my soul! The Sun of righteousness had arisen upon me, and all nature seemed to rejoice in the brightness of its rising. The trees that waved their lofty heads in the forest, seemed to bow them in adoration and praises. The living stream of salvation flowed into my soul.... I felt a love for all mankind, and reproached myself for having been such a fool as to live so long in sin and misery when there was so much mercy for me."[3] By this time, Methodist and Presbyterian revivals, precursors to the predominantly Methodist camp meetings of the nineteenth century, had been rocking that part of the frontier for more than ten years. They adapted several traditions of outdoor worship in ways that would bring personal and social transformation across the continent and beyond.

Not long after Cane Ridge, came the first camp meeting in Canada in 1805, organized by the young circuit rider Nathan Bangs, with the help of William Case and Henry Ryan, also circuit riders. Worshipers gathered "on the Hay Bay shore, and near the chapel in Adophustown," Upper Canada, on the Bay of Quinte.

> Its announcement beforehand excited great interest far and near. Whole families prepared for a pilgrimage to the ground. Processions of wagons and of foot passengers wended along the highway. With two of his fellow-evangelists, our itinerant had to take his course from a remote appointment through a range of forest thirty miles in extent. They hastened forward, conversing on religious themes, praying or singing, and eager with expectation of the moral battle-scene about to open. They arrived in time to commence the meeting on the 27th day of September, though only about two hundred and fifty people had yet reached the ground. "The exercises began with singing, prayer, and a short sermon on the text 'Brethren, pray.' Several exhortations followed, and after an intermission of about twenty minutes another sermon was delivered on 'Christ, our wisdom, righteousness, sanctification, and redemption.' Some lively exhortations again followed, and the Spirit of the Lord seemed to move among the people. After an interruption of an hour and a half a prayer-meeting was held, and toward its close the power of God descended on the assembly, and songs of victory and praise resounded through the forest. The battle thus opened, the exercises continued with preaching, exhorting, and singing, until midnight, when the people retired to their booths. The night was clear and serene, and the scene being new to us, a peculiar solemnity rested upon all minds. The lights glowing among the trees and above the tents, and the voice of prayer and praise mingling and ascending into the star-lit night, altogether inspired the heart with emotions better felt than described. During this day six persons passed from death to life."

---

[3] W.P. Strickland, ed. *Autobiography of Rev. James B. Finley (etc.)*. Cincinnati: Methodist Book Concern, 1855, 166-170; Noah Webster. An American Dictionary of the English Language (etc.). Springfield, MA: George and Charles Merriam, 1848, 90.)

Nathan Bangs

Bangs went on to describe in detail the events of that meeting, including the growing crowd, the celebration of Holy Communion, and the often dramatic transformation of lives. Then, in recalling the people leaving after the meeting had ended, he shows us the depth and power of this great event:

> "The preachers, about to disperse to their distant and hard fields of labor, hung upon each other's necks weeping and yet rejoicing. Christians from remote settlements, who had here formed holy friendships which they expected would survive in heaven, parted probably to meet no more on earth, but in a joyful hope of reunion above. They wept, prayed, sang, shouted aloud, and had at last to break away from one another as by force. As the hosts marched off in different directions the songs of victory rolled along the highways. Great was the good that followed. A general revival of religion spread around the circuits, especially that of the Bay of Quinte, on which this meeting was held. I returned to Augusta circuit and renewed my labors, somewhat worn, but full of faith and the Holy Ghost."[4]

---

[4] Neil Semple. *The Lord's Dominion: The History of Canadian Methodism.* Montreal & Kingston; London & Buffalo: McGill-Queens University Press, 1996, 129; George F. Playter. *The History of Methodism in Canada (etc.)*. Toronto: Anson Green, 1862, 85; Abel Stevens. *Life and Times of Nathan Bangs,* D.D. New York: Carlton & Porter, 1863, 148; 154 & 155.

The awareness that camp meetings, with their depth of friendship and love, must come to an end, was painful indeed, but there was also "the joyful hope of reunion above," which sustained those who "marched off in different directions..." Heaven was that place "where congregations ne'er break up, and Sabbaths never end."[5]

The experience of leaving and remembering camp grounds points to their spiritual status as holy ground, often related back to the words of Jacob concerning Bethel: "How awesome is this place! This is none other than the house of God; this is the gate of heaven."[6] Powerful experiences of God interacting with his people could be thought of and remembered in similar ways, on camp grounds as in other places. Some became destinations for pilgrims, seeking their own connection with that same God. Some would be enshrined in memory, like the place of Paul's last meeting with leaders of the church at Ephesus, where they knelt and prayed, the elders knowing "they would never see his face again."[7]

Each campground came to be seen as holy, and those whose lives had been impacted by an encounter with God there, would return to that special place, either in person or in memory. For example, Laurence K. Mullen wrote a history of Beulah Camp in New Brunswick, so people would always have a record of what has taken place "on these sacred grounds." A young woman attended camp with her husband early in their marriage, at what began as a United Brethren gathering place. She has attended every year since, and she is now 100 years old. Some who have been blessed by the ministry at Beulah have traveled far afield, including one who became president of Houghton College – Dr. Shirley Mullen. A Free Methodist pastor looks back fondly at early memories of Cattaraugus Camp Ground in western New York. Year after year, sometimes over generations, people and families return to Eaton Rapids in Michigan, or Sychar in Ohio; to Mount Carmel in South Carolina, or Berwick Camp Ground in Nova Scotia.

Camp meetings spread quickly after the explosion at Cane Ridge, hence the meeting on the Bay of Quinte. Encouraged by Francis Asbury and William McKendree, they could be found across the West, so that in 1808

---

[5] J.B. Packard. "Jerusalem," in W. McDonald & S. Hubbard, eds. *The Wesleyan Sacred Harp (etc.)*. Boston: John P. Jewett; Cleveland: Jewett, Proctor & Worthington; New York: Sheldon, Lamport & Blakeman, 1856, 85.
[6] Genesis 28:17, NIV.
[7] Acts 20:38, NIV.

McKendree took part in camp meetings in Missouri and Illinois.[8] Camp meetings spread to the longer settled eastern states and provinces, as well as the western frontier, attracting both intense participation and intense criticism. Those for whom camp meetings brought a life-transforming encounter with God could scarcely contain or mute their enthusiasm, while those who were repelled by what they heard or witnessed could be extravagant in their rejection. One Anglican clergyman in Canada said, "You can have almost no conception of their excesses…. They will bawl twenty of them at once, tumble on the ground, laugh, sing, jump, and stamp, and this they call the working of the spirit [sic.]." Those who found blessings in these gatherings were undeterred by their critics, and their churches grew exponentially across North America.[9]

Charles Giles, who described himself as "young and green" at the time, related his own introduction to camp meetings as he first encountered one in New York State, early in the nineteenth-century. "Though unacquainted with camp meetings, I had no prejudices to counteract; I was delighted with the enterprise." He was especially intrigued "that the celebrated Lorenzo Dow would be at the meeting, and officiate in his own peculiar way, which awakened a curiosity in my mind to enjoy the opportunity, though I had seen him once, and heard him preach." Giles traveled with a friend, finding that "the interchange of thoughts on the way" made their "journey … pleasant and profitable: with bounding hearts we moved along over the rough road, reflecting on the past, and cogitating on the events to come. So the time passed away till we arrived at the place we were so anxious to gain." This kind of traveling fellowship and exchange of experiences, hopes, and ideas was a vital part of traveling to and from the great event, as it was – and still can be – when colleagues and fellow delegates made their way to Annual or General Conferences, or to the Quarterly Meetings that were once inspiring parts of every circuit's life. Next, Brother Giles describes the appearance of the camp meeting as he first saw it:

> According to our expectations, we found the forest converted into holy ground, and, temple-like, consecrated to the worship of God. Rough seats, arranged with due design, were prepared to accommodate the worshipping assembly. On one side of the ground an elevated platform appeared, built of logs and floored, which was designed merely for the sacred rostrum.

---

[8] Robert Paine. *Life and Times of William M'Kendree (etc.).* Nashville: Southern Methodist Publishing House, 1869, i: 206-209.

[9] Scott McLaren. *Pulpit. Press, and Politics: Methodists and the Market for Books in Upper Canada.* Toronto, Boston, London: University of Toronto Press, 2019, 36 & 37.

> The forest trees, like lofty columns, stood in the order in which nature had placed them, whose wide-spread arms, intersecting, formed verdant arches high over the hallowed ground, waving gently as the winds played among the branches. The place was delightful. And there, in accordance with my wishes, I found, in company with other ministers, the Rev. Lorenzo Dow, who was looked upon as an oracle. ... Good order prevailed on the consecrated ground; and, to my view, the scene was solemn and interesting. The native wildness of the place, the sound of human voices uttering devout supplications, and singing the songs of Zion, produced a strange effect on the listening ear; and the exciting tones of the heralds of salvation, bringing good news to lost sinners, echoed delightfully through the wilderness.[10]

An 1853 another camp meeting took place among Primitive Methodists in Blenheim Township, Upper Canada. A letter from that time describes the preparations that made this gathering possible:

> The place selected was a lovely spot in the woods. Here a number of warm-hearted friends had assembled a day or two before to erect their tents. There was a large square inclosed and well-seated. In front was the preacher's stand and tent, and on each side the tents of our friends. At each corner of the area a high stone was erected, on which was placed a quantity of pitch pine. When the fire was applied to it in the dusk of the evening, it produced a most brilliant light in our leafy temple. All our dear friends around took a lively interest in the work. They gave their time, their talents and substance freely on the occasion to make the season interesting. It was a faint picture of the early Christians at Jerusalem where they had all things common. ... It seemed like a little worshipping village. ... A number of conversions were the fruits of these meetings....

When it was time to head for home, "There was much weeping. We thought some of us will never meet again until we meet in heaven." Although other branches of Canadian Methodism had been holding camp meetings since 1804, "We believe this is the first regular and efficient camp meeting held in Canada, at which our people [Primitive Methodists] dwelt in the bush by day and by night."[11] Sister Hopper also recalled what it was like traveling to a summer time "field meeting:"

> The branches are cracking and twisting about the wheels. You cannot escape the holes in the road because it looks level, being filled with leaves; you may as well hold on as the road is very uneven. You want a place to tie the horse in the shade, and now you are in sight of the worshippers sit-

---

[10] Charles Giles, *Pioneer* (etc.). New-York: G. Lane & P.P. Sandford, 1844. 94&95; 97.

[11] Jane Agar Hopper. *Old-Time Primitive Methodism in Canada: 1829-1884.* Toronto: William Briggs, 1904, 122&123.

ting on plank seats, improvised for the occasion by rolling three logs into position: two to rest the ends of the planks upon and one for a support in the middle. The pulpit is probably a farmer's market wagon drawn there for the purpose, and a few seats placed in it for the preachers; the service has begun, and we get a seat, our boots nearly buried in the dead leaves at our feet.[12]

Joseph Hilts compared spiritual growth to the grandeur of old growth trees on the Flamboro, Ontario Circuit's camp ground:

As the sun was climbing up the eastern sky, the tall majestic trees would send their shadows clear across the encampment, as if to give us puny mortals the measure of our littleness. And while we were engaged in worship at their base, they lifted their cone-shaped heads half a hundred yards above us, as if to show us how far they had got ahead of us in the upward journey. But like haughty upstarts everywhere, they overlooked the humility of their origin and the smallness of their beginning. They ignored the fact that they once had been so little that a dewdrop falling on them would have bent them, or a fawn stepping on them might have broken them. And another encouraging thought is this. Their present altitude has been gained only after centuries of growth. Give us time to grow, and we, too, shall rise above our present moral and spiritual standard.[13]

Minuette Floyd remembers traveling to camp meetings in the 1960s. She and her family took part in several such gatherings "in North Carolina that originally were Methodist or African Methodist Episcopal, but now often have an interdenominational flavor." She remembers "traveling the back roads for more than an hour through farmland and heavily forested areas. Then we parked across the street from the campground in a large dirt field so that cars would not block us in. People who lived in the surrounding neighborhoods often walked to camp meeting, though car traffic was heavy too." License plates from other states showed the distances that some were willing to travel. Once they arrived,

There was always a large crowd of people near the entrance, hugging and catching up. Despite the dust, women wore colorful hats and dresses, and some wore high heels too. Many of the men wore dark suits with white shirts, hats, and shiny dress shoes. When camp meeting attendees stopped at a store on their way home, people who saw their nice shoes all dusty would guess that they had been to the campgrounds.

---

[12] Jane Agar Hopper. *Old-Time Primitive Methodism in Canada: 1829-1884.* Toronto: William Briggs, 1904, 119.

[13] Joseph H. Hilts. *Experiences of a Backwoods Preacher.* Wiarton, ON: Bruce County Historical Society (Reprint), 1986, 105&106.

Inside the grounds, the arrangement showed little change since their nineteenth-century beginnings. The "arbor" provided the necessary focal point, where community worship was held. Nearby were "the 'tents.' That name has carried over from the early days of makeshift canvas structures, but actually these are small, hand-built dwellings, usually of unstained wood, where families stay during religious services." These tents "all have front porches facing the arbor. Waving to people on the porches, we could now hear singing and the sounds of preaching or testifying up ahead."[14]

Peter Jones

Peter Jones, a Mississauga Indian who was to become a prominent Methodist preacher in Canada, recorded his encounter with a camp meeting at Ancaster, Upper Canada, in 1823. Jones had been "prompted by curiosity to go and see how the Methodists worshipped the Great Spirit in the wilderness." Here is his account of his experience on the camp ground:

> On the Sunday, June 2nd, several sermons were preached, and prayer-meetings were held during the intervals. By this time I began to feel sick in my heart, but did not make my feelings known. I thought the black-coats knew all that was in my heart and that I was the person addressed. The burden of my soul began to increase, and my heart said, "What must I do to be

---

[14] Minuette Floyd. *A Place to Worship: African American Camp Meetings in the Carolinas.* Columbia, SC: University of South Carolina Press, 2018, 3&4.

saved?" for I saw myself to be in the gall of bitterness and bond of iniquity. The more I understood the plan of salvation by our Lord Jesus Christ, the more I was convinced of the Christian religion and of my need of salvation. In spite of my old Indian heart (which repudiated tears as womanish) tears flowed down my cheeks at the remembrance of my sins.

While Jones looked back on this experience through Christian eyes and expressed his feelings in Christian terms, the crisis and subsequent resolution he felt reflected both the path he had taken to that point, and the new path he would follow. While his conversion was distinctively his own, it paralleled the experience of countless others in any number of cultures and individual life stories. The next day, Peter experienced the anguish that often weighed people down before release from sin and victorious salvation. He went deep into the woods to pray, then sought the prayers of others at the meeting. When he learned that his sister Mary had found the Lord, and was "apparently as happy as she could be," he "fell on my knees and cried for mercy." Surrounded by the prayer of his sister and others at the meeting, "at the dawn of day I was enabled to cast myself wholly upon the Lord, and to claim the atoning blood of Jesus. That instant my burden was removed, joy unspeakable filled my heart, and I could say, 'Abba Father.' Everything now appeared in a new light, and all the works of God seemed to unite with me in uttering the praises of the Lord."

When William Case noticed Jones with the new converts, "he exclaimed, 'Glory to God ... now is the door opened for the work of conversion among his nation!'"[15]

To these dimensions of camp meetings we might add arrival by steamship at Wesleyan Grove on Martha's Vineyard, or by canoe from one nation or settlement to another along the Great Lakes – and more besides. Many of the details differ according to place and time, yet there are elements of these experiences that still unite these very different camp meetings, elements that connect their deepest purposes with people's deepest needs.[16]

Since camp grounds tended to be located away from, yet accessible to cities and larger towns, travel and time away from home were both necessities and blessings. Many elements in the camp meeting experience were as true of African Americans as of whites. People came anticipating

---

[15] Case's prophetic words were abundantly fulfilled in Peter Jones' ministry as evangelist, translator, and advocate for his people. John Carroll. *Case and His Cotemporaries*. Toronto: Wesleyan Conference Office, 1869, Vol. 2, 411-414.

[16] H. Vincent. *History of the Camp-Meeting and Grounds at Wesleyan Grove, Martha's Vineyard (etc.)*. Wilmore, KY: First Fruits Press; Peter Jones. *Life and Journals of Keh-ke-wa-guo-na-ba (etc.)*. Toronto: Anson Green, 1860.

particular speakers. "The roads leading to the grounds literally overflowed with people on horseback, on foot, and traveling in wagons. Some of the travelers were just lonely or curious. But most came excited and anxious to hear the word of God."[17]

One such element is the participants' sense that the camp ground itself was a sacred place, a meeting place between God and his people, where monumental milestones in a spiritual journey would always be gratefully remembered. Joseph Hilts looked back at the camp ground where he was converted in 1832. He mentions the presence of "two of the Ryersons, James and Richardson, one of the Evans, and other preachers both Canadian and American." The camp ground in this case included "a camp of Indians" and "a square enclosure" for prayer meetings. "The singing was after the manner of happy children whose hearts were full of joy and their souls full of melody, rather than the cold, majestic performances of some of the stately choristers of our times." After a time of struggle common to these events, Hilts found his "soul was full of light and my heart was filled with joy unspeakable." He expressed his joy in the words of several hymns, closing with:

> O! sacred hour; O! hallowed spot,
> Where love divine first found me;
> Whate'er shall be my distant lot,
> My heart shall linger round thee.
> And when from earth I rise to soar
> Up to my home in Heaven,
> Down will I cast my eyes once more,
> Where I was first forgiven.[18]

George Peck left an account of camp meetings where the grounds, the weather, or the accommodations were far less than ideal by normal standards. Yet even these became places of glory and transformation for those who persevered. Many who made their way across Cobb's mountain to a Pennsylvania meeting found their camp meeting experience worth the difficult journey:

> A camp-meeting was held, early in September of the year [1818], in Salem, which, on the invitation of the presiding elder, we attended. We

---

[17] Minuette Floyd. *A Place to Worship: African American Camp Meetings in the Carolinas.* Columbia, SC: University of South Carolina Press, 21.

[18] William Hunter, "The Hallowed Spot," in Joseph H. Hilts. *Experiences of a Backwoods Preacher*. Wiarton, ON: Bruce County Historical Society [Reprint], 1986, 96-99. Identification of composers and titles has been done here and in several other places by consulting Hymnary.org.

crossed Cobb's mountain in a considerable company of men and women on horseback, led by our magnificent presiding elder on a mammoth horse. All in all it was a novel scene to us, and there was a sprinkling of romance in the train of travelers on saddles, composed of men and women, old and young, climbing the mountain and clambering over rocks.... Many of them crossed this mountain on foot, we were well mounted; they traveled in peril of their lives, we in safety.

The encampment was small, the ground rough, and the tents poorly built. Everything was rude and primitive, but God was there. ... We were happy in subsequent years to find some who were there brought to God, bright and shining lights in the Church.

Another camp meeting showed similar challenges, with similar results:

"In September last we held a camp-meeting on Litchfield circuit, the season being cold and rainy, rendered our situation in the tented wilderness very unpleasant; but these gloomy circumstances did not impede the work of grace: both preachers and people were zealously affected in the good cause from day to day. At the close of the meeting about one hundred souls were found who professed to know that their sins were forgiven. Indeed, all our camp-meetings have been attended with glorious consequences: hundreds are now rejoicing that they ever saw those consecrated grounds, where they were awakened to see their vileness, and where they first felt the renovating power of grace."[19]

Peck also tells us that camp meetings could have an effect beyond the actual time and place in which they were held. After one meeting, he says, "The work spread over the circuit, and extended to adjoining charges." In another, "A blessed influence went out from this meeting, and a revival of religion extended to several parts of the circuit."[20]

Joseph Long told of an Evangelical Association camp meeting in Ohio, in which the same effect radiated outward, from the camp ground to the circuit in which the meeting was held, to a larger area nearby:

The holy fire then spread over the whole circuit, the meetings everywhere became interesting and many a precious soul was hopefully converted to God." ...

The influence of this revival also spread over the other circuits of the district, and the brethren labored with great success everywhere during

---

[19] George Peck. *Early Methodism within the Bounds of the Old Genesee Conference (etc.)*. New York: Carlton & Porter, 1860, 319; 392.

[20] George Peck. *Early Methodism within the Bounds of the Old Genesee Conference (etc.)*. New York: Carlton & Porter, 1860, 433; 459.

the year. There is no doubt that the presiding elder's powerful preaching greatly contributed to this blessed success."[21]

Jacob Gruber told in a letter a story that illustrates the sacredness of a camp ground. At one of his camp meetings, a woman "who was in declining health desired that she be taken to the camp ground that she might go to heaven from that spot. She was accordingly taken, and 'in transports of joy she went up to join the song of the redeemed.'"[22] The power and meaning in a camp ground came directly from the interactions of God and his people in that place. The connection between the camp ground, eternal life, and the experience of heaven in the midst of worship was something people came to anticipate, without ever taking it for granted. So for the woman in Gruber's story, the camp ground was the perfect place to transition from this world to the next.

Ellen Eslinger has pointed out what she calls "religious neglect" in late 18th century America. "Most late-eighteenth-century American churchmen agreed that the secular, rationalistic thinking of the Enlightenment was a major factor in a general decline of religion." Some churches were stronger than others, depending on the colony or state. The frontiers saw waves of settlement, often leaving the churches to catch up with their westward movement. Disorder, spiritual lethargy, skepticism, or indifference weakened any attempts to minister. In describing the situation of mid-18th century churches, Richard Hofstadter said that "surprisingly large numbers in the English continental colonies enjoyed little or none of the amenities and comforts of a religious community, and many seemed not to be trying very hard to get them."

However, as Eslinger tells us, "This general, persistent sense of malaise ... made religious leaders more receptive to experimentation with new forms of worship."

---

[21] R. Yeakel. Bishop Joseph Long: the Peerless Preacher of the Evangelical Association. Cleveland: Thomas & Matill, 1897, 45.

[22] W.P. Strickland, ed. *The Life of Jacob Gruber*. New York: Carlton & Porter, 1860, 43.

Freeborn Garrettson

Freeborn Garrettson provides an example of this "general decline of religion," in this account of a conversation he had – or tried to have - with a stranger in 1779:

> I suppose the people in this part of the country had scarcely ever heard any kind of preaching.... I met a man one day, and asked him if he was acquainted with Jesus Christ. "Sir," said he, "I know not where the man lives." Lest he should have misunderstood me, I repeated my question, and he answered, "I know not the man."

The camp meeting would provide an extremely effective response. It was new and exciting, yet with a long and somewhat diverse tradition. It was innovative and adaptable to what were often very different North American communities, yet solidly based in the ancient traditions of Christian orthodoxy. "Traditional belief and practice provided the core," that would direct its emotion and mass appeal to constructive ends. "It brought together a diverse and divided society and created a model of Christian society." While the evangelical culture symbolized by the camp meeting was never universal, it was large, energetic, and amazingly successful in its influence and leadership. It lived in various denominations, uniting them, perhaps more than they realized, in its basic theology and spirit.

> The result, largely unintended and certainly unforeseen, was a very different sort of evangelical experience, one which resonated deeply with a

generation disoriented by a war for independence, geographic relocation, a more competitive economy, and a disturbingly partisan political culture.
...

To members of a society severely divided by culture, economic differences, and political ideology, the camp meeting seemed to exert a miraculous unifying power over the crowd of participants.[23]

Weighing the various observations and reactions to camp meetings, James Finley wrote: "Much may be said about camp meetings, but, take them all in all, for practical exhibition of religion, for unbounded hospitality to strangers, for unfeigned and fervent spirituality, give me a country camp meeting against the world."[24]

---

[23] Ellen Eslinger. *Citizens of Zion: The Social Origins of Camp Meeting Revivalism.* Knoxville: University of Tennessee Press, 1999, 180-185; 224; Richard Hofstadter. *America a 1750: A Social Portrait.* New York: Vintage, 1971, 180; Nathan Bangs. *The Life of the Rev. Freeborn Garrettson (etc,).* New-York: T. Mason & G. Lane, 1839, 84&85.

[24] W.P. Strickland, ed. *Autobiography of Rev. James B. Finley (etc.).* Cincinnati: Methodist Book Concern, 1855, 315.

2

Overview

"Celebrate the Festival of Tabernacles for seven days.... Be joyful at your festival.... For seven days celebrate the festival to the Lord your God at the place the Lord will choose. For the Lord your God will bless you in all your harvest and in all the work of your hands, and your joy will be complete."[1]

"Oh, if dere be one seeking mourner here dis afternoon,
if dere be one sinking Peter,
if dere by one weeping Mary,
if dere be one doubting Thomas,
won't you be so pleased to come and deliber them?"[2]

Early Nineteenth Century Camp Meeting

---

[1] Deuteronomy 16:13-15, NIV
[2] African American camp meeting song, sung by Nancy Brooks, quoted in Albert J. Raboteau. *Slave Religion (etc.)*. Oxford, et al: Oxford University Press, 1978, 265.

Camp meetings go a long way toward explaining early Methodism's rapid growth and formative impact. Along with class meetings, quarterly meetings, and other growthful gatherings, these instruments of revival came to represent the heart of the Wesleyan movement. They fueled its expansion across North America and the radical transformation of its people. Thomas Rankin tried to put into words an experience at a 1775 quarterly meeting where the presence of God moved in ways similar to many camp meetings. His description helps place camp meetings in their larger context.

> At ten our love-feast began. There were such a number of whites and blacks as never had attended on such an occasion before. After we had sung and prayed ... the power of the Lord descended in such an extraordinary manner as I had never seen since my landing at Philadelphia. All the preachers were so overcome with the divine presence, that they could scarce address the people; but only in broken accents saying, "This is none other than the house of God, and the gate of heaven." When any of the people stood up to declare the loving-kindness of God, they were so overwhelmed with the divine presence, that they were obliged to sit down, and let silence speak his praise.[3]

The experience of being "overcome with the divine presence" and finding oneself at "the gate of heaven," several years before the earliest camp meetings and sixteen years before Cane Ridge, offers us a window into a growing spiritual movement that would soon provide enormous power for church expansion and personal – and social - transformation.

Camp meetings, especially in the early nineteenth-century, present to some, as they did to many in that day, forms of prayer and worship that may well come across as bizarre and even off-putting. It may be hard to imagine participating in such gatherings. We may wonder how those early experiences connect to our own. We may, at first glance, be glad those "primitive" days are over. But camp meetings were much more than strange spectacles of an overheated, exotic spirituality. They played several important roles in the lives of Christians and others, addressing human needs we share in common. So for us it is important to understand the specific purposes they served, and how they can help us accomplish similar purposes in our very different age. We also need to recognize *similarities* between the spirituality and worship of early camp meetings and the experiences of many churches today. For those who recognize such similarities, the strangeness will not be as noticeable, even though time has brought about significant changes.

---

[3] Thomas Rankin, Journal, in P.P. Sandford. *Memoirs of Mr. Wesley's Missionaries to America*. New-York: G. Lane & P.P. Sandford, 1843, 231.

The nineteenth-century camp meeting may seem to have sprung *de novo*. But in fact, the spiritual explosion seen in camp meetings had roots extending back hundreds of years, even to events in Scripture. Nor can camp meetings be relegated to a quaint and distant past, as if nothing of the kind exists today. In reality, several tributaries poured into the river of life that was the early camp meeting, and its impact continues to influence Christian life and churches today. There are still ongoing camp meetings across North America, and while they may have undergone significant changes over time, they continue to fulfill most or all of their original purposes.

This book will explore some of the experiences that led to the classic camp meeting, and some of the ways camp meetings have developed since that early time. Most of all, we will see the specific needs they addressed, so that they can teach us something about addressing similar contemporary needs.

We can chart the course of camp meetings from the late eighteenth-century through today, but especially throughout the nineteenth-century. Among their contributions, they enabled people to break away from their normal routines in order to focus on God and his role in their lives. B.W. Gorham wrote in 1854,

> Camp Meetings are believed to owe much of their success to the following considerations: They call God's people away from their worldly business and cares for several successive days, thereby securing time for the mind to disentangle itself of worldly care, and rise to an undistracted contemplation of spiritual realities.

Gorham realized, as we must, that "The great facts of the human character and of human condition have not changed." Therefore, "there will always be a call for an annual resort to the tented grove."

As we look at the purposes and accomplishments of camp meetings, we could well ask ourselves, as Gorham did the people of his day, "But do you not need, just now, a protracted season of rest from worldly care, and of devotion to God?" The same reasons that produced the vacation, were and continue to be addressed by camp meetings, and because they offer not only rest and recreation, but spiritual growth in the refreshing presence of God, they can go much farther in meeting this very real human need. Even before camp meetings took on the shape of seaside or lakeside resorts, they offered a healthy alternative to the harried, unhealthy life of the world from which its participants often came.[4]

Dan Young echoed this theme as he reflected on camp meetings he had known:

> I attended a number of camp-meetings in New England, all of which were more or less seasons of divine power and grace. One great reason why these meetings are attended with such happy results is that those who go to them for the most part arrange their business and worldly concerns to leave them for some days in succession, and give their attention to devotional exercises and feelings. I have noticed in myself, that one day after another my religious enjoyment in those meetings has become higher and higher, till I would almost seem to have a look into paradise; and when the meeting has closed, I have felt a reluctance to going again into the drudgery of worldly cares, and have rather wished that I could find Jacob's ladder.[5]

Not everyone could, or wished to, stay for a full week, yet even shorter times on the camp ground could work miracles in their lives, as we have seen in the case of James Finley, whose fairly brief time at Cane Ridge set the direction for his life and ministry. Short stays can also serve as introductions that grow into annual commitments.

Today the loss of a dependable, shared day off, including anything like a day of worship and rest, has forced more and more people into a "24/7" existence. What looks to some like freedom, especially freedom to shop any time of the day or week, has brought chains of its own. The advance of communications technology has meant that many can rarely, if ever, escape their enforced connection to work and other responsibilities. It was hard two hundred years ago, for people to close a shop, leave a farm, or vacate their homes for a week or more each summer in order to "rise to an undistracted contemplation of spiritual realities." It may well be harder today. Tethered to cell phones and every day preoccupations, many must remain instantly available to re-enter the world they so much needed to leave behind.

---

[4] B.W. Gorham. *Camp Meeting Manual, etc.)*. Boston: H.V Degen, 1854, 17; 22&23; 45; 64&65.

[5] W.P. Strickland, ed. *Autobiography of Dan Young (etc.)*. New York: Carlton & Porter, 1860, 170.

Gilbert Haven

(Methodist Episcopal) Bishop Gilbert Haven was a great advocate for, and participant in, camp meetings at a time when many were questioning their continued usefulness. He noted not only the ancient heritage of outdoor worship, but the universal need to get away from the world's gravitational pull. "They [camp meetings] have united and uplifted the Church; they have recalled the wandering, and awakened the slumbering Christian." Camp meetings offered an opportunity for people enmeshed in "fatal surroundings" to regain clear perspective, reclaim threatened values, and find needed rest. Bishop Haven said, "As long as sinners are steeped in worldliness, so long will special means [such as the camp meeting] be needed to arouse them. This earliest and still most attractive method should never be abandoned." Churches, as well as individuals, needed the renewal offered in Jesus' invitation to "Come with me by yourselves to a quiet place and get some rest." It is true that camp meetings were often noisy, tumultuous, even exhausting events, yet through them God offered "refuge and strength" to world-weary pilgrims. They captured attention, overcame skepticism, and ushered people into the very presence of God.[6]

---

[6] Gilbert Haven, Introduction to George Hughes, *Days of Power in the Forest Temple (etc.)*. Boston: John Bent, 1873, 5&6; Mark 6:31, NIV; Psalm 46:1, NIV.

Camp meetings, whether on the frontier, or near a major city, were always set in natural surroundings, away from distractions, chosen and built as temporary sanctuaries. There God spoke his Word and the Spirit moved with power; ordinary people saw heaven open so that on that holy ground God refreshed and transformed his people. Commitments were made and lives reoriented as the power of God's Spirit poured out upon the gathered congregation. It was essential that such events took place outdoors, distinct from established communities, so that Christian community itself could be extended beyond what people might experience at home. Gilbert Haven described the camp meeting as "a temporary occupancy of the summer woods for sacred worship; it is a sanctification of the green tree and the high hill to their true Creator and Lord."[7]

Joseph Long

Joseph Long recalled a camp meeting from early in his ministry, where in spite of annoying disruption from rowdies, "heaven was opened and blessings came upon us in showers...." Regardless of the specifics of any given camp meeting – good or bad weather, disturbance and disruption, the size of a crowd or the location of the camp ground – often – very often, participants would report a rending of the separation between earth and

---

[7] Gilbert Haven, Introduction to George Hughes, *Days of Power in the Forest Temple (etc.)*. Boston: John Bent, 1873, 4&5.

heaven, and an outpouring of the Holy Spirit in waves of transforming grace. Such experiences offered people a vision of the God who loved them, and the destiny that awaited them.[8]

"Camp Meeting" John Allen died in 1887, at a camp meeting in East Livermore, Maine. He first attended a camp meeting as an adult in 1825, this time in Industry, Maine, where he joined other seekers In serious prayer, was converted, and began his journey into ministry. "Ever after, the camp-meeting seemed to him the next place to heaven." As part of his long life of ministry, Allen found in each camp meeting a new infusion of "Divine grace," which led him further along the road of spiritual growth and ministry as an exhorter and, later, as a local preacher. Eventually he was given an appointment as an ordained itinerant, continuing to take part in camp meetings and other forms of evangelism. "He was a great lover of camp-meetings, and during his fifty-seven years of his religious life, he attended three hundred and sixty-seven such meetings. On these occasions, he was specially at home." Not surprisingly, Allen was part of the first National Association camp meeting, at Vineland, New Jersey. "From that time onward he retained a deep interest in this subject and delighted especially in attending meetings when the subject of holiness was the leading topic."[9]

Benjamin Titus Roberts

---

[8] R. Yeakel. *Bishop Joseph Long: the Peerless Preacher of the Evangelical Association*. Cleveland: Thomas & Mattill, 1897, 40; D. Gregory Van Dussen. *Circuit Riders on the Road to Glory*. Lexington, KY: Emeth, 2020, 89-100.

[9] Stephen Allen. *The Life of John Allen (etc.)*. Boston: B.B. Russell, 1888, 11; 21; 47; 63&64; 43&44.

Free Methodist Bishop B.T. Roberts believed that camp grounds must be chosen specifically and exclusively for their godly purpose. Camp meetings "should not be held on grounds used by others as pleasure grounds," for to such places "people come ... not to be instructed, but to be entertained." They should be located so as to be accessible, without losing their sacred purpose and atmosphere. Each one serves as a Bethel, "the gate of heaven." Minuette Floyd points out that "the feeling of spiritual illumination" is "the core of the experience at every camp ground." Dr. Floyd speaks from her participation in camp meetings in recent years, as well as their nineteenth-century origins. She says,

> The campgrounds are a truly mystical place. They are set aside from everyday life so that attendees have time to reflect on how good God has been to them. That happens in heightened moments of worship, when we clap our hands and stamp our feet more expressively than we might in a modern, air-conditioned church.[10]

Camp meetings offered connection and fellowship beyond one's local church and community. They drew people together for a common, spiritual purpose, and that purpose provided their sense of belonging. They would often stay in family and church groups, but their worship took them beyond these limited associations. They connected with others in the Wesleyan tradition, ending their local isolation. Their fellowship could also extend to worshipers of other denominations. In some cases people were so caught up in the presence of God and the spirit of revival, they could transcend barriers of age, gender, and race in an inspired unity that was sadly temporary. Even those who might come to mock or disrupt could be swept up or struck down by the power of God and become unlikely members of Christ's one body. Ministers would renew their camaraderie as they worked together in this common endeavor. Some, such as New England's "Camp Meeting" John Allen, would attend more than one such event in a single season.

Alongside the spiritual purpose drawing like-minded people together, there was in those early years a more general magnetism that drew all sorts of people to what they might see as a special social time, perhaps an antidote to loneliness. Dickson Bruce wrote, "The camp meeting was a major social event of frontier life, inasmuch as it offered an unparalleled

---

[10] William B. Rose, ed. *Pungent Truths: Being Extracts from the Writings of The Rev. Benjamin Titus Roberts, A.M.* Chicago: Free Methodist Publishing House, 1912, 15; Genesis 28:17, NIV; Minuette Floyd, *A Place to Worship: African American Camp Meetings in the Carolinas.* Columbia, SC: University of South Carolina Press, 2018, 8; 10.

occasion for all the people in a territory to gather for several days of social activity, unencumbered by a need to work."[11]

Camp meetings were annual celebrations of faith, reorientation, and spiritual growth. Like the ancient Feast of Tabernacles and the Eucharistic occasions of Presbyterian Scotland, such events spoke, and still speak, to a basic human need for landmark events and seasons. B.W. Gorham wrote, "The truth is, human life needs to be dotted over with occasions of stirring interest. The journey asks its milestones, its watering places along the way. … Our nature requires the recurrence now and then, of some event of special interest; something that shall peer up from the dead level of existence, - an object of hope to rest upon in the future – an oasis in the desert of the remembered past."[12]

Those who were active participants and advocates of camp meetings realized the inevitable disconnect between God's kingdom and every worldly dream. Those who responded in faith to the power of God, experienced through worship, fellowship, and creation, found life changed, often dramatically. These meetings, along with all the other means of grace, built the Methodist movement through the radical transformation of people's lives. As James Finley noted, "Many were converted that would not have heard the Gospel; besides, backsliders were reclaimed, and believers were quickened and built up in Christian faith." Describing an 1813 camp meeting at Deer Creek in Ohio, Finley noted the presence of thousands "from all parts of the country," led by those he regarded as the most gifted preachers in his conference.

> While one after another of these pioneer preachers would hold forth the word of life to listening, attentive thousands, the Spirit would apply the truth with demonstrative power to the heart, and hundreds were awakened and converted to God. Many that came out of curiosity had an interest awakened in their hearts, to them before unknown, while many who came to curse and oppose the cause of God, remained to pray and unite with the faithful in carrying it on.[13]

---

[11] Dickson D. Bruce, Jr. *And They All Sang Hallelujah: Plain-Folk Camp-Meeting Religion, 1800-1845*. Knoxville: University of Tennessee Press, 1974, 54.

[12] B.W. Gorham, *Camp Meeting Manual (etc.)*. Boston: H.V. Degen, 1854, 31&32.

[13] W.P. Strickland, ed. *Autobiography of Rev. James B. Finley (etc.)*. Cincinnati: Methodist Book Concern, 1855, 294; W.P Strickland, ed. *Sketches of Western Methodism … Rev. James B. Finley*. Cincinnati: Methodist Book Concern, 1855, 209.

Hannah Reeves

The change in someone's life could be personal, deeply felt, and gratefully remembered. This was the case in the ministry of Hannah Reeves, who learned about changes in a certain family and community, sometime after the camp meeting where they took place. Hannah and her husband and fellow minister William Reeves were headed from conference to begin a second year at their appointment in Youngstown, Ohio.

> On returning home to prepare for new efforts to extend the Redeemer's kingdom, they were much encouraged to go forth with renewed energy, by information received from a brother concerning the good done in his family at a camp-meeting ... under Hannah's ministrations, more than one year ago. He likewise conveyed the information that a number of others in his same neighborhood, now happy subjects of saving grace, were the fruits of her labor of love.[14]

The key components or purposes of camp meetings explored and encouraged throughout this book are these:

1 – Camp meetings seek, most of all, to provide a place and time of worship, in which people are encouraged and empowered to experience

---

[14] George Brown. *The Lady Preacher:, or, the Life and Labors of Mrs. Hannah Reeves (etc.)*. Philadelphia: Daughaday & Becker; Springfield, OH: Methodist [Protestant] Publishing House, 1870, 181.

the reality and power of God and to grow closer to their fellow worshipers – in fact, to all Christians and "everyone else," even those who do not yet claim Christian identity.[15] In worship we receive a glimpse of heaven as present encouragement and as a vision of our destiny in Christ.

2 – Camp meetings provide a place away from the pressures and distractions of everyday life, work, and responsibilities, so that participants can focus on growing closer to God in a context of Christian community. In order to accomplish this essential purpose, participants, including preachers and other leaders, are encouraged to remain on the ground for as long as possible, preferably for the entire length of the camp meeting. However, a shorter stay can still be spiritually beneficial, and beneficial to the camp community, so long as the participant is fully engaged in the program while at camp. All of us can take to heart Jesus' words to his friend Martha: "you are worried and upset about many things, but few things are needed – or indeed only one."[16]

3 – Camp meetings provide a place of worship and community within a natural surrounding that maintains the beauty of God's creation. Campgrounds should be designed so that the natural world is prominent and human creations (streets, walkways, tents, cottages, auditoria, recreational areas, etc.) are in harmony with the environment.[17]

4 – Camp meetings seek to provide a context and community within which participants encounter God so that they are moved by the Spirit to commit their lives to God, to begin their spiritual journey in Christ, and experience grace-empowered transformation to become like Christ. This journey of faith results in changed attitudes and changed behavior as each person travels through this life and makes the transition to eternal life.[18]

5 – Camp meetings are designed to bring Christians together in one place from a larger area than their own local congregations and communities. This can strengthen the ties of fellowship across churches and communities and limit the isolation sometimes found in local congregations. This can take place mainly within a tradition or ecumenically, but in the movement and examples studied here, it generally takes place within the tradition broadly called Wesleyan or Methodist (or Wesleyan Holiness), yet very much open and hospitable to the participation of others. Camp

---

[15] I Thessalonians 5:15, NIV.

[16] Luke 10: 41&42, NIV.

[17] "The earth is the Lord's, and everything in it, the world, and all who live in it." - Psalm 24:1, NIV.

[18] "And we all ... are being transformed into his image with ever-increasing glory, which comes from the Lord, who is the Spirit." - II Corinthians 3:18, NIV.

meetings are further designed to bring pastors and leaders together for collaboration, fellowship, and mutual encouragement – beyond what usually happens in local or denominational settings – which mobilizes their shared gifts and downplays competition, misunderstanding, and mistrust. For "in Christ we, though many, form one body, and each member belongs to all the others."[19]

6 – The message of a Wesleyan camp meeting takes its authority from the Bible. Scripture is the foundation for all teaching, and for the way of life of speakers, leaders, and participants. The truth of Scripture must be presented in a clear and compelling way. While styles and externals will inevitably change over time, the truth does not. There must be a consistency between the doctrine of this year's camp meetings and that of our earliest precursors. The form of a camp meeting without the Spirit and without the truth of God's Word, is empty. In the Bible, God has given us, as John Wesley put it, "the way to heaven."[20]

7 – Camp meetings, like the churches themselves, are best rooted in their tradition, aware of the road traveled and the inheritance of faith handed down across the generations. This kind of rootedness allows for mid-course corrections whenever a present practice, decision, or course of action is measured against the camp's original purpose. Tradition can be a deep and rich resource of experience, wisdom, and inspiration, built up over time and available to present day leaders and participants. As God said through the prophet Jeremiah, "Stand at the crossroads and look; ask for the ancient paths, ask where the good way is, and walk in it…"[21] Camp meetings in the Wesleyan tradition will reflect Wesley's teachings, especially regarding grace, conversion, and holiness.

8 – Camp meetings are designed to strengthen each participant, and the families, churches, and ministries in which they live out their sanctification and discipleship. Many organizations and activities drain people's spiritual energies. Camp meetings should offer rest, healing, and revitalization. Here we experience what Jesus promised when he said, "you will find rest for your souls…."[22]

9 – Camp meetings inspire us for mission. They move us forward on "the path of life," with "joy in [his] presence," which is not fleeting or

---

[19] Romans 12:5, NIV.

[20] John Wesley, Preface to the Sermons, in Albert C. Outler, ed. *The Works of John Wesley*. Nashville: Abingdon, 1984, i: 105. "Heaven and earth will pass away, but my words will never pass away." (Mark 13:31, NIV.

[21] Jeremiah 6:16, NIV.

[22] Matthew 11:29, NIV.

selfish, but filled with "eternal pleasures." Filled to overflowing from the outpouring of his love, we are inspired to share with others in our needy world.[23]

Quotations used in this book come from a wide variety of times and writers, sometimes using spellings or grammar unlike those we would normally use today. I have retained the original forms, using *sic* sparingly, thus allowing the original writers to speak in their own way. On some occasions, I have used a mid-19th century American dictionary to define a term no longer in use.

The sources used here come from several Methodist denominations active in Canada and the United States. Some of the Canadian churches were, for a time, joined to U.S. denominations. Even so, day-to-day realities could be similar or different on either side of the border. Larger denominations have left more extensive records, so that their representatives are likely to be cited more than others. However, every attempt has been made to include a diversity of voices and experiences. There are examples from indigenous and African American Methodists as well as European Americans. Preachers whose names appear on these pages range from well-known to obscure, from bishops and other prominent figures to those with whom the reader may be unfamiliar. While each person and denomination contributes something of importance to the general picture, the similarities are remarkable and were seen as such by many early on. Although precursors of Methodist camp meetings reach back centuries and many of the camp meetings themselves continue to this day, most of the focus will begin with Cane Ridge (1801) and extend to the late 19th century.

Even so, since this book argues the relevance of camp meetings to the present and future, especially for churches in the Wesleyan family, it will be important to understand and evaluate experiments and adaptations already attempted. How much change can a camp meeting endure before losing its identity? Is it possible for a camp meeting and a vacation resort to occupy the same ground? How well have people maintained the essential character of camp meetings while adding to or modifying their programs? Is it possible to steadfastly hold on to the past until it becomes an oddity, fit only for museums? Or if we succeed in drawing enormous crowds through extensive use of essentially secular entertainment, have we gained the world at the expense of our soul? Can a ministry that once involved hard work and sacrifice survive intact amid abundant creature

---

[23] Psalm 16:11, NIV.

comforts? Can an event that once offered a break from work and worry make a similar promise to those who are tethered by their cell phones?

Some of the "exercises" of early camp meeting attendees come across as bizarre today, and while they are not among the key or essential components of camp meetings themselves, they did serve essential purposes in their own contexts. It will be important to distinguish between strange, time-bound forms and important, enduring results.[24]

Charles Giles described a camp meeting held on his district in New York State, where he was serving as the Presiding Elder. His account is extremely useful due to his clarity and the depth of his reflections, which he shares with openness and maturity. Giles notes various ways camp meeting leaders, of which he was one, dealt with distraction brought there by rowdies, and signs that this event was accomplishing its essential spiritual purpose:

> At a certain time we were holding camp meeting in the eastern part of my district; the exercises from day to day had been conducted with great regularity and solemnity, but no extraordinary excitement had marked the progress of the meeting till on one afternoon. It was ascertained that there were irreligious persons in the congregation....

Giles continues to illustrate how he dealt with emotions and challenges that week.

> ...I conversed with a lady who was inconsolable – quite on the verge of despondency: she had been under powerful temptations for some time. When the congregation was called together to engage in a praying exercise. I requested the despairing lady, and likewise all the penitents, to come into the central place before the stand: soon a number of seats were filled with broken-hearted penitents:- a moving spectacle for a pious eye to behold. Then I requested the Christian brethren to come in next, and form a circle around the penitents; which being done, the rest of the assembly gathered round on the outside of the circle. ... After the conclusion of a short address, and the singing of an appropriate hymn, I requested the penitents, along with the pious part of the assembly, to kneel before the Lord, and call on him for mercy and grace – expecting that the usual order would be observed; that one would follow another in vocal prayer. But after I had ut-

---

[24] See D. Gregory Van Dussen, *Circuit Riders on the Road to Glory*. Lexington, KY: Emeth, 2020, 125-133. Some camp meeting behaviors were seen as questionable or unacceptable even at the time, by critics within and beyond Methodism. For example, see the 1819 publication entitled *Methodist Error, or Friendly, Christian Advice to those Methodists, who Indulge in Extravagant Religious Emotions and Bodily Exercises*, written by an anonymous British Wesleyan (Trenton, NJ: D.& E. Fenton, 1819).

tered a few sentences in my prayer, my vocal tones were lost in a swelling roar of mingled voices from the excited multitude. The sound was solemn, impressive, and awfully grand; like the organ of nature when playing a wild storm-anthem in the orchestra of the cloud-wrapped heavens. While the wavy sound rolled over the hills and reverberated through the wilderness, I realized that there was a holy charm in it, which seemed to produce an overwhelming and subduing influence:- the Holy Ghost was evidently among the people.

Giles did not see or hear a spiritual cacophony, but instead was reminded of worship in heaven as it appears in the Book of Revelation.

I saw no discord or confusion discoverable in the commingled tones of these devout worshipers on the camp ground. They were all united in feeling, action, and design; and their suppliant voices sounded harmoniously.... So the various tones which bore their holy aspirations, played, in concert, on the vibratory nerve of the listening ear, and rolled upward to meet the bending heavens. An awful solemnity reigned throughout the assembly during this unusual exercise. Indeed, the irreligious part of the congregation stood and gazed with wonder and amazement. The power and grace of God were manifested in such a wonderful manner, that Satan was expelled from the soul of the desponding lady, and many others were healed who were afflicted with spiritual plagues. Hence there was joy among the angels in heaven, and peace and good will upon earth – melody in hearts, melody in songs, which filled the wilderness with melody.

The good that Giles found in this camp meeting gave him a new perspective on the conduct of such events, and he encouraged other leaders on the camp ground to focus on the spiritual transformation happening there, instead of overemphasizing rules and restrictions:

When I have seen the operations of the Holy Spirit exciting surprise and wonder, by passing over some lines marked out by established rules and modes, this thought has occurred. Perhaps we spend too much time in hewing and polishing stones for the Lord's altar, and rest too much on the externals of religion. The operations of divine power are not confined to our plans and local views. While observing the form of godliness, we should be looking for the coming of the Holy Ghost to impart to us the spiritual baptism.

He writes, specifically about emotion in worship:

Many are inclined to believe that feeling, zeal, and ardour, belong, appropriately, to worldly concerns; and hence are not consistent with piety and religion. [He lists examples in secular professions.] But the preacher, the ambassador of Jesus Christ, it seems, must be unmoved himself, and be careful not to raise any excitement among the people of God. Alas! is not this carefulness to suppress excitements, and to keep religion confined to mere mechanical ceremonies, the cause why careless sinners are so little interested in the house of worship? Being trained to this sameness, the minister appears to be afraid to move one step out of the beaten track, fearing he might possibly produce a degree of pious friction, and by that means some sparks of sacred fire might be elicited, and ignite the sleepy, stupid assembly; so set the neighborhood on fire. Indeed, it is a lamentable fact, that some preachers are too deficient in zeal and pathos to make the house of worship an interesting place.[25]

M.E. Bishop L.L. Hamline had a similar concern from his observation of Methodist worship and its critics. He was encouraged to learn that in New Hampshire some of the preachers "are warm and sunny and fiery, and can weep and shout," prompting him to write this reflection: "Oh, I bless God for religion and for Methodism. But when Methodism affects the dignity and silence and stiffness and corpse-like aspect of formalism, it makes me weep. I want to see it the warm, breathing thing it was in the days of [early American Methodist preacher Benjamin] Abbott, and not a statue."[26]

U.B. preacher W.M. Weekley put it this way:

One serious hindrance to the work [of revival] is the fact that too many profess to have found a "new way." They counsel moderation, and would have us go about the business with that cold, mathematical precision which the astronomer employs in measuring the heavens. As the result, many of our revival efforts turn out to be very *moderate* affairs. They are self-constituted appointees to shut off steam and put down the brakes, and they succeed. What we need is more steam; that is, purpose, push, and power.[27]

The 19th century camp meeting contributed to the astonishing growth of the Methodist movement, a pattern we have not seen in a very long time. Could the essentials of the camp meeting contribute to a new era in growth? Casting about for new theologies, enthusiastic promotion of cultural conformism, and seeking "the next thing" while forgetting our iden-

---

[25] Charles Giles, *Pioneer* (etc.). New-York: G. Lane & P.P. Sandford, 1844, 298-302.

[26] F.G. Hibbard. Biography of Rev. Leonidas L. Hamline, D.D. (etc.). Cincinnati: Hitchcock & Walden; New York: Phillips & Hunt, 1880, 154&155. With similar appreciation, Richard Allen called his friend and colleague Benjamin Abbott "that great and good apostle" and "one of the greatest men that I ever was acquainted with." Richard S. Newman. Freedom's Prophet: Bishop Richard Allen, the AME Church, and the Black Founding Fathers. New York & London: New York University Press, 2008,145; See John Ffirth. *Experience and Gospel Labors of Benjamin Abbott (etc.)*. New York: J. Emory & B. Waugh, 1830.

[27] W.M. Weekley. *Twenty Years on Horseback, or Itinerating in West Virginia*. Dayton, OH: United Brethren Publishing House, 1907, 131.

tity and purpose – all have been tried and, no matter what they promised, have failed to provide us with "hope and a future."[28] What if we looked, not to the arcane and brittle shell of our past, but to the living power that made us who we were, and for whom the possibilities are endless? There are some parallels between the "malaise" and disorder of the late 18th century and our own. Could the combination of solid tradition and adaptability speak to a continent and world many believe has lost its way?

Many camp meetings still operating in our own time are much more than relics of a bygone era or objects of holy nostalgia. The needs of people and society that were addressed by camp meetings long ago are just as real and pressing today. The resources of grace which God offers are just as powerful and relevant as in earlier times. While there may be elements of style and custom that no longer seem to work well in connecting us with God and each other in transforming worship, these may need to be revised or superseded, but the essential purposes that drove these gatherings in the past remain just as important now. The people of God still, as much as ever, need the Bethels and Mounts of Transfiguration he provides; places and events where outpourings and upwellings of grace set us free and empower us to be the people he created us to be.

---

[28] Jeremiah 29:11, NIV.

3

Roots and Precedents

"About eight days after Jesus had said this, he took Peter, John and James with him and went up on a mountain to pray."[1]

"A rest where all the soul's desire / Is fixed on things above; Where fear and sin and grief expire, cast out by perfect love."[2]

North American camp meetings are often traced back to the massive revival at Cane Ridge (1801), led mainly by Presbyterians but with participation and limited leadership by Methodists and Baptists. Certainly Cane Ridge spurred Methodists to adopt and develop camp meetings, so that while others used this form, Methodists found it perfectly suited to their theology, spirituality, and evangelistic purpose. Yet Cane Ridge had its own ancestors in the often large Communion occasions held by Presbyterians in Scotland. These in turn can be seen as inheriting outdoor preaching, festivals, and celebrations extending back to and beyond the Reformation, all the way back to Old and New Testament models.

Methodists related their worship in the forest to the outdoor preaching of the Wesleys and their movement in Britain and Ireland, and also to American Methodist outdoor events extending back into the late 18th century. The elements of singing, preaching, Communion, and love feast were also part of the early quarterly meetings that brought Methodists together from districts and nearby regions. Richard Boardman wrote in 1769 to John Wesley, saying, "There appears such a willingness in the Americans to hear the word, as I never saw before. There is no preaching

---

[1] Luke 928, NIV.
[2] Ralph C. Horner & J.V. MacDowell, eds. *Gospel Tent Hymns*. Toronto: W. Briggs; Montreal: C.S. Coates; Halifax: F.F. Huestis, 1889, #58.

in some parts of the back settlements. I doubt not but an effectual door will be opened among them." Indeed there would, and the early ministries of "Wesley's missionaries" helped prepare the ground. Chief among them would be Francis Asbury, who would maintain an exhausting schedule in order to lead and organize ministry, often in those "back settlements." By 1808 he knew very well the role camp meetings would play in every part of the continent, even in the most remote parts of the frontier: In his journal for August 24, he wrote, "I rejoice to think there will be perhaps four or five hundred camp-meetings this year; may this year outdo all former years in the conversion of precious souls to God."[3]

The German denominations in our tradition held "great meetings" long before Cane Ridge. Henry Spayth mentions ten such gatherings among United Brethren in Pennsylvania during the 1800 conference year. Great meetings in Virginia "were attended with the rich effusions of divine power and grace. At some of these, the people fell like mown grass before the Lord. The cry and distress of souls manifested, was great, and great was the succeeding joy." Behney and Eller's definition helps us to see these great meetings as precursors, along with others, to the camp meetings to come:

> Great meetings had been taking place in rural areas since the first one was held in 1724. The members of the Church of the Brethren, especially, were active in holding them. An announcement would be spread abroad that a great meeting would be held at some available place, a farm or grove. People from many miles around would come bringing with them provisions to last several days. They spent the nights in nearby homes or barns or in hastily erected rude shelters. Preachers of different denominations attended the great meetings and preached wherever they could get a crowd to gather about them within voice range. Often several preached at the same time at different places within the great meeting area. The great meetings were heavily attended because they afforded people who lived in lonely, remote places the opportunity to hear the gospel and to enjoy social contacts. Most of the people were German, although English-speaking people, both ministerial and lay, also attended.[4]

As with Methodist quarterly and camp meetings, Holy Communion and love feasts were part of United Brethren great meetings. Spayth lists nineteen of these events in 1802.

---

[3] P.P Sandford. Memoirs of Mr. Wesley's Missionaries to America. New-York: G. Lane & P.P. Sandford, 1843, 19; 158.

[4] Kenneth W. Krueger, ed; J. Bruce Behney & Paul H. Eller. *The History of the Evangelical United Brethren Church.* Nashville: Abingdon, 1979, 38&39.

They afforded an enlarged field of action, and a wider spread of the knowledge of true religion, and a fit opportunity to enforce the practice of its [United Brethren] moral precepts. Hundreds, and we may say thousands, by these means came to hear, who in the ordinary way of holding religious or divine worship would not have been brought under the saving influence of this dispensation of life. Prejudices which had taken possession of the minds of many, accompanied by a sectarian spirit, were thereby more or less removed or shorn of their strength, and the best of all was, many experienced a change of heart.

As the United Brethren and Methodists grew to know each other better, they recognized their common doctrine, mission, and spiritual life, "hence they were drawn and flowed together. A mutual friendship and confidence ensued. This friendship, this pure disinterested love, was of great advantage to the cause of religion, and the extension of the reign of grace." As they saw and shared in their parallel ministries, they "saw powerful conversions, and extraordinary displays of the outpouring of the spirit [sic] of God upon many people, as a result of their united labors."[5]

Cane Ridge (1801) arose most directly from Scottish Presbyterian sacramental meetings, British Methodist outdoor evangelism, and American frontier revivals under both Presbyterian and Methodist leadership. One of its leaders, Richard McNemar, explained the spiritual dynamics at work in the great "Kentucky Revival." McNemar, "whose spirit was in it from the beginning," was an eyewitness and leader at Cane Ridge, and though his future took him and others far from the evangelical mainstream, his descriptions give us a picture of what actually took place at that formative meeting.

> It first began in individuals who had been under deep convictions of sin, and great trouble about their souls, and had fasted and prayed, and diligently searched the scriptures, and had undergone distresses of mind inexpressibly sore, until they had obtained a comfortable hope of salvation. And from seeing and feeling the love of Christ, and his willingness to save all that would forsake their sins and turn to God through him; and feeling how freely his love and goodness flowed to them, it kindled their love to other souls, who were lost in their sins; and an ardent desire that they might come and partake of that spiritual light, life, and comfort, which appeared infinite in its nature, and free to all.

While many reacted negatively to the depth and power of emotions among worshipers at Cane Ridge, others saw the power of God at work

---

[5] Henry G. Spayth, *United Brethren in Christ*. Circleville, OH: United Brethren in Christ, 1851, 88; 84; 80&81.

in a way that attracted thousands. What seemed to some as bizarre and excessive behavior, impressed others as persuasive evidence that God was working in ways that were real and effective. Where ordinary worship might touch only the surface of a worshiper's consciousness, here was an experience in which God and his preachers could go deeper, to the heart and soul, in such a way as to begin a thoroughgoing transformation.

> The news of these strange operations flew abroad, and attracted many to come and see; who were convinced, not only from seeing and hearing but feeling; and carried home the testimony, that it was the living work of God. This stirred up others, and brought out still greater multitudes. And these strange exercises still increasing, and having no respect to any stated hours of worship, it was found expedient to encamp on the ground and continue the meeting day and night. To these encampments the people flocked in hundreds and thousands, on foot, on horseback, and in wagons and other carriages.

This spiritual wildfire spread to nearby communities, attracting both commendation and condemnation along the way. At one point, McNemar described the wonder of thousands of people, mostly strangers to each other, singing and praying in unrehearsed harmony:

> No one, who has not been an eyewitness, can possibly paint in their imagination the striking solemnity of those occasions, on which thousands of Kentuckians were convened in one vast assembly, under the auspicious influence of the above faith. How striking to see hundreds who never saw each other in the face before, moving uniformly into action, without any preconceived plan, and each, without intruding upon another, taking that part assigned him by a conscious feeling, and in this manner, dividing into bands over a large extent of ground, interspersed with tents and wagons. Some uniting their voices in the most melodious songs; others in solemn and affecting accents of prayer: some lamenting with streaming eyes their lost situation, or that of the wicked world; others lying apparently in the cold embraces of death: some instructing the ignorant, directing the doubtful, and urging them in the day of God's visitation, to make sure work for eternity: others, from some eminence, sounding the general trump of a free salvation, and warning sinners to fly from the wrath to come: the surrounding forest at the same time, vocal with cries of the distressed, sometimes to the distance of half a mile or a mile in circumference.

> How persons, so different in their education, manners, and natural dispositions, without any visible commander, could enter upon such a scene, and continue in it for days and nights in perfect harmony, has been one of the

greatest wonders that ever the world beheld.[6]

James McGready reflected on the mystery and unexpectedness of this great revival (really a series of related revivals), though it is also true that this event had its precedents and preparation. In a sermon called "Vindication of the Exercises in the Revival of 1800," McGready said, "Whenever Christ has appeared for the salvation of sinners, it has been in a manner contrary to the expectations of a blind world – and in a way too humbling to the pride of the carnal heart." He gives examples from the past, especially Jesus' incarnation. He will not leave criticism and disbelief unanswered: "And thus it has been in every period of the church since his resurrection and ascension, - when in a day of power he comes for the salvation of sinners. And still he appears and works widely contrary to the expectations of the carnal mind, and in a way humbling and abasing to the proud heart of man."

Then McGready brings his point to bear on the strange goings on, "exercises" that would become an oft repeated and oft rebuked part of the coming decades of Methodist camp meetings:

> Well, my brethren, Christ's coming at the present day in the power of the Godhead to visit his church with the outpouring of his Spirit, is marked with circumstances equally unreasonable in the opinion of the proud and worldly minded. They think the noisy tumult and uproar is mad confusion, and cannot believe this falling down, and shrieking, and crying for mercy – the praising, shouting, and rejoicing, to be the glorious work of the Eternal God – that it is that revival of religion – that day of God's power, for which christians [sic] have been longing and praying.

Far from mere "mad confusion," he sees in all this the same divine source as the Day of Pentecost.[7]

Methodist preacher John McGee believed that some of his Presbyterian colleagues at Cane Ridge and its associated Communion occasions were initially shaken by the explosive worship they saw there. McGee, on the other hand, who thrived in this [to him] familiar environment, "came forward and without hesitation, entered on the most heart-stirring exhorta-

---

[6] Richard McNemar. *The Kentucky Revival (etc.)*. n.c.: Trumpet Press, 2012 (orig. 1808, 7; 23; 36&37.

[7] James M'Gready. The Posthumous Works of the Reverend and Pious James M'Gready, etc. n.c.: n.p., 1833, 449&450; 471.

tion, encouraging the wounded of the day never to cease striving ... until they had obtained peace in their souls."[8]

The Communion at the center of the entire gathering followed the pattern of similar events in Scotland. At its heart was a belief and awareness of Christ's "spiritual presence," as understood in the Presbyterian tradition. Paul Conklin sees this doctrine as "perhaps the most powerful and moving conception of the divine presence in any Christian tradition." Actually it would be similar to that held by Methodists, coming from their own Anglican tradition, which in turn carried an appreciation of the Eucharist influenced by ancient as well as reformed sources. Presbyterians would have come to Cane Ridge seeing Communion as "the most important of all the rituals in the church year," the centerpiece of a revival lasting several days. Communion gatherings became not only great spiritual events, but also "a proper time for courtship, for the formation of new friendships, and for various reasons a time of joy and celebration. For most devout Presbyterians, Communion was usually the peak experience of the year; at some communions it could be the peak experience of a lifetime." Of course, it was not the Lord's Supper, but the size and spectacle that received both acclaim and notoriety. Conklin describes what such a Communion was like and stresses that "little if anything that happened in this great revival was new, without precedents that stretched back through two centuries, to Carolina and Virginia, to Pennsylvania, and ultimately to Ulster and Scotland."[9]

When North American camp meetings drew similar objections to those McGready was addressing, the Methodist evangelist James Caughey offered some wisdom from John Wesley. On one occasion, when Wesley was questioned about the way some people responded to Methodist preaching, he [Wesley] replied with this perspective: "I have ... thought it best to leave the whole with God; thinking it much better to have a little false fire mixed with the true, than to have none at all."[10]

Cane Ridge inherited a long tradition and then handed it on to a new generation, in a form that would sweep over North America with astonish-

---

[8] Thomas Rankin, quoted in Ellen Eslinger. *Citizens of Zion: The Social Origins of Camp Meeting Revivalism.* Knoxville: University of Tennessee Press, 1999, 195.

[9] Paul K. Conklin. *Cane Ridge: America's Pentecost.* Madison, WI: University of Wisconsin Press, 1990, 16-18; 63; 89&90. See also James R. Rogers. *The Cane Ridge Meeting House.* Wilmore, KY: First Fruits, 2019.

[10] Ralph W. Allen & Daniel Wise, eds. *Helps to a Life of Holiness and Usefulness ... Selected from the Works of The Rev. James Caughey, etc.* Boston: James P. Magee, 1859, 276.

ing results. The story of Cane Ridge has been told often, and from many vantage points. It was a transition from one form of dramatic, outdoor worship to another. The Methodist preachers who played a part there received and reshaped that tradition so that while others would hold their own such gatherings, Methodism would be its chief sponsor and beneficiary.

Peter Cartwright

Cane Ridge's best known Methodist attendee was the famed circuit rider, Peter Cartwright, who included an account of the event in his autobiography. His description is classic.

Begun as "a sacramental meeting by some Presbyterian ministers," Cane Ridge revealed "the mighty power of God ... displayed in a very extraordinary manner." In ways that would become common in Methodist camp meetings, "many were moved to tears, and bitter and loud cries for mercy."

> Ministers of almost all denominations flocked in from far and near. The meeting was kept up by night and day. Thousands heard of the mighty work, and came on foot, on horseback, in carriages and wagons. It was supposed that there were in attendance at times during the meeting from twelve to twenty-five thousand people. Hundreds fell prostrate under the mighty power of God, as men slain in battle. Stands were erected in the woods, from which preachers of different Churches proclaimed repentance before God and faith in our Lord Jesus Christ, and it was supposed, by eye

and ear witnesses, that between one and two thousand souls were happily and powerfully converted to God during this meeting. It was not unusual for one, two, three, and four to seven preachers to be addressing the listening thousands at the same time from the different stands erected for the purpose. The heavenly fire spread in almost every direction. It was said, by truthful witnesses, that at times more than one thousand persons broke out into loud shouting all at once, and that the shouts could be heard for miles around.[11]

Cartwright thought of Cane Ridge as "the first camp meeting ever held in the United States," though the origins of camp meetings, some led by Methodists, extend back more than a decade earlier. Nevertheless, significant elements of what quickly became standard North American camp meetings were certainly present at Cane Ridge, and the explosion of that event, as Cartwright said, "kindled a religious flame that spread all over Kentucky and through many other states." Cartwright lamented that just as the spiritual outpouring at Cane Ridge was contagious, the same event also precipitated divisions and even heresies among its participants and the people they influenced. But for the ever-expanding Methodist movement, Cane Ridge provided a launching place and, to some extent, a model for what became the great tradition of camp meetings, which were quickly and enthusiastically adopted by its leaders. Thus, "evidently a new impetus was given to the work of God, and many, very many will have cause to bless God for this revival of religion throughout the length and breadth of our Zion."

Cartwright himself experienced a radical conversion and reorientation of his life at a meeting that followed soon after Cane Ridge. Still in 1801, the Presbyterian minister James McGready called another sacramental meeting "about three miles north of my [Cartwright's] father's house." McGready "invited the Methodist preachers to attend," and Cartwright remembered John Page as prominent among those who accepted the invitation: "Accordingly, he came, and preached with great power and success." Cartwright's conversion was much like those that would follow in Methodist camp meetings, wherever they were held.

> The power of God was wonderfully displayed; scores of sinners fell under the preaching, like men slain in mighty battle; Christians shouted for joy.
>
> On the Saturday evening of said meeting I went, with the weeping multi-

---

[11] (W.P. Strickland, ed. *Autobiography of Peter Cartwright, the Backwoods Preacher*. New York: Carlton & Porter, 1856, 30&31.

tudes, and bowed before the stand, and earnestly pleaded for mercy. In the midst of a solemn struggle of soul, an impression was made on my mind, as though a voice said to me, "Thy sins are all forgiven thee." Divine light flashed all round me, unspeakable joy sprung up in my soul. I rose to my feet, opened my eyes, and it really seemed as if I was in heaven; the trees, the leaves on them, and every thing seemed, and I really thought were, praising God. ... I have never, for one moment, doubted that the Lord did, then and there, forgive my sins and give me religion."

Soon after, Cartwright joined the Methodist Episcopal Church, 'which I have never for one moment regretted." He would become a minister in that church, and among his efforts would be preaching and leading many camp meetings.

We can be thankful that Cartwright and others preserved accounts of those early camp meetings, which took the spiritual energy displayed at Cane Ridge across North America, where they came to characterize the common experience of Methodists in several denominations. For a time, "Presbyterians and Methodists in a great measure united in this work, met together, prayed together, and preached together." In time, Presbyterians would face serious division within their denomination over the theology and practice of these meetings. Methodists came to dominate the movement, though preachers of other churches would sometimes participate and people of many denominations, or none, would attend. Lasting ingredients would include sizable congregations, with the forest as their meeting place; simple, makeshift "tents" (which could be wooden sheds or actual canvas tents); the preaching stand or stands; the extended time, commonly a week but sometimes longer; and many preachers, with preachers and congregations coming from across a considerable region. Most importantly, the power of God would shake people to the depths of their being, causing both lamentation over sin and shouts of victory in the experience of salvation. Some of these elements were carried over from the Presbyterian sacramental meetings. The celebration of the Lord's Supper was a regular part of the camp meeting schedule – though not as central as it was for the old Scottish festivals. Conversion, renewal, and fellowship in the presence of the living God continued and developed as the central purposes for these events. The forest setting and duration of meetings were also critical for these purposes to be accomplished. There would be modifications, but the essential experience would remain the same for decades, in all parts of the continent.[12] Unlike today, when the term "religion" is often used in a

---

[12] W.P. Strickland, ed. *Autobiography of Peter Cartwright, the Backwoods Preacher*. New York: Carlton & Porter, 1856, 37&38; 45&46.

negative, institutional sense, in the 19h century its first meaning involved "a belief in the being and perfections of God, in the revelation of his will to man, in man's obligation to obey his commandments," etc. But a further definition better describes the way Cartwright and other evangelicals used it: "true piety of life, with the practice of all moral duties," and fulfilling these duties arose "from love to God and his law." Further, for evangelicals, getting religion equated to the conversion and new spiritual life at the heart of the revival experience.[13]

B.W. Gorham traced the ancestry of camp meetings as special, extended, outdoor events to times long before Cane Ridge and its immediate predecessors in North America and Scotland. He saw in the Old Testament celebrations of Passover, Pentecost, and Tabernacles "the principle that the church needs her seasons protracted and extraordinary of rest from worldly care and devotion to God."

The New Testament also offered precedents for such events. "The practice of the Saviour, in holding protracted religious meetings in places remote from the Synagogue or the Temple, and in the uninhabited portions of the country, is, as we feel, a full sanction of the principle involved in the holding of Camp Meetings." John the Baptist also held large gatherings outdoors and away from (yet accessible to) Jerusalem and other population centers. As Christianity spread across the known world, "Out-door meetings were common in the Apostles' times...." Gorham mentions also the outdoor ministries of Wesley and Whitefield, and, in a more ecumenical age, might have mentioned the work of Franciscan and Dominican friars in the late middle ages.[14]

The outdoor meetings of Wesley and Whitefield were not camp meetings, but occasional gatherings, often very large, and sharing some of the spiritual and emotional characteristics that would become well known in North American camp meetings. Whitefield also took part in the great 1742 Cambuslang sacramental meeting, near Glasgow in Scotland, which brought together congregations estimated in the tens of thousands. Whitefield's preaching there represents a fascinating link between these Scottish gatherings and the camp meetings that drew on their tradition.[15]

---

[13] Noah Webster. *An American Dictionary of the English Language (etc.)*. Springfield, MA: George & Charles Merriam, 1848, 932.

[14] B.W. Gorham. *Camp Meeting Manual (etc.)*. Boston: H.V. Degen, 1854, 289; 38&39.

[15] Arthur Fawcett. *The Cambuslang Revival (etc.)*. Edinburgh, UK & Carlisle, PA: Banner of Truth, 1971, 114-122.

Albert Raboteau explores the African roots and American development of Christian music among slaves, including songs used in outdoor settings in general and camp meetings in particular. African influences may well have influenced the form Christianity took in these communities, and some theorize that African American worship may be partially responsible for the more "unrestricted religious behavior" of many white worshipers. While many factors have been cited to explain this way of worshiping, including such things as "the need of an oppressed class to release pent-up tension," Raboteau looks to Africa, saying, "the slaves tended to express religious emotion in certain patterned types of bodily movement influenced by the African heritage of dance." He also makes it clear that African influences do not negate the reality of Christian faith among slaves. "Despite the African style of singing," for example, "the spirituals, like the "running spirituals" or ring shout, were performed in praise of the Christian God. ... African style and European hymnody met and became in the spiritual a new, Afro-American song to express the joys and sorrows of the religion which the slaves had made their own.[16]

Robert Danielson, following Kenneth O. Brown, says "It is difficult to assess if there was a 'first camp meeting.'" He believes that camp meetings predated Cane Ridge, which has often been seen as the origin for the movement. Danielson cites six such gatherings, all taking place during the 1790s in Georgia and the Carolinas, and all led by Methodists. (See cover for a 1790 camp meeting in Kentucky.) Brown says,

> ...the mighty Great Revival did not birth the camp meeting. The spiritual inferno in Kentucky simply provided the medium whereby the camp meeting quickly gained national publicity and notoriety, but evidence suggests encampments had already become popular in the Carolinas and Georgia, perhaps a decade or more before Cane Ridge.

Brown then provides substantial information about several of those earlier camp meetings and their Methodist leaders, going back into the 1780s.

---

[16] Albert J. Raboteau. *Slave Religion (etc.)*. Oxford, et al. Oxford University Press, 1978, 60&61; 74; Hortense Powdermaker. *After Freedom*. New York: Atheneum, 1969, 259&260.

Nathan Bangs, depending in part on the contributions of a leader at Cane Ridge, Methodist preacher John McGee, also describes a considerable cluster of smaller meetings culminating in Cane Ridge.[17]

The Presbyterian sacramental meetings that led to Cane Ridge and provided many of the components of Methodist camp meetings did not originate in Appalachian America. They were brought by Scottish immigrants and represent a very old tradition in Presbyterian Scotland. Leigh Eric Schmidt has traced that tradition's history and shown its importance for the camp meeting culture in North America and its contribution to the larger Scottish diaspora.

For Scottish Presbyterians, "religion and culture, communion and community, piety and sociability" came together in these annual Communion occasions. In a church and society purged of the festivals of an earlier era, they became "an engaging combination of holy day and holiday." Centered around the Lord's Supper, these Eucharistic festivals replaced the Roman Catholic calendar and its many celebrations with a single event, to which ordinary church life pointed and from which individual and congregational piety took shape and nourishment. The replacement of earlier Catholic feasts and commemorations with Communion occasions began in the late 1500s. Schmidt says that the new ritual was welcomed and adopted more easily than might have been the case because of the centrality of Communion for Catholics, and because the departure of older celebrations left an emptiness and longing in people's lives. "The rise of festal communions … suggested that the old rhythm that went along with the popular festivals of late medieval Catholicism was not as easily eradicated as the early reformers had hoped." In fact, "In an ironic twist the evangelical Presbyterians, the most Puritan group in Scotland, wound up recovering much of the eucharistic festivity of late medieval Catholicism in their own sacramental occasions."[18]

Actually, a line can be drawn connecting the importance given to Communion in Catholicism, through the Eucharistic theology of Calvin, to Anglican and Methodist views of the Sacrament, especially in the theology

---

[17] Robert Danielson. Tenting by the Cross: The History and Development of the Methodist and Holiness Camp Meeting. Wilmore, KY: First Fruits, 2019, 6; Kenneth O. Brown. Holy Ground, Too: A Study of the American Camp Meeting. New York: Garland, 1992, 28-34; Nathan Bangs. A History of the Methodist Episcopal Church. New-York: Mason & Lane, 1839, II: 101-105.

[18] Leigh Eric Schmidt. *Holy Fairs: Scottish Communions and American Revivals in the Early Modern Period.* Princeton: Princeton University Press, 1989, 3&4; 15-17; 19&20.

of John and Charles Wesley. Schmidt details the similarities in Catholic and Reformed thought on the subject, and much has been written on Holy Communion's importance to Wesleyan theology, spirituality, and practice.[19]

Some of the characteristics of early Scottish Communion events provide both contrast and connection to the Methodist camp meetings that would flourish across North America. These included,

> ...outdoor preaching, great concourses of people from an extensive region, long vigils of prayer, powerful experiences of conversion and confirmation, a number of popular ministers cooperating for extended services over three days or more, a seasonal focus on summer, and unusually large numbers of communicants at successive tables."

James Kirkton believed "there were more souls converted to Christ at that time than in any season since the Reformation." Among the reasons are the great anticipation and prayer leading up to the occasion, the encouragement of a large company of believers, and the length of time and attention given to repentance, forgiveness, and conversion. The transformative power of these gatherings was generally greater than the more conventional worship taking place in local churches.

Another observation points to the powerful presence of the living God during worship, similar to descriptions by Methodists who would later attend camp meetings. Thomas Hog said that at a Sacramental gathering at Kiltearn in the late 1650s, *"The Lord bowed his Heavens and came down,* and displayed his saving Power on the Occasion most comfortably and signally."

During the 18th century, when emigrants were leaving for North America, and the Wesleyan revival was unfolding in Britain and Ireland, there were massive Communion revivals in Scotland, some with participants numbering in the thousands. There were political factors, with tragic clashes involving churches, whose relevance would fade in the new world. Still, the crowds demonstrated how important these events were,

---

[19] For example, Winfield Bevins. *Marks of a Movement: What the Church Today Can Learn from the Wesleyan Revival.* Grand Rapids: Zondervan, 2019. Timothy J. Crouch, ed. J. Ernest Rattenbury. *The Eucharistic Hymns of John and Charles Wesley* Cleveland: OSL, 1990; Lorna Khoo. *Wesleyan Eucharistic Spirituality (etc.).* Adelaide, Australia: ATF, 2005; Rob L. Staples. *Outward Sign and Inward Grace: The Place of Sacraments in Wesleyan Spirituality.* Kansas City, MO: Beacon Hill, 1991; James B. Scott & Molly Davis Scott. *The Medicine of Immortality: The Sacrament of Jesus.* Dallas: Provident, 2013; Daniel B. Stevick. *The Altar's Fire: Charles Wesley's Hymns on the Lord's Supper (etc.).* Peterborough, UK: Epworth, 2004.

even when distracting issues are left to one side. The heart of it all was "an evangelical synthesis of conversionist preaching and Eucharistic practice," indicating that "salvation and the sacrament were intimately related, even inseparable." Schmidt uses the helpful image of a journey: "The new birth was the great point of entry into a long journey heavenward.... The communion season drew people into the pilgrimage and kept them going once on the journey." When their journey in faith and life took them across the Atlantic, they took this practice with them. As early as 1724, New Hampshire "evangelicals, scattered on the frontier and dispersed in small agrarian hamlets, came together and reaffirmed who they were and what they believed." Farther South,

> In the middle colonies, where Presbyterian immigration was much heavier than in New England, sacramental occasions were proportionately larger and more pronounced. The communion seasons – prevalent, powerful, and well-attended - figured prominently in the religious life of the Presbyterian immigrants throughout the region.

They very naturally provided the form for the revivals that would join other tributaries to produce the great camp meeting tradition of 19th century North America, even as they also continued for a time in communities of Presbyterians who had come from Scotland and the North of Ireland.[20]

In 1742 in Cambuslang, near Glasgow, crowd estimates reached as high as fifty thousand. Cambuslang would in some ways parallel Cane Ridge as the most impressive single example of this tradition. Since George Whitefield was one of the preachers there, Cambuslang becomes an especially relevant precursor to the great outdoor gatherings of Methodism.

The great revival at Cambuslang is well documented by the local Presbyterian pastor at that time, William McCulloch, a colleague, James Robe, and by lay participants. McCulloch served the Cambuslang congregation for forty years (1734-74), amid a farming region with a small population that included coal miners and linen weavers. Coal miners lived and worked much like slaves. The people in that area had been part of the volatile, sometimes violent interplay of religion and politics that had long been part of life here. "McCulloch's ministry began among a people who had had direct, and in some cases personal experience of suffering for their faith." The parish included some who were very poor.

Cambuslang took prayer seriously, in an organized way. Many eagerly read the Bible and other Christian books, and tried to encourage each

---

[20] Leigh Eric Schmidt. *Holy Fairs: Scottish Communions and American Revivals in the Early Modern Period.* Princeton: Princeton University Press, 1989, 24; 36; 49-51; 54&55; 63; 65.

other in the faith, some of them in prayer groups like those established by Whitefield and Wesley. All of this helped prepare the community for revival. On an earlier visit to the area (1741), Whitefield preached "to a very thronged assembly. After I had done with prayer, and had named my text, the rustling made by opening the Bibles all at once, quite surprised me – a scene I had never witnessed before."[21]

By the time Whitefield reached Cambuslang in 1742, the revival was well under way. On one July day he preached three times, followed by McCulloch. Whitefield's description of the reaction sounds like what was to come in North America:

> For about an hour and a half there were scenes of uncontrollable distress, like a field of battle. Many were carried into the manse like wounded soldiers. "Mr. M ['Culloch] preached after I had ended, till past one in the morning, and then could scarce persuade them to depart. All night in the fields, might be heard the voice of prayer and praise."

Cambuslang would be an experience in superlatives for Whitefield, McCulloch, and the many thousands of others who were there. Its powerful influence would be felt across the evangelical world, in Scotland and beyond. Together with other, smaller occasions during that century, it would form the background and model for Communion revivals on the American frontier. These events in Scotland must join with the circumstances in the Appalachians to help explain how a gathering like the giant meeting at Cane Ridge could have happened. As amazing and perplexing as they were and are, they were and must continue to be seen as the result not merely of human efforts and the particular settings of Scotland or North America. For while any given confluence of people, forces, and events can lend itself to revival – even massive, sweeping revival, lasting many years, only the outpouring of God's Spirit can work through it all to produce something as transformative as these were.[22] One central part of these Communion occasions was, of course, the much anticipated, outdoor celebration of the Lord's Supper. While Communion would be a staple component of Methodist camp meetings, one which carried great importance for participants, there were significant differences between Communion occasions and camp meeting Communion.

---

[21] Arthur Fawcett. *The Cambuslang Revival: The Scottish Evangelical Revival of the Eighteenth Century*. Carlisle, PA: Banner of Truth, 1971, 4-7; 31-33; 36; 45; 57-93; 81 [quote from Luke Tyerman, *Life of George Whitefield*, I, 508.

[22] Arthur Fawcett. *The Cambuslang Revival: The Scottish Evangelical Revival of the Eighteenth Century*. Carlisle, PA: Banner of Truth, 1971, 114 [including Whitefield quote]; 119&120.

First, admission to the (literal) table was restricted in the Presbyterian occasions. There were expectations as to sincerity and depth of faith, honesty in repentance, and reliability of one's participation in a parish community. All of this was symbolized by the metal token each communicant had to bring as the sign of eligibility to take part. Communion was the high point of the days of prayer, sermons, and reflection, and it required serious, prolonged spiritual preparation, which would take place at the site of the gathering and during the weeks leading up to this time. People took the granting of tokens seriously, and the number of actual communicants would be much smaller than the total of all attending the revival.[23]

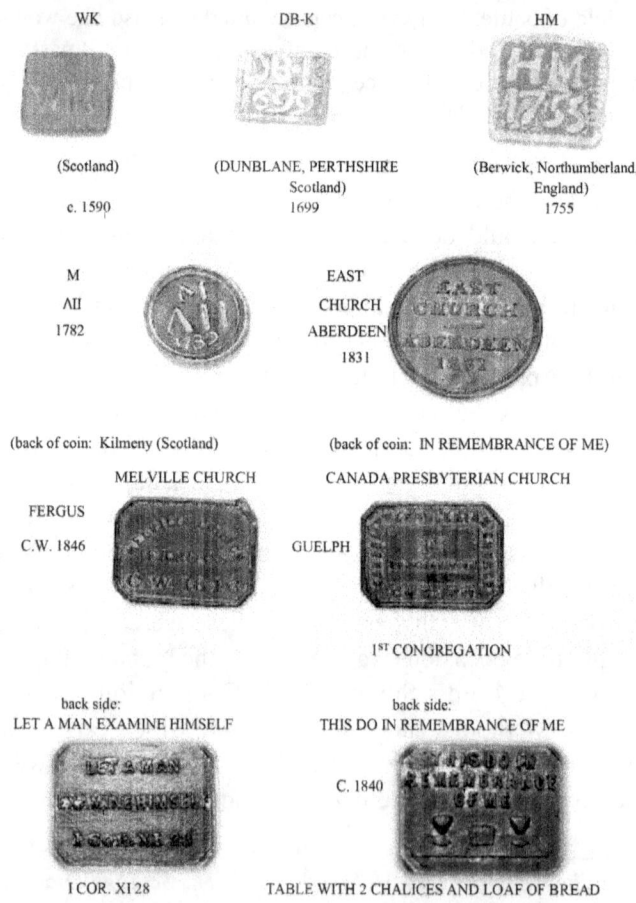

---

[23] Arthur Fawcett. The Cambuslang Revival: The Scottish Evangelical Revival of the Eighteenth Century, Carlisle, PA: Banner of Truth, 1971, 118.

The tokens authorizing individuals to take part in Communion make for a fascinating study in themselves, and their use identifying members in good standing bears some resemblance to Methodist tickets. Various Methodist denominations issued class or quarterly tickets for the purpose of identifying active members of a class or local church. One function of these was to admit the bearers to love feasts at quarterly meetings, just as the Scottish tokens admitted people to Presbyterian Communions.[24]

Communion tokens were usually made of inexpensive metals. Their value, both originally and now for collectors, is in their meaning, markings, and design. Early tokens, from the 1500s, were simple, usually featuring letters identifying a particular minister, church, parish, or denomination. They were used commonly in Scotland, but also in England, Ireland, North America, and other parts of the British Empire to which Scottish Presbyterians had migrated. Tokens from United States churches were used less often and are therefore harder to find. Due to limitations on the frontier, they were few and extremely simple. The earliest tokens made in what is now the United States were produced in the mid-18th century. The first Canadian token bears the date 1772 and comes fom Nova Scotia. It remains possible to find and purchase Communion tokens today. They were made in various shapes and in time came with more elaborate designs. More recent tokens may include a relevant verse from Scripture, along with the name and location of the church that issued them. The photo on page 50 shows sample Communion tokens from Scotland, England, and Canada and with a variety of dates.[25]

James McGready observed something in the celebration of Communion at these festivals, something very similar to the experience of countless attendees at Methodist camp meetings: "At the table of the Lord ... they appeared to feel heaven upon earth." Leigh Eric Schmidt says, "These sacraments, most all agreed, were tokens of heaven, if not quite outright transports there." McGready reflected on the experience of Communion as being "at the gate of heaven," or "the threshold of heaven." Schmidt's conclusion: "the saints found that the transformational power of the sacramental season allowed them inklings of final transcendence."

An important part of this was its implications for unity and fellowship among participants. As Methodists would soon discover in their quar-

---

[24] https:?//myprimitivemethodists.org.uk; https://catalog.gcah.org>publicdata>gcah5247; https://findingaids.library.emory.edu.

[25] Michael S. Shutty. *Communion Tokens: A Guide for Collecting Scottish, Canadian, and United States Tokens*. Shelbyville, KY: Wasteland, 2013, 25; 31; 48; 101; 109-113.

terly and especially camp meetings, these regional gatherings provided "the power ... to promote community" as they brought "together people in great numbers from over a wide area." Even in their travel to the Sacramental meeting, they felt "a sense both of spiritual expectancy and enlarged camaraderie." Traveling to their mutual destination, "people could grow closer to God and to each other through pilgrimage. Singing, talking, praying, and socializing along the way, the saints experienced increased piety as well as heightened love and union."

Worship involved singing and everyone was expected to take part. So many things – travel, conversation, shared expectation, prayer, and preaching – built a unity among the people, but Communion itself was the chief unifier. McGready saw in this celebration a realization of what the Apostles' Creed calls "the communion of saints," including all who were present at the event, and extending across all the generations whose faith united them. "The Lord's Supper, more than any other part of the sacramental season, was understood as the consummate ritual of community." There were times – yet another similarity to Methodist camp meetings – when the worshiping community was so lifted up as to transcend, whether for a moment or longer, any earthly disunity. Categories of gender, race, and age, for example, could be set aside as people testified, exhorted, sang, prayed, and even preached.

Also like Methodist camp meetings, Communion festivals had to contend with "distraction and diversion" among participants. Human nature was not suspended entirely. Thoughts could stray, temptations might surface, concerns and responsibilities at home could undermine people's prayers, thoughts, and interactions. Thoughts of work left behind and the rigors of the meeting's schedule could be exhausting. Profound reflections were sometimes derailed by superficialities. "Solemnity and sociability freely intermingle."[26]

Several factors led to what Schmidt calls "The Autumn of the Sacramental Season." Division among Presbyterians, including a theological critique based upon Calvinist orthodoxy, resulted in disunity among ministers and presbyteries, and even breakaway groups that formed new denominations. All of this contrasted with the unequivocal enthusiasm of Methodists toward what quickly became their own institution. Satirical portrayals, especially that of Robert Burns, sought to make what he called

---

[26] Leigh Eric Schmidt. *Scottish Communions and American Revivals in the Early Modern Period.* Princeton: Princeton University Press, 1989, 93-99; 102-107; 129-131; Albert J. Raboteau. *Slave Religion (etc.).* Oxford, et al: Oxford University Press, 1978, 128-138.

"holy fairs" appear ridiculous. Others saw the spirituality of the Sacramental occasions as irrational, or contrary to their view of what Christianity is or should be. Still others replaced the "awe and mystery" of the (annual) Lord's Supper as it was practiced in these summer events, with greater frequency and a more ordinary presentation in ordinary parishes. Hard as it may be to understand, the multifaceted attack on the tradition of large, spiritually powerful, outdoor Communions succeeded to the point where many Presbyterians today are unaware that such a practice ever existed. Many critics saw these gatherings as a waste of time, leftovers from an increasingly outmoded past, or in serious need of reform.[27]

Methodist camp meetings, however, preserved much of the essence of the Sacramental occasions, including the gathering of people from a distance for a time of revival lasting several days, where people could draw nearer to God and to each other in ways that built up and strengthened the churches. At the heart of these camp meetings was the experience of the powerful presence of God and an opportunity for ordinary people to see and even enter the kingdom of heaven. In this experience they would find inspiration for the present and power for the road ahead. They also incorporated the German American (Evangelical Association & United Brethren in Christ) tributary flowing from "great meetings," the African American gatherings that met "with [their] face to the rising sun," and the Wesley/Whitefield tributary of outdoor evangelism and Eucharistic revival. These Methodist camp meetings flourished across North America and among Wesleyan people of many large and small denominations. There would come a time when many of the same forces that brought down the Scottish sacramental festivals would seek to end, or at least domesticate, the North American camp meeting. But camp meetings, and the venerable tradition of which they are a part, continue in various forms to this day. Since the needs they have addressed and the purposes they have served are significant, pressing, and universal, the wisest course for today's Church, and especially for the Wesleyan tradition churches, is to take a careful look at those needs and purposes, and then to restore *and* refashion a response that will take present and future generations to what James McGready

---

[27] Leigh Eric Schmidt. Scottish Communions and American Revivals in the Early Modern Period. Princeton: Princeton University Press, 1989, especially 169-182; Charles A. Johnson. *The Frontier Camp Meeting: Religion's Harvest Time*. Dallas: Southern Methodist University Press, 1955, 4.

called "the threshold of heaven," where we and they can see, feel, and live "heaven upon earth."[28]

All these tributaries flowed into Cane Ridge, Kentucky, whose giant gathering brought Presbyterians, Methodists, and Baptists together for a common purpose and launched the camp meeting portion of the Second Great Awakening. The remaining monument at Cane Ridge is the Presbyterian log meeting house, constructed of ash logs by area settlers. Leaders included Presbyterians William McGee, Barton Stone, and James McGready, along with Methodist minister John McGee, William's brother. Other preachers, such as Methodist circuit rider William Burke, fit in where they could and multiplied the outreach to the enormous audience. While this cooperative effort brought people together, it also set in motion the fragmentation that formed the Cumberland Presbyterians and the movement that became the Disciples of Christ. Within the main body of Presbyterians, there would be a hardening division between those sympathetic to the revival and those who could not accept it.[29]

Cane Ridge "has been estimated to have drawn between 20,000 and 30,000 people." Since it remains hard to visualize all that happened there, or how it might have felt to be there, we are greatly assisted by the recollections of some who were there. Along with Peter Cartwright's account, we have that of James Finley (See pp. 1-3 in chapter 1), who saw Cane Ridge as "a young man of twenty who lacked a conversion experience" and who would be turned around in dramatic fashion at Cane Ridge.

Presbyterian pastor Barton Stone wrote of the unity he perceived among preachers at Cane Ridge, across denominational lines.

> The Methodist and Baptist preachers aided in the work, and all appeared cordially united in it – of one mind and one soul, and the salvation of sinners seemed to be the great object of all. We were all engaged in singing the same songs of praise – all united in prayer – all preached the same

---

[28] "Let Us Break Bread Together," *African Methodist Episcopal Church Hymnal*. Nashville: African Methodist Episcopal Church, 1984, #530; Carlton R. Young. *Companion to the United Methodist Hymnal*. Nashville: Abingdon, 1993, 463; Albert J. Raboteau. *Slave Religion (etc.)*. Oxford, et al: Oxford University Press, 1978, 67; 223-226; Minuette Floyd. *A Place to Worship: African American Camp Meetings in the Carolinas*. Columbia, SC: University of South Carolina Press, 2018.

[29] James R. Rogers. *The Cane Ridge Meeting House*. Wilmore, KY: First Fruits, 2019.

things – free salvation urged upon all by faith and repentance.[30]

Cane Ridge and its associated revivals "continued for some time" as joint ventures, "the Presbyterians and Methodists uniting together as one army of the Lord." While there were mixed opinions among some observers – especially Presbyterian concern over disorder and the Arminian theology implicit in their appeal – the Methodists generally saw these as continuous with their own prior experience. Finley wrote, "To all but Methodists the work was entirely strange." Some of the peculiarities had been witnessed before by the preachers, and they were enabled to carry it on. As we have already seen, there were earlier camp meetings among frontier Methodists prior to Cane Ridge. But the numbers and intensity of Cane Ridge brought this form of revival worship into public view to the point where, generally under Methodist leadership, it became a standard mechanism for reaching multitudes with the gospel of Christ, and for opening believers to the gracious gift of sanctifying grace. Many of the essentials of the camp meeting experience could be seen at Cane Ridge – worship in the outdoors by people from across a large territory; transformational spiritual experiences in response to high energy sermons and exhortations; the importance of singing and prayer; separation from home and work routines; a clear focus on people's connection with God; a strong sense of fellowship, and basic Christian teaching, with an emphasis on universal availability of saving grace.

On the other hand, Finley wrote,

> There is a mistaken opinion with regard to this meeting. Some writers of late represent it as having been a camp meeting. It is true that there were a number of wagons and carriages, which remained on the ground night and day; but not a single tent was to be found, neither was any such thing as camp meetings heard of at that time. Preaching in the woods was a common thing at popular meetings, as meeting-houses in the west were not sufficient to hold the large number of people that attended on such occasions.

A contrasting report appears in Nathan Bangs' account, where, relying on John McGee's remembrance, he describes "a range of the tents," and in another gathering from around that time, "The people came with horse and wagons, bringing provisions and bedding, and others built temporary huts or tents," giving the impression that Cane Ridge was indeed a camp meet-

---

[30] Barton Stone, from *The Biography of Eld. Barton Stone (etc.)*, quoted in Robert Danielson. T*enting by the Cross: the History and Development of the Methodist and Holiness Camp Meeting*. Wilmore, KY: First Fruits, 2019, 10.

ing. It is probably best to see Cane Ridge as part of the earliest development of what was quickly recognized as a proper camp meeting. Perhaps such contrasting recollections reflect a fluid, quickly developing reality, where practical concerns are being cared for along the way.[31]

It was difficult, if not impossible, to remain aloof, detached, or anonymous in such gatherings, for they swept people, even unwillingly, into their high intensity spirit and actions. James Finley described at length the often strange, confusing behavior that characterized Cane Ridge and many subsequent meetings, but also the genuine transformations that occurred. For these events were "unequaled for power and for the entire change of the hearts and lives of so many thousands of men and women." The enthusiasm and sometimes bizarre behavior was, in Finley's view, accomplishing the rebirth and revitalization of people who might otherwise have remained lost – separated from God and bound for hell. Nothing less was at stake. Finley recorded his recollection of what Cane Ridge was like for participants. A session "opened with a sermon or exhortation...." In response,

> ...there would be a universal cry for mercy, some bursting forth in loud ejaculations of prayer or thanksgiving for the truth; some breaking forth in strong and powerful exhortations, others flying to their careless friends with tears of compassion, entreating them to fly to Christ for mercy; some, struck with terror and conviction, hastening through the crowd to escape, or pulling away from their relations, others trembling, weeping, crying for mercy; some falling and swooning away, till every appearance of life was gone and the extremities of the body assumed the coldness of death. These were surrounded with a company of the pious, singing melodious songs adapted to the time, and praying for their conversion. But there were others collected in circles round this variegated scene, contending for and against the work.

The increasingly chaotic, lawless, hopeless, and unchristian nature of the West required and flourished with such measures, though other regions saw similar responses to the Gospel and to their own needs and social contexts.

> Upon the whole, this revival in the west was the most extraordinary that ever visited the Church of Christ, and was peculiarly adapted to the cir-

---

[31] W.P. Strickland, ed. *Sketches of Western Methodism ... James Finley.* Cincinnati: Methodist Book Concern, 1855, 77&78; Nathan Bangs, *History of the Methodist Episcopal Church.* New York: Mason & Lane, 1839, 109; 103; Cf. Ellen Eslinger. *Citizens of Zion: The Social Origins of Camp Meeting Revivalism.* Knoxville: University of Tennessee Press, 1999, 196.

cumstances of the country. Infidelity was triumphant, and religion at the point of expiring. Something of an extraordinary nature was necessary to arrest the attention of a wicked and skeptical people, who were ready to conclude that Christianity was a fable and futurity a dream. This great work of God did do it. It confounded infidelity and vice into silence, and brought numbers beyond calculation under the influence of experimental religion and practical piety.[32] Methodist preachers were not the only people who were concerned or appalled by conditions in the West. Ely Parker, Seneca Chief, engineer, and later general in the Union army, was assigned to serve as an engineer in Galena, Illinois. "He had wanted to go west for years, but once there, he found that the West was not at all as he had expected. His first impression was that it was a 'dark and benighted part of the globe' with no society or amusements 'unless it be drinking whiskey, and plugging one's fist into somebody else's mug.' He was critical of the greed, the 'abundant use, in every expression or remark made in any company, of hard epithets,' and 'the practice of cheating & bare faced lying and unconsciously swindling a neighbor.'" Parker soon found there were more and better things about the West, but his initial impression must have been similar to those of many itinerants who rode circuits there.[33]

Robert Paine summarized Bishop McKendree's view of "religious excitement" and genuine Christian faith:

> As might be expected in so wide-spread and general a state of religious excitement, there were excesses and irregularities among some of the subjects. The exercises known as *jerks* and *dancing* appeared, although discountenanced generally by the more intelligent and sedate part of the ministers and members. A great deal of enthusiasm was excited, and doubtless some fanaticism also; yet a vast amount of good was accomplished, and many who seemed to act from impulse, and ran into excesses in manifesting their emotions, became steady and consistent Christians, and closed life in peace and hope. The Churches had a fresh baptism, and were united in fraternal love.[34]

---

[32] W.P. Strickland, ed. *Autobiography of Rev. James B. Finley (etc.)*. Cincinnati: Methodist Book Concern, 1855, 169; 366; 368&369.

[33] William H. Armstrong. *Warrior in Two Camps: Ely Parker, Union General and Seneca Chief*. Syracuse: Syracuse University Press, 1978, 62.)

[34] Robert Paine. *Life and Times of William M'Kendree (etc.)*. Nashville: Southern Methodist Publishing House, 1869, I; 153&154. For other observations, see D. Gregory Van Dussen. *Circuit Riders on the Road to Glory*. Lexington; Emeth, 2020, 125-133.

William McKendree

Whatever explanation or evaluation we might give for the strange and controversial aspects of early camp meetings, this form of worship and evangelism succeeded in reaching and transforming vast numbers of people. They experienced, at close range, the power of God to turn people from selfish, destructive, aimless ways of life to become new creatures in Christ. Suddenly people could see life from God's perspective, and by his power, change the direction of their lives and envision a new, eternal destiny. Here they received and shared a divine purpose that often propelled them into ministries of one kind or another. Here they saw glimpses of heaven; of life as it was meant to be; of the people and nature around them as reflections of God's glory, goodness, and love. "For a few days, people from every possible sort of background joined together to form a temporary community ruled by principles of harmony, virtue and unity." Though unconventional elements in worship created concern for many and opposition from some, "Proponents of the revival defended the emotional behavior as the mighty power of God breaking through a dense atmosphere of deism, infidelity, and indifference." With this new identity and purpose, motivated by God's love and filled with a vision for this world, they were propelled into every part of North America with a light they could not hide.[35]

The shared message of the Cane Ridge revival separated many Presbyterians and Baptists from the conventional, and, especially among Presbyterians, staunchly Calvinist mainstream of their churches, leading some to blaze new trails in ministry and denominational connection.

While others would develop their own camp meetings, Methodist Bishops Francis Asbury and William McKendree, with many others, would take the tradition in their own direction, so that soon camp meetings became a staple characteristic of Methodism and largely identified with the various Wesleyan churches. Kenneth O. Brown says, "By 1810... it became almost exclusively a Methodist tradition." Wesleyan theology was lived and promoted in camp meetings, as in other forms of ministry, led by the ever-spreading network of itinerant and local preachers across the frontiers of the United States and Canada. Calvinist theology continued to raise questions and concerns about revival, and, in turn, was constantly opposed and even ridiculed in Methodist preaching and literature.

The Wesleyan way of salvation, delivered by the circuit system and energized in camp meetings and other forms of revival, resulted in what Baptist historian Winthrop Hudson called "the triumph of Methodism" in the 19th century. Neil Semple made the same point within the Canadian context:

---

[35] Ellen Eslinger. *Citizens of Zion: The Social Origins of Camp Meeting Revivalism.* Knoxville; University of Tennessee Press, 1999, 214; 221.)

The essence of revivalism stood in stark contrast to perceptions of election and predestination and drew evangelical Protestants to an Arminian position which stressed the universality of God's saving grace. This freedom was not based on a totally free will since God initiated the process, but it did permit, if not demand, a more active participation in spiritual reformation and affirmed a hopes for immediate conversion and growth in grace. The impact of the element of revivalism was so profound that as the nineteenth century progressed, it became increasingly difficult even for Calvinists to preach predestination and its implications were either abandoned or ignored.[36]

James Finley watched as some non-Methodists fragmented over their theology and even embraced familiar heresies of that day. He also saw them as responsible for the most outrageous excesses of revival behavior. Heresies and the new religion of the Shakers carried people away from the orthodox message of mainstream revival. "The new isms that followed the great revival were many, and it seemed as if Satan had taken advantage of the excitement to drive the bewildered into darkness and the sanguine into error and folly."[37]

Many of the essential ingredients of the Methodist camp meeting could be seen, at least in a rudimentary state, at Cane Ridge – worship in the outdoors by people coming from a large territory; transformational spiritual experiences in response to high energy sermons and exhortations; the importance of singing and prayer; separation from home and work routines; a clear, compelling focus on people's connection with God; a strong sense of fellowship, and clear, basic Christian teaching with an emphasis on the universal availability of saving grace.[38]

Camp meeting hymnals/songbooks were – and are, where these meetings continue today – a vital part of camp meeting worship and fellow-

---

[36] Kenneth O. Brown. *Indian Springs Holiness Camp Meeting: A History of "the Greatest Camp Meeting in the South."* Hazleton, PA: Holiness Archives, 2000, 8; Among the many works against Calvinism, perhaps the most colorful is included in W.S. Hooper, ed. Peter Cartwright. *Fifty Years as a Presiding Elder*. Cincinnati: Jennings & Graham; New York: Eaton & Mains, n.d. 108-193; Winthrop S. Hudson. *Religion in America*, New York: Macmillan, 1987 (4th ed.), 168-171; Neil Semple. *The Lord's Dominion: The History of Canadian Methodism*. Montreal & Kingston, London & Buffalo: McGill-Queens University Press, 1996, 144.

[37] W.P. Strickland, ed. *Autobiography of Rev. James B. Finley (etc.)*. Cincinnati: Methodist Book Concern, 1855, 373.

[38] For more on the transition from Communion occasion to camp meeting, see Ellen Eslinger. *Citizens of Zion: The Social Origins of Camp Meeting Revivalism*. Knoxville: University of Tennessee Press, 1999, 197; 206.

ship. Nathan Bangs highlights the musical contribution of John Alexander Grenade, who "became distinguished among his brethren as the 'western poet,' and the 'Pilgrim's Songs' were among the most popular hymns which were sung at these camp meetings, and perhaps became the fruitful source whence sprung the numerous ditties with which the Church was, for some time, almost deluged." As involved as he was in camp meetings and revivals, Bangs looked down on some of the music he found there, but also understood something of their value. "These songs," he wrote, "though they possessed but little of the spirit of poetry, and therefore added nothing to true intellectual taste, served to excite the feelings of devotion, and keep alive that spirit of excitement which characterize the worshipers in those assemblies."[39]

There were times when Methodist singing seemed to some to be more noise and emotion than substance and rational understanding. The words of the English evangelical William Wilberforce offer a wise and necessary corrective to this view. After quoting, for example, Deuteronomy 6:5 on loving God with all one's heart, he says, in part:

> We can scarcely indeed look into any part of the sacred volume without meeting abundant proofs that it is the religion of the Affections which God particularly requires. Love, Zeal, Gratitude, Joy, Hope, Trust, are each of them specified; and are not allowed to us as weaknesses, but enjoined on us as our bounden duty, and commended to us as our acceptable worship. Where passages are so numerous, there would be no end of particular citations. Let it be sufficient, therefore, to refer the reader to the word of God. There let him observe, too, that as the lively exercise of the passions towards their legitimate object is always spoken of with praise, so a cold, hard, unfeeling heart is represented as highly criminal. Lukewarmness is stated to be the object of God's disgust and aversion; zeal and love, of his favour and delight; and the taking away of the heart of stone and the implanting of a warmer and more tender nature in its stead, are specifically promised as the effects of his returning favour, and the work of his renewing grace.[40]

The explosion of revival songs helped to prompt Methodist Episcopal bishops to include in the denomination's early, official hymnals, a plea like

---

[39] Nathan Bangs. *A History of the Methodist Episcopal Church.* New-York: Mason & Lane, 1839, ii: 109; 103; 105.

[40] William Wilberforce. *A Practical View of the Prevailing System of Professed Christians ... Contrasted with Real Christianity.* London: T. Cadell, 1830, 54&55. An excellent revision of this can be found in William Wilberforce. *Real Christianity Contrasted with the Prevailing Religious System.* Portland, OR: Multnomah, 1982, 29&30.

the one in 1831. After stating the principles on which the official hymnal was assembled and edited; even mentioning that profits from its sale will go to charity, the bishops "earnestly entreat" Methodists, "if you have any regard for the authority of the Conference, or of us, or any regard for the prosperity of the Church of which you are members and friends, to purchase no Hymn Books but what are published by our own agents, and signed with the names of your Bishops."[41] Many denominational hymnals did *not* include this kind of appeal, and some denominations, including the M.E. Church, published their own song books for such occasions. In fact,

> Among the most enthusiastic proponents of camp-meeting songs were the German denominations of Pennsylvania: the United Brethren, Evangelicals, and others. The used the familiar camp-meeting spirituals in German translations and partial borrowings and were among the first to publish camp meeting songsters.[42]

It may be that the M.E. bishops were thinking only, or mainly, of hymnals used in local churches. But if they also had in mind the extraordinary means of grace called camp meetings, their plea had little effect – especially given the flow of songs between the venues in which they were sung. The world of camp meetings and other evangelistic ministries produced an explosion of song books, often compiled and edited by preachers and others heavily involved in those same ministries. Here is a sampling of such books from Methodist sources and/or used in Methodist meetings:

B.W. Gorham, ed. *Choral Echoes (etc)*. Boston: Henry V. Degen, 1864.

Joseph Hillman, ed. *The Revivalist (etc.)*. Troy, NY: Joseph Hillman, 1872.

Ralph C. Horner & J.V. MacDowell. *Gospel Tent Hymns*. Toronto: W. Briggs; Montreal: C.W. Coates; Halifax: S.F. Huestis 1889.

John Inskip, ed. Songs of Triumph: Adapted to Prayer Meetings, Camp Meetings, and All Other Seasons of Religious Worship. Philadelphia: National Publishing Association for the Promotion of Holiness, 1882.

C.C. McCabe & D.T. MacFarlan, eds. *Winnowed Hymns: A Collection of Sacred Songs, Especially Adapted for Revivals, Prayer and Camp Meetings*. New York, Chicago: Biglow & Main; New York: Nelson & Phillips; Philadelphia: National Publishing Association for the Promotion of

---

[41] A Collection of Hymns for the Use of the Methodist Episcopal Church (etc.). New York: Emory & Waugh, 1831, 4&5.

[42] Ellen Jane Lorenz. Glory, Hallelujah! The Story of the Campmeeting Spiritual Nashville: Abingdon, 1978, 45.

Holiness, 1873. [Note that C.C. McCabe was one of the M.E. bishops for the late 19th century, which may explain why the book was published by Nelson & Phillips, the Methodist Book Concern, and also by the National Publishing Association for the Promotion of Holiness.)

William McDonald & Stephen Hubbard, eds. *The Wesleyan Sacred Harp. (etc.)*. Boston: John P. Jewett; Cleveland: Jewett, Proctor & Worthington; New York: Sheldon, Lamport & Blakeman, 1856.

Ira D. Sankey, James McGranahan & George C. Stebbins, eds. *Gospel Hymns, Nos. 1 to6 Complete (etc.)*. Cincinnati, New York, & Chicago: John Church; New York & Chicago: Biglow & Main. 1894.

Orange Scott, ed. *The New and Improved Camp Meeting Hymn Book*. Published by Compiler, 1830.

Charlie D. Tillman, ed. *The Revival* [Several volumes]. Atlanta, Cincinnati, Kansas City: MO: Charlie D. Tillman, n.d. For more on camp meeting music in the United States, see Ellen Jane Lorenz. *Glory, Hallelujah! The Story of the Camp Meeting Spiritual*. Nashville: Abingdon, 1978. For camp meetings, hymns, and songbooks in Canada, see Scott McLaren. *Pulpit, Press, and Politics: Methodists and the Market for Books in Upper Canada*. Toronto, Buffalo & London: University of Toronto Press, 2019.

Reactions against camp meeting songs could be strong, but not as strong as the impulse behind them. A study of camp meeting songbooks demonstrates that any generalization alleging poor writing and overdone repetition is wide of the mark. But the strictures some placed on the appropriateness of writing songs at all indicates a standard of excellence did not appear to take into account either the specific focus of camp meetings, or the tremendous emotion surrounding experiences of conversion and significant spiritual growth. Even when the dynamics of conversion are recognized, critics could posit a need for speedy movement in the direction of order, dignity, and concern for appearances.

An 1819 publication called *Methodist Error* offers such a critique. While the author is anonymous, he identifies himself as a "Wesleyan [British] Methodist" and is clearly familiar with the writings of the Wesleys, John Fletcher, Adam Clarke, and others whom he believes argue against the kind of worship then developing in North American camp meetings. In the matter of music, he quotes Clarke as saying "never to sing hymns of your own composing in public, unless you be a first rate poet, such as can only occur in every ten or twenty *millions* of men; for it argues incurable vanity." Our anonymous author immediately applies this judgment: "Such singing as has been described, has we know, been ordinarily sung in most of our prayer and camp meetings...."

In another place, he describes,

> ...a growing evil, in the practice of singing in our places of public worship, *merry* airs, adapted from old *songs*, to hymns of our composing, often miserable as poetry, and senseless as matter, and most frequently composed and first sung by the illiterate *blacks* of the society. Thus instead of inculcating sober christianity [sic] in them who have the least wisdom to govern themselves; lifting them into spiritual pride and to an undue estimation of their usefulness: overlooking too the counsel of Mr. Wesley, who has solemnly expressed his opinion in his book of hymns, as already amply sufficient for all our purposes of rational devotion: not at all regarding his condemnation of this very practice....

The derogatory reference to "blacks" is one of several, indicating a bias against the poor in general, but especially slaves and others of African descent. He goes on to speak with disdain for "the people of Wales, singing the same verse over and over again with all their might 30 or 40 times, "to the utter discredit of all sober Christianity." Returning specifically to camp meetings, our author speaks of "musical feelings, and consonant animal spirits." He is particularly concerned about what he sees as "the tolerance of at least the rulers of our camp meetings" for the kind of singing he attributes to African Americans when they meet as a group during a racially mixed camp meeting:

> In the *blacks'* quarter, the coloured people get together, and sing for hours together, short scraps of disjointed affirmations, pledges, or prayers, lengthened out with long repetition [sic] *choruses*. These are all sung in the merry chorus manner of the southern harvest field, or husking-frolic method, of the slave blacks; and also very greatly like the Indian dancers.

Having spoken dismissively about these groups, he describes whites' use of music in prayer tents within "some camp meetings," where,

> ...from 50 to 60 people crowd into one tent, after the public devotions had closed, and there continue the whole night, singing tune after tune ... scarce one of them which were in our hymn books. Some of these from their nature, (having very long repetition [sic] choruses and short scraps of matter) are actually composed as sung, and are indeed almost endless.

Part of the problem, as he sees it, arises from his observation that "those who sing so long, and so incessantly" are "frequently ... very young and inexperienced persons." And his objections extend to movement as well, believing that worshipers who "jump and scream ... clap their hands, and thump and pat the floor, either by stamping or by *stepping* the music, or to see-saw their bodies to and fro,' actually create a "house of confusion" instead of a decent house of prayer, a discredit to the Gospel, and an embarrassment before better behaved Christians.[43]

But the enthusiasm of others drove the tidal wave of camp ground music, and while it could not silence the critics, it reflected people's actual experience of revival - the shared power and glory of God's presence - assuring this genre, and many individual songs, of a lasting place among God's people. Here, for example, is A.P. Mead's position on the subject:

> The music of the camp meeting! who, that has ever heard it, has not paused to drink the rich melody into his soul? It comes with a grandeur, a softness and sweetness, that can be heard nowhere else. In the measured strains of a multitude of voices, uttered in charming melody, and unbroken by walls, it swells in solemn grandeur and rolls deliciously through the forests, awaking re-echoing cadences on every hand.[44]

Ellen Jane Lorenz tracks these songs from oral tradition to established publication. "For a long time the *music* was unpublished, transmitted only orally as preachers went from one camp meeting to another. The *words*, however, found a home almost at once, in little wordbooks, or 'songsters,' which sprang to life in each area where the campmeeting fever struck."

Hymns written by Charles Wesley, Isaac Watts, and others, retained an important place at camp meetings, but were supplemented by newer revival songs that expressed the emphases and culture of these events. Lorenz explains,

> Watts and Wesley and other eighteenth-century English hymnists had written hymns that expressed the emotions of the newly converted, and those were wholeheartedly adopted. But new hymns, and especially new tunes, had to be found that equally conveyed the sense of the exhilaration, even the ecstasy, which newborn souls needed to express.

Lorenz says of songsters and early camp meeting songs, that some were "written by anonymous campmeeting versifiers" and "uneducated clergy of the frontier," whose songs show "the lack of polish and the poor grammar of the uneducated itinerant. But the spirit of the camp meeting is present, and even some of the physical details of the meetings are occasionally revealed in the verses." She reconstructs the process by which

---

[43] Anon. Methodist Error, Or Friendly, Christian Advice to Those Methodists who Indulge in Extravagant Religious Emotions and Bodily Exercises. Trenton, NJ: D.&E. Fenton, 1819, 28-34.

[44] A.P. Mead, in Ellen Jane Lorenz. *Glory, Halleluljah! The Story of the Campmeeting Spiritual*. Nashville: Abingdon, 1980, 28.

tunes were chosen for new words, often derived from ethnic and secular sources – "any tunes they knew ... to express their newfound joy." With their power to encapsulate and share people's experience in a way that was easily accessible and often memorizable, "campmeeting spirituals spread like the kudzu vine, and soon covered the country with their catchy, fervent melodies."

In the late 19th century, the holiness theme of massive national and regional camp meetings dominated the Methodist songbooks of the era, often with lyrics celebrating "heaven and the pilgrimage there." No amount of pleading from Methodist Episcopal bishops, or criticism from musical aristocrats could stop "the persistence of the spirit of camp meetings and their songs." They combined the core theology and spirituality of the Wesleyan movement with the everyday experience of their singers, in a way that was "singable." When they could not transcend limits of region or culture, their premises were transferable to new contexts.[45]

The lasting vitality of these songs reflects the power of camp meetings to bless, grow, and transform people and churches. Nathan Bangs tells us that after Cane Ridge, "these meetings spread through all the settlements of the western country; and such was the eagerness of the people to attend, that the roads were literally crowded with those who were pressing their way to the grove; so much so that entire neighborhoods would be forsaken, for a season, of their inhabitants." This was a brief period of transition from the enlarged sacramental meetings in which Presbyterians ministered with others in common cause, to the predominantly Methodist camp meeting movement.

> And as the Methodists and Presbyterians were generally united together in these meetings, they took the name of *"General Camp Meetings."* By these means they spread all through Tennessee, Kentucky, and some parts of Ohio, carrying with them fire and destruction into the enemy's territories, and bowing the hearts of God's people as the heart of one man to the yoke of Jesus Christ. Of their subsequent progress, and the influence they have exerted on society, I need not here speak, as these things are known to all.

Bangs made it clear that these camp meetings were *adopted* and pressed into service by the Methodists.

> Indeed, they did not originate with the Methodists, but upon a sacramental occasion among the Presbyterians, at which time there was such an outpouring of the Divine Spirit in the people as inclined them to protract

---

[45] Ellen Jane Lorenz. *Glory, Hallelujah! The Story of the Campmeeting Spiritual*. Nashville: Abingdon, 1980, 14; 41&42; 45; 56; 78.

their exercises to an unusual period; and then this being noised abroad brought others to the place, and finally so many that no house could hold them; this induced them to go out in the fields, and erect temporary shelters for themselves, and to bring provisions for their sustenance; and finding God so abundantly blessed them in these meetings, they were led to continue them, until they at length became very general among the Methodists throughout the country.[46]

As the premier historian of mainstream Methodism in the United States in his day, and as one with considerable experience in ministry, early camp meetings included, Nathan Bangs could with authority argue for the genuineness and spiritual benefit of these meetings. Authority and leadership in this regard also rested with Methodism's first bishops. W.P. Strickland recounts the time when Bishops Asbury, Whatcoat, and McKendree were traveling together after a session of the Western Conference. One after another they spoke to a large gathering in Nashville. Soon they would play a decisive role in the transition to Methodist camp meetings.

> While in Tennessee they attended a meeting which had been in progress four days. It was one of those remarkable meetings called sacramental occasions, held by Presbyterian ministers, and which, on account of the great numbers that attended them, gave rise to camp-meetings. At this meeting, Asbury, Whatcoat, and M'Kendree were invited to participate, and it was continued several days longer. The following graphic description of this meeting we find in his [Asbury's] Journal: "The stand was in the open air, embosomed in a wood of lofty trees. The ministers of God, Methodists and Presbyterians, united in their labors, and mingled with the childlike simplicity of primitive times. Fires blazing here and there dispelled the darkness; and the shouts of the redeemed captives, mingling with the cries of precious souls struggling into life, broke the silence of midnight. The weather was delightful, as if heaven smiled, while mercy flowed in abundant streams of salvation to perishing sinners."

---

[46] Nathan Bangs. *A History of the Methodist Episcopal Church*. New-York: Mason & Lane, 1839, ii; 110-112. Although there were several Methodist camp meetings prior to Cane Ridge, it was the size and power of Cane Ridge that introduced camp meetings to people across the continent and convinced the Methodists of their surpassing usefulness in bringing salvation and holiness to the multitudes.

Francis Asbury

By means of these meetings great revival prevailed in the South and West, and extended to the Middle and Eastern States. So great were the multitudes, collected far and near from the surrounding country, that from ten to fifteen thousand persons have been estimated to be present at a single encampment. The congregation being so immense it was impossible for the voice of one preacher to reach them, and stands were erected at different points, where ministers of different denominations, but all in the same spirit, and animated by the same motives, held forth to the listening thousands the words of life. So great was the excitement which pervaded the encampment at times, that hundreds if not thousands might have been seen prostrate upon the earth at once in the greatest distress, or wild with joy, on their feet, shouting the praises of God.

Strickland goes on to detail the spread of Methodist camp meetings to Virginia, North Carolina, Maryland, and the Territory of Mississippi, where similar events resulted in hundreds of conversions and where revival had radiated outward to nearby communities. He encourages his readers to follow the story further, through the writings of James Finley and Jacob Young, "both of whom were present at the meetings."[47]

---

[47] W.P. Strickland, ed. *The Pioneer Bishop: Or, the Life and Times of Francis Asbury*. New-York: Carlton & Porter, 1858, 327&328; Jacob Young. *Autobiography of a Pioneer (etc.)*. Cincinnati: Cranston & Curts; New York: Hunt & Eaton, 1857; W.P. Strickland, ed. *Autobiography of Rev. James B. Finley (etc.)*. Cincinnati: Methodist Book Concern, 1855.

While Presbyterian revivalists were facing criticism and challenges from many in their own denomination, Methodists were enjoying virtually unanimous enthusiasm within theirs, an enthusiasm supported by spiritual results most of all, but also the uncontrolled expansion of their ranks. New converts, as well as believers experiencing sanctifying grace, were forming or expanding congregations, and among them was a steady stream of new preachers, ready to add their own voices, experiences, and leadership to the ever-expanding map of preaching places, circuits, congregations, districts, and conferences.

Dickson Bruce sought to make sense of the impact of this movement in the southern Appalachians, taking into account both the character of Methodism and the context of the frontier:

> The Methodists were the most interested in, and the most successful at, gaining converts. Much of the success of the Methodists was due to their theology and organization, but it was also due in large measure to their exploitation of the frontier's unique contribution to Christian practice, the camp meeting.

Bruce recounts the origins of this kind of worship with the Presbyterians, under the particular conditions of the frontier, though he acknowledges that "outdoor preaching is as old as Christianity itself." He recalls the work of James McGready, including the 1800 revival at Gasper River in Kentucky, and moving on to Cane Ridge in 1801. He mentions the Methodist involvement at Cane Ridge and the cooperation between denominations in its immediate aftermath. He also notes the massive attendance at Cane Ridge – "Estimates ranged from ten to twenty-five thousand, with people coming from Kentucky, Tennessee, and even the territory north of the Ohio River."

Bruce then acknowledges the support of Bishop Asbury and the rapid spread of the movement under Methodist auspices: "Asbury reported some four hundred camp meetings during 1811 alone." Later he writes that by the mid-1840s, many were finding camp meetings increasingly out of step with a maturing society.

> As some Methodists and Baptists became more affluent and more "responsible," sectarian practices such as those of the camp meeting were no longer thought appropriate. ... The denominations were no longer concerned with providing an alternative world and an alternative life because their leaders and many of their members had succeeded in terms of the world as it was.

For Bruce, the camp meeting "belonged only to the marginal folk of the frontier," so the passing of that frontier threatened the camp meeting itself. "Its association with the frontier folk was so complete that when the churches ceased to be devoted to that group, the camp-meeting ceased to play a significant role in church practice." The weakness in this thesis arises from too narrow a focus on one social context and one time period in the development of churches and the people they served. Camp meetings flourished all across North America, in very different social, cultural, economic, and political settings. While, by the 1840s, many people across America were criticizing camp meetings as outmoded, their demise was a long way off, and the last chapter has yet to be written. Just to give one example, what does Bruce's frontier-based thesis say about the massive camp meetings about to appear on the Atlantic shores of the northeast – even if the newer models looked very different? Why should the purposes of conversion, sanctification, and the building of God's kingdom become irrelevant because a region or nation attains a degree of prosperity or self-satisfaction? Is the measure of a camp meeting – or any religious practice - its reception by a given social class, or its charter in the foundational documents of the Church or denomination (in this case, the Bible and the writings of John Wesley, for starters)? Is a particular cultural example of a camp meeting a sufficient criterion for evaluating the entire phenomenon?[48]

In assessing the meaning and value of camp meetings, It is important to remind ourselves of their power – really God's power, working in a particular setting (remembering that God is working in many other settings as well) to reach the depths and inspire the transformation of a person's soul. For example, John Seybert saw this happening right before his eyes, and while his experience was common among camp meeting preachers and participants, examples like his keep the reality fresh, as when he experienced it. It is also important to point out that Seybert represents a distinct ethnic, demographic, and denominational identity: German, rural, Pennsylvania, Ohio, and wherever else Evangelical Association people migrated.

---

[48] Dickson D. Bruce, Jr. *And They All Sang Hallelujah: Plain-Folk Camp-Meeting Religion, 1800-1845*. Knoxville: University of Tennessee Press, 1974, 51-53; 59&60.

John Seybert

In one of these German camp meetings, Seybert was amazed that, not long after the meeting had started, "the altar was crowded with seekers of salvation, already at the first service, many of whom received pardon the same night. Upon this he exclaims, 'What do you think of that?'" Later during that same meeting, "'the throng of seekers was so great,' Brother Seybert says, 'one might almost be led to think, the straight gate might be over-crowded'." That camp meeting was then extended by another day.

Seybert preached again on the morning of the added day: "The gracious Spirit continued to work all day mightily. The spiritual tide did not ebb and flow, but remained high. The meeting that evening had to continue all night, until the morning dawned. It was so impressive and powerful, that Seybert never forgot it."[49]

In a similar way, AME preacher Charlotte Riley spoke at a South Carolina camp meeting, where "her hearers were both white and colored," An AME report on this event said, "The sermon was the best preached during the day, and had considerable merit to it. 'It was good Gospel' all the way through, and set the congregation all a-shouting." The impact of her sermon is shown not only by the shouting, but also by "the overjoyous ones,"

---

[49] S.P. Spreng. *Life of Bishop Seybert, First Bishop of the Evangelical Association*. Cleveland: Lauer & Mattill, 1888, 154&155.

who after worship had ended, "went into a trance and were carried out to their tents." Again we have a different culture, preacher, and constituency. Sister Riley could rejoice to say: "Now, good reader, you see the result of the woman 'preaching Christ, with Christ, to the glory of His Name. Amen. Amen'."[50]

---

[50] Crystal J. Lucky, ed. *A Mysterious Life and Calling: From Slavery to Ministry in South Carolina*. Madison: University of Wisconsin Press, 153.

4
Breaking Away from Routine and Distraction

"Come with me by yourselves to a quiet place and get some rest."[1]

"From busy scenes we now retreat,
 That we may now converse with thee;
O Lord, behold us at thy feet,
Let this the gate of heaven be."[2]

Camp meetings were and are designed and located to offer and require a temporary break from routine thinking and action. Even local church or community revivals "do not, like Camp Meetings, call the people away for successive days from their business and cares." For this and other reasons, even the largest, most spacious of churches could not replicate a camp meeting, either in its basic purpose or its practical arrangements. One key value of camp meetings is that "They offer the church an admirable break upon the worldliness of summer," the season in which most of them take place.[3]

Camp meetings called for a single-minded focus on spiritual matters. Away from normal routines and responsibilities, preachers and participants alike could give prolonged time and attention that might otherwise be lost or diluted amid the pressures and preoccupations of everyday life – even for the most committed Christians. As early as Cane Ridge, some

---

[1] Mark 6:31, NIV.

[2] Thomas Kelly, "How Sweet to Leave the World Awhile," in William McDonald & Stephen Hubbard, eds. *The Wesleyan Sacred Harp (etc.)*. Boston: John P. Jewett, et al., #38.

[3] B.W. Gorham, Camp Meeting Manual (etc.). Boston: H.V. Degen, 1854, 18.

leaders "correctly sensed that removing people from daily life increased the likelihood of personal transformation." B.W. Gorham, who led and attended decades of camp meetings, especially across the northeastern states, expressed this purpose in his *Camp Meeting Manual*:

> Camp Meetings are believed to owe much of their success to the following considerations:
>
> 1. They call God's people away from their worldly business and cares for several successive days, thereby securing time for the mind to disentangle itself of worldly care, and rise to an undistracted contemplation of spiritual realities.
>
> 2. Camp meetings are well adapted to exercise the powers of faith and prayer in the church, and they therefore greatly strengthen these powers.[4]

While this insight clearly applied to all who carried responsibilities for families, farms, churches, and businesses, James Finley found it especially true for the Wyandott Indians with whom he ministered in Ohio. In them he saw a remarkable capacity for giving undivided attention to spiritual, as well as other matters, enabling them to break away from everything else in order to focus on their relationship with God. Here is his description of an 1828 camp meeting, in which both indigenous people and white settlers took part:

> It is characteristic of the Indian to devote exclusive attention, for the time being, to whatever pursuit or employment he may take in hand. If it be fishing, or hunting, or sugar making, or corn planting, nothing else is allowed to interfere in the time allotted to these things. So in regard to religion. The time devoted to God was the most sacred, and no people could unite with greater sincerity than they in singing those appropriate lines:
>
> "Far from my thoughts vain world begone [sic],
> Let my religious hours alone,"
>
> Soon [after arriving at the camp ground and setting up their tents,] the Christian chiefs, and queens, and all, were formed into a circle, and the voice of praise and prayer made the forest arches sing. After singing one of their Christian songs, only as Indians can sing, they fell simultaneously upon their knees and lifted up their faces toward heaven, as if they ex-

---

[4] Ellen Eslinger. *Citizens of Zion: The Social Origins of Camp Meeting Revivalism.* Knoxville: University of Tennessee Press, 1999, 196; B.W. Gorham, *Camp Meeting Manual, A Practical Book for the Camp Ground (etc.).* Boston: H.V. Degen, 1854, 17&18.

pected to see the Great Spirit descend in blessings from the parted skies. ...

So it was in this instance, for while they were praying the Spirit came down upon them, and the power of God was manifested in the awakening and conversion of souls. As the shaking of the leaves in the tops of the mulberry trees was an indication to the prophet of the presence of God, so the excitement of the multitude engaged in prayer, and indicated by the tears, and groans, and shouts, was a sign that the Great Spirit was at work upon the hearts of these sons and daughters of the forest, and presently the tents of the whites were forsaken, and many might have been seen mingling with their red brethren and sisters in the exercises of the hour. From this hour, though so early in the meeting, the work of the Lord began, and continued to increase and spread as the meeting progressed, till Saturday night, when the whole encampment was in a flame of religious excitement.

All of this was possible when people would "follow the leading of the Spirit," so that their worship "was interrupted only – if indeed it may be called an interruption – by the loud cries for mercy, which rose from the burdened hearts of the kneeling penitents, or the louder shouts of praise to God for delivering grace...." Such transformation came as people gave their full attention, for many hours, over a period of several days, to the God who had called them away from lesser things and brought them together under a canopy of grace, in an experience that "will never be erased from our memory."[5]

Minuette Floyd describes the need of African Americans to have a break from hard work back home. "Celebrating their release from the toil and isolation of farm work, they gathered to commune with nature under the stars, and to fulfill a deep and abiding need." This need to get away and experience renewal is universal for humanity, but the ability to actually meet that need is uniquely and effectively met on camp meeting grounds.

John McGee noted this crucial part of the camp meeting experience in describing a participant in an early Kentucky gathering: "He had left his worldly cares behind him, and had nothing to do, but attend on divine service." A key aim and purpose of a camp meeting preacher was, as James Finley said of Peter Massie, to be "an instrument of great good wherever he went, scattering the holy fire." Camp meetings live on the light and warmth of that "holy fire," preparing people to carry that fire into the dark and cold places of daily routine and responsibility. "Holy fire" is what missionaries carried "to the ends of the earth." (Acts 1:8, NIV) An example

---

[5] W.P. Strickland, ed. *Sketches of Western Methodism ... by Rev. James B. Finley*. Cincinnati: Methodist Book Concern, 1855, 517-519.

is Daniel Poe, who "was born again at a camp meeting," and eventually became what James Finley called him, "this intrepid young missionary."

Camp meetings maintain many characteristics they have carried over from an earlier time, yet they have also had to change aspects of their life, we hope without compromising anything essential. Music may be played with modern instruments; schedules may change, and society may force speakers and prayer leaders to apply Gospel principles to new situations. African Americans may need to reaffirm their Christian and ethnic identity in unexpected new ways. All people who take part in camp meetings will have to distinguish between permanent essence and temporary forms, without at the same time uncritically buying into new forms that in some unforeseen way undermine the essence. Children, families, and newcomers may need special programs or ways to "grow into the tradition."

Nor are present day camp meetings merely a quaint, outdated phenomenon of the distant past. Many camp meetings continue to serve their original purposes. Minuette Floyd has given us a lavishly illustrated book on a cluster of African American camp meetings in which she herself is a participant. Tom Stanley, in his introduction to Floyd's book, writes: "Part holiday, part revival, part family reunion, camp meeting sites are still tucked away in rural fields and governed by common purpose and familiar rules. They are alive and well." While their roots anchor them in valued tradition, that tradition is itself a response to compelling, enduring need.

> Contemporary camp meetings are phenomenal events. People come to these spirit-filled gatherings to get to know God, to receive blessings, to pray, to testify, to reflect upon their lives, to renew old friendships, and to build new ones. For many participants the reasons for attending camp meetings have not changed since Francis Asbury and Harry Hosier rode the circuit together. They come seeking spiritual transformation, and they are rarely disappointed. As the elders say, you never leave camp meeting the way that you came.[6]

Floyd carefully describes "the many ways in which camp meetings allow participants to stop the whirlwind of daily activity, look one another in the eye, and focus on things that really matter. For most participants that requires a conscious shift of priorities." Many things change in mov-

---

[6] Minuette Floyd, *A Place to Worship: African American Camp Meetings in the Carolinas*. Columbia, SC: University of South Carolina Press, 2018, 21; 29; 33; 53; 66-68; 76-79; John McGee, quoted in Ellen Eslinger. The Social Origins of Camp Meeting Revivalism. Knoxville: University of Tennessee Press, 1999, 234; W.P. Strickland, ed. *Sketches of Western Methodism ... by Rev. James Finley*. Cincinnati: Methodist Book Concern, 67; 501.

ing from home and work to the camp ground. "But the biggest switch in priorities is the one that allows participants to connect with the divine."[7]

The early circuit rider John Collins shared this sense of breaking away in order to spend undistracted time with God and his people, when "they would leave their houses, and the cares of the world, to worship, for several days, in some beautiful grove." This is one of the enduring factors that made camp meetings such a powerful force in the lives of individuals, families, and local congregations. Collins mistakenly believed that a growing population would need such gatherings less than a dispersed, rural, frontier situation. B.W. Gorham and the other organizers of holiness camp meetings with larger, eastern constituencies, would disagree. They knew that people who were caught up in the speed, complexity, and demands of life and work in urban communities, would need just as much the opportunities to put it all aside in order to restore their first love and deepest priorities.[8]

One of the obstacles to camp meetings today is the transportation revolution, which enables people to enter or leave the camp ground, perhaps more than once, making it difficult to gain the needed distance to allow for renewing our connection with God and regaining endangered priorities. These require unhurried time, walks in the woods, catching up with long-time friends, and taking stock of our lives. They need expanses of time, space, and focus not usually allowed us in our everyday lives. Leaving and returning to the camp ground tends to leave us with a fragmented, compartmentalized existence where God has a hard time breaking through and capturing our attention.

Equally problematic is the communication revolution, which allows people to be physically on the camp ground, while several times a day connecting with the work and world they had left behind. Time away is a rare and precious thing, offering freedom, slowing our pace, redirecting our energy, and fostering perspective. When we compromise that time away with frequent return trips, we run the danger of losing what we came to receive. There can be emergencies and time sensitive calls, but they should not be used to justify regular or continual disruptions in a time set aside for things like prayer, healing, rest, inspiration, reflection, fellowship, and spiritual growth.

---

[7] Minuette Floyd. *A Place to Worship: African American Camp Meetings in the Carolinas*. Columbia, SC: University of South Carolina Press, 2018, xiii; 33.

[8] *A Sketch of the Life of Rev. John Collins (etc.)*. Cincinnati: Swormstedt & Power, 1850, 115.

These concerns for presence, what is sometimes called mindfulness, need to remind us to give ourselves fully to the camp meeting experience. We need time to read, to ponder, to go well beyond the surface of relationships - especially our relationship with God. The need to break away, slow down, and gain perspective is especially important in the lives of pastors. When a pastor comes on to the camp ground in a harried or distracted condition, finds it hard to concentrate, or frequently leaves to make or receive calls, the need for this breakaway experience is particularly clear. When the pastor or lay person does these things without seeing the problem; when workaholism or the unforgiving demands of the world are allowed to intrude and even control a person's life, something has to change, and camp meeting is one of the rare, effective ways to set a new direction. The changes in ourselves that begin or grow at camp meeting are more than wishes. They are more than good intentions; more than those fruitless times when we say, "I know I should ...." Real and significant change will come as we hear God's voice, cooperate synergistically with his initiatives, and live by his power. None of this is likely when we allow ourselves to get so busy we can't slow down, can't really listen; can't receive the gifts of peace, joy, and hope that God offers us.

The experience of being with God in camp meeting worship has been called the outskirts of heaven or the coming together of heaven and earth. Camp meeting should offer us at least a momentary glimpse of heaven, and allow us to pour that glimpse into the meaning of a line in the Lord's Prayer: "on earth, as it is in heaven." Christian holiness calls us to reflect in our lives the character of the God we worship. Christian life on earth should also reflect the character of heaven as it is revealed to us. D.D, Davisson once wrote a sermon called "The Christian's Legacy." He closes the sermon with a short, but powerful glimpse of what heaven is like. In that glimpse, may we see what we might be like, if indeed God's kingdom is found "on earth, as it is in heaven:"

> Things to come – in heaven. It implies a most perfect state of soul, gloriously enlightened, enlarged, ennobled, exalted – being made glorious in holiness, inasmuch as it will be conformed to God, the being admitted into glorious society, even that of patriarchs and prophets, evangelists and apostles, saints and angels. This also must be a source of honor, and pleasure, and improvement – the having free, constant, uninterrupted communion with the Father of glory through the Lord of glory, and by the glorious Spirit.[9]

---

[9] W.P. Strickland, ed. D.D. Davisson. *Practical Sermons on Various Subjects.* Cincinnati: Methodist Book Concern, 1854, 227.

Charlotte Riley

Camp meetings allow us a glimpse, a taste, of that "free, constant, uninterrupted communion," an unhurried, deep, and growing fellowship with God, a time in the midst of time, when heaven and earth are one.

5

Finding God in Creation

"God saw all that he had made, and it was very good."[1]

"Beautiful day, lovely thy light;
Holy each ray, nothing like night;
Cloudless the sky; peaceful my stay
Here in the sunlight of beautiful day."[2]

In his introduction to A.P. Mead's book extolling camp meetings, J.B. Wakeley wrote,

> There is a peculiar charm about camp meetings. We worship in God's great Cathedral, in nature's magnificent temple, arched over with brilliant heavens and floored with the beautiful green earth – under the foliage of trees, planted by God's own hand. There is a kind of grandeur about such a temple that accords with man's noble origin and destiny….
>
> It was when Jacob was in such a temple he exclaimed, "How dreadful is this place! This is none other than the house of God, this is the gate of heaven."

For those who worship there, "The camp ground is a hallowed place. Every tree seems clothed with richer verdure, and sacred. We worship in

---

[1] Genesis 1:31, NIV.
[2] Wiliam Kirkpatrick, "Beautiful Day," in John S. Inskip, ed. *Songs of Triumph: Adapted to Prayer Meetings, Camp Meetings, and All Other Seasons of Religious Worship*. Philadelphia: National Publishing Association for the Promotion of Holiness, 1882, #47.)

the shady grove with peculiar emotions. The places where camp meetings are held, are consecrated. We feel that we are treading on holy ground."[3]

When Charles Giles entered a camp ground early in his ministry, he saw its arrangement, but also the way its natural setting suited it for a divine purpose:

> According to our expectations, we found the forest converted into holy ground, and, temple-like, consecrated to the worship of God. Rough seats, arranged with due design, were prepared to accommodate the worshipping assembly. On one side of the ground an elevated platform appeared, built of logs and floored, which was designed merely for the sacred rostrum. The forest trees, like lofty columns, stood in the order in which nature had placed them, whose wide-spread arms, intersecting, formed the verdant arches over the hallowed ground waving gently as the winds played among the branches. The place was delightful.

Charles Giles

---

[3] J.B. Wakeley, Introduction to A.P. Mead. *Manna in the Wilderness; or, The Grove and its Altar (etc.)*. Philadelphia: Perkinpine & Higgins, 1860, ix&x.

At a camp meeting near Seneca Lake, in New York State, Giles felt a powerful, metaphorical connection between that place and the outdoor places where Jesus had taught and prayed, including the Mount of Transfiguration:

> It was truly cheering to meet the disciples of Jesus there, to offer vocal adoration to Heaven in the desert.... Though we were not in Bethlehem, not on the shore of the Sea of Tiberias, not on the mountain where Jesus preached, nor in the desert where he fed the multitudes, still we were on the globe which was formed by his own creative power, and under the leafy trees which were planted by his hand. The same sun shone there that illuminated the road where Jesus walked. Such air as Jesus breathed, while praying in the gloomy garden, encircled us there; and breezes similar to those which fanned his sacred form, while it was bathed in sweat and blood, played lightly over us as we were worshipping at his throne. But what was more to us, a thousand times more than anything else, the Lord displayed his gracious power, and wrought some wonderful things among us, which touched the harps of heaven, and made the saints rejoice, and say, as Peter said to Jesus on the mountain, "Lord, it is good for us to be here"....
>
> There is a solemn pleasure in ruminating on the past; in calling up the usage of primitive days, when the saints lived in tents, and worshipped at altars built of stone, unchanged by art, within the shade of some hallowed grove. The native simplicity of the camp-meeting scene represented, in some degree, those days of antiquity.[4]

Henry Boehm recorded his visit to "the first camp-meeting on the [Delmarva] peninsula," 1805. There he saw "multitudes of tents," for "thousands came to the feast of tabernacles." It was in such places that people made life-giving contact with the God of creation. "Worshiping in nature's magnificent temple, the preachers and the people got new inspiration."[5]

---

[4] Charles Giles. Pioneer. New-York: Lane & Sandford, 1844, 95; 112&113.
[5] J.B. Wakeley. *The Patriarch of One Hundred Years ... Henry Boehm*. New York: Nelson & Phillips; Cincinnati: Hitchcock & Walden, 1875, 128&129.

Henry Boehm

Nathan Bangs, along with Henry Ryan and William Case, led Canada's first camp meeting (1805), at Adolphustown, on the Bay of Quinte in Upper Canada. He left us this impression of night time on the camp ground: "The night was clear and serene, and the scene being new to us, a peculiar solemnity upon all minds. The lights glowing among the trees and above the tents, and the voice of prayer and praise mingling and ascending into the star-lit night, altogether inspired the heart with emotions better felt than described."[6]

Mary Woods Apess was a Native American whose husband (also Native American) was a Methodist Protestant preacher. Her account of her own experience at a camp meeting reveals its profound impact on her life. She also paints a compelling picture of the camp ground as a meeting place between heaven and earth.

> One day upon the camp ground, there was a light from heaven shone into my soul, above the brightness of the sun. I lost sight of all earthly things – heaven was open to my view, and the glory of the upper world beamed upon my soul. My body of clay was all that hindered my flying up to meet Jesus in the air. How long I remained in this happy frame of mind I do

---

[6] Abel Stevens. *The Life and Times of Nathan Bangs, D.D.* New York: Carlton & Porter, 1863, 151.

not know. But when I came to my recollection, my Christian friends were around me singing the sweet songs of heaven; and I thought I was in the suburbs of glory. And when I saw them, they looked like angels, for they were praising God. I felt the love of God like a river flowing into my soul.[7]

Russell E. Richey roots the camp meeting experience in the larger – and sometimes earlier – context of outdoor worship. "Accustomed to reaching crowds by preaching in fields, on greens, and in public squares, British Methodist missionaries to the new world found that very different settings – in the woods, under spreading oaks, in shady groves – would congregate Americans. So began the saga of Methodism in the American woodland."

After a time, the Wesleys and other British Methodists were excluded from preaching in regular parish churches. Outdoor preaching places gave them opportunities to reach people who were, for whatever reason, unable or unwilling to worship in those churches. There was little in the way of structures or laws to limit the size of the crowds that would gather. Richey sees that experience as preparation for ministry in America. This new wilderness became the venue for evangelism and worship. There were dangers in these forests, and considerable work in preparing a camp ground, but many of the earliest preachers, such as William Colbert, found the wilderness to be "pleasingly romantic." There "the Lord displayed his power."[8]

Canadian preacher Joseph Hilts reflected on the role of nature in making camp meetings so valuable to their participants. Like many others, Hilts had a sacramental appreciation of these meetings and their settings, for they were capable of lifting people to an experience of heaven.

> If there is any place on this earth that is more like heaven than a good live camp-meeting, I should like to hear from it. I would be pleased to know where it is, and on what grounds the claim is made. To commune with nature is, to a devout mind, a precious privilege. To commune with good people is a blessed means of grace. And to commune with God is a greater blessing than either or both of these. To hold converse with nature, tends to expand the intellect and quicken the sensibilities. To hold friendly intercourse with the good elevates, refines, and stimulates the social and moral elements of our being. And to commune with God purifies and exalts our whole nature, and inspires us to a holier life and a fuller consecration to the service of God.

---

[7] Barry O'Connell, ed. *William Apess, A Son of the Forest and Other Writings* (1831). Amherst, MA: University of Massachusetts Press, 1997, 81&82.

[8] Russell E. Richey. *Methodism in the American Forest*. New York: Oxford University Press, 2015, 4; 35.

> In the original idea of the camp-meeting we are at the same time, and in the same place, brought in converse with nature, in religious fellowship with the good and in sweet communion with God. I know of no place where the ethical, social and spiritual wants of humanity are more fully provided for than at the camp meeting. There some of the most soul-inspiring scenes that earth can furnish may be witnessed. When a strong religious influence is felt by the assembled worshippers as, with cheerful voices they ring out the melody of their gladdened hearts, where is the soul so dead as not to feel an impulse drawing heavenward. The trees that surround this leafy temple seem to catch the spirit of song and send back to the ears of the happy worshippers in pleasing echoes the very words they are giving utterance to. The leaves upon the forest trees as they are swept by the ascending currents of air that are heated by the 'light stand' fires, seem to vie with the human singers as they rustle to the praise of Him who gave to them their numbers and their beauty. Even the shadows cast by the trees and limbs that intercept the lights of the camp-fires seem to enter into the spirit of the occasion, and point upward to a realm where darkness is unheard of and shadows are unknown.[9]

Even when the natural venue looked unattractive, or the weather challenging, the camp ground remained a holy place, a place where people came together in the presence and power of God. George Peck described such a place near Truxville, Pennsylvania, in 1825: "The ground was rough and unpromising, but it was soon made evident that, like the place where Jacob laid his head upon a pile of stones, it was 'the house of God and the gate of heaven.'"[10]

African American camp meetings also looked to "rural, sparsely populated areas" as the proper environment for these gatherings, for practical as well as symbolic, spiritual reasons.

> Water and pasture land were needed to support a large crowd, as well as a place to park wagons and carriages, and a place for horses and mules to graze. The site was usually located in a large grove, where smaller trees could be cleared and larger trees could provide a sheltering canopy.

These camp grounds became important gathering places for African Americans to share faith and common experiences; to break away from arduous work and loneliness. "But most came excited and anxious to hear the word of God." Like those attending camp meetings across the continent, but from situations distinctly their own, "they gathered to commune

---

[9] Joseph H. Hilts. Experiences of a Backwoods Preacher. Wiarton, ON: Bruce County Historical Society (Reprint), 1986, 95&96.

[10] George Peck. *Early the Bounds Methodism within of the Old Genesee Conference (etc.)*. New York: Carlton & Porter, 1860, 432.

in nature under the stars, to renew their spirits, and to fulfill a deep and abiding need."[11]

In our own time the connection between creation and worship may be downplayed or taken for granted, and this is a serious mistake. It may be more difficult for churches that have minimal green space around them, but even in such cases it may be possible to create a small garden, courtyard, or display area to give natural elements a greater presence. Yet nothing can replace the immersion in the outdoors offered by camp grounds.

Michigan's Eaton Rapids Camp Meeting has long given people an inspired and renewing experience in its setting of great natural beauty, captured in a 1950 poem by Marjorie Louise Snell. In a way familiar to many at camp meetings, nature points people to God, and God deepens our experience of nature. Here the Creator gives peace and joy in "The beautiful camp ground," and in turn his presence gives her "eyes to see / The wonders of His land!"

> 'Mid towering oaks our cottage stands
> Upon a wooded knoll.
> And from the spacious porch we view
> The Grand's majestic roll.
> When winter's bound the river in
> And ground is bleak with snow,
> It makes me sad to see this place
> Where in the summer's glow
> The hills are thick with woodland flowers
> And bird's song fill the air.
> Where sky is blue and hearts are light.
> And joy is everywhere.
> When winter's cold has left the land,
> A call the breezes bring;
> I leave the city far behind
> And go to meet the spring.
> I stand among the scented pines,
> My heart so gay and bold;
> I watch the awe inspiring sight
> When buds first light behold.
> I want to cry, or laugh and sing,
> And throw my arms around
> The whole of the enthralling scene
> The beautiful camp ground!
> I love it so, for one can be

---

[11] Minuette Floyd. *A Place to Worship (etc.)*. University of South Carolina Press, 2018, 19.

So close to nature there;
My heart is filled with peace and calm,
I lift to God a prayer.
The Father up above us all
With His all-powerful hand,
Has given me eyes with which to see
The wonders of His land![12]

---

[12] David & Marybeth Baggett. With Joelee Bateman. *At the Bend of the River Grand (etc.)*. Lexington, KY: Emeth, 2016 131&132.

6

Expanded Fellowship

"...that you and I may be mutually encouraged by each other's faith."[1]

"And when we there [heaven] arrive / Our parting will be o'er.
We'll join the saints above the skies / And shout forever more,
'All glory to the Lamb.' / 'Til then let us endure
And help each other on our way / Toward that happy land."[2]

Camp meetings were never intended to replace or undermine the work of local churches or alternative forms of revival. They served to strengthen the ordinary ministries of the church as they renewed and refreshed its ministers and people. Each form of ministry was designed to work cooperatively with the others so that the whole Church would fulfill its converting and sanctifying mission.

Protracted meetings were seen by some as rivals or even replacements to camp meetings. These local events allowed people to remain in their homes and at their work even as they devoted parts of successive days to the cause of revival. B.W. Gorham wrote in his *Camp Meeting Manual*, that there is a place for both protracted and camp meetings. There is no reason to abandon one to make room for another – they have different roles to play that complement each other.

> It often happens that the fire is kindled on the Camp Ground, and burns in the form of a blessed revival carried forward by means of the Protracted Meeting all winter. On the other hand, if extensive revivals have prevailed over a district of country during the winter, and added many to the church,

---

[1] Romans 1:12, NIV.
[2] Anon., early American Methodist hymn, found in Lester Ruth. *Early Methodist Life and Spirituality: A Reader*. Nashville: Abingdon, 2005, 273.

what better thing can she and her children do, than to retire from the cares of the world, for a week, and renew their vows and brighten their hopes just at that period of the year when the faith of the faithful is likeliest to wane, and when the half fledged piety of the young converts has oftenest yielded to worldliness."

Gorham pointed out that even protracted meetings, held in local churches for an extended period, seeking similar spiritual ends, "do not amount to anything like a general convocation of the membership of the church from an extended territory, to labor and pray together for the general good." The focus of protracted meetings remains local, within a congregation or cluster of congregations, without providing the necessary change of environment and without the larger fellowship drawn together for camp meetings.[3] Camp meetings gathered large numbers of ministers and church members from across a given region or beyond, to celebrate something they held in common, something central and motivational in their lives – something that could easily be lost amid the responsibilities, temptations, and distractions of daily life. They offered a sense of belonging to a larger body of Christians than they would ordinarily encounter in their local churches, communities, and even circuits. "By calling large numbers of our ministers and people together, to labor and enjoy in concert, they improve the bonds of Christian union among us."

A.P. Mead argued that camp meetings, in a way different from *any* other denominational meeting or conference, could break through the isolation and competitiveness of the clergy who took part.

> Our modern quarterly meetings, where indeed we continue to have them at all, usually call together but two of us, the Presiding Elder and the pastor. Our District meetings, which are far from universal, are not even intended to meet the want alluded to. Our Annual Conferences are seasons of exhausting toil and care. And, in a word, with all the other usages of Methodism, there is still wanting some season of great and general interest, that shall convoke these men of God in considerable numbers, and permit them, disburthened of all worldly care, to drink together at the fountain of mercy, to cement their friendships at the foot of the cross, and to lose their selfishness, and pride, and unholy ambition, while bathing together in a

---

[3] In focusing on an earlier time, it often seems natural and appropriate to use past tense, just as present tense best serves conversation about today's reality. However, since insights and observations of both often run parallel to each other, along a continuum they both share, it will be important to avoid unnecessary compartmentalization, just as it is important to recognize principles and experiences that have endured over time. B.W. Gorham. *Camp Meeting Manual* (etc.). Boston: H.V. Degen, 1854, 32-37.

common ocean of love.[4]

While it could be questioned whether a camp meeting could accomplish this task completely, Mead's point is well taken and might well address a similar situation among pastors in our tradition today. If, for example, the annual conferences of Mead's time were, or could be, "seasons of exhausting toil and care," how much more these same events have become in ours! But camp meetings, along with ministries derived from them, have a very different reason for being, one that actually nourishes and empowers the body of Christ.

The gathering of so many people, preachers among them, away from their usual activities, in the beauty of creation, sharing a single, well understood purpose, in the power of the Spirit, could restore ministers and lay people alike to the depth of their original calling and the bonds of their essential fellowship. There, on the sacred ground where so many found new life in Christ and new purpose in life, blurred vision could be brought to clarity and new steps could be confidently taken on "the path of life."[5] There both familiar hymns and songs newly written could lift people's hearts to God in thanksgiving and praise. There the Word of God could be alive, inspiring, and motivating, without its impact being blunted by a tendency to move too quickly back into an old habit, or forward into whatever "next thing" demanded people's attention.

The official summary of the 1861 season at Wesleyan Grove in Massachusetts made the same point for all participants. There are other events that bring laity and clergy together over the course of a year. "The camp-meetings, however, afford the greatest facilities for making and renewing acquaintances with large numbers of the membership of the churches and societies."[6]

One of the facts of life for many of today's churches is a sense of isolation, unless ways can be found to bring people together for a common purpose or celebration. The reality of the universal body of Christ, even of one's own denomination, can be lost or obscured by this isolation. Young people may not recognize fellow Christians at school who happen to belong to other churches. The sense of being part of something larger than oneself can be compromised by lack of familiarity. In our time, distrust and a wholesale breakdown of shared identity makes it difficult for people

---

[4] A.P. Mead. *Manna in the Wilderness, or the Grove and its Altar (etc.)*. Philadelphia: Perkinpine & Higgins, 1860, 35.

[5] Psalm 16:11, NIV.

[6] H. Vincent. *History of the Camp-Meeting and Grounds at Wesleyan Grove, Martha's Vineyard (etc.)*. Lee & Shepard, 1870, 71.

to find common ground even within their own traditions. In my experience, several kinds of events have overcome some or all of this, to reveal the richness of shared faith and outreach. Included here are pilgrimages to the Holy Land, Paul's Greece, and Wesley's England; cross-cultural missions in Northern Ireland and the island of Andros; Christian concerts and conferences, and Family Bible Camp, located at The Camp at Findley, Findley Lake, New York, which continues the camp meeting tradition.

Early camp meetings also attracted curious onlookers, "opposers," skeptics, "rowdies," and even persecutors, some of whom went home changed people. "Multitudes hear the gospel at Camp Meetings who rarely or never attend church services elsewhere; and of those attracted to the place as they have been, by the singularity of the occasion, thousands have been converted to God." Those who argued that local churches and protracted meetings could or should supersede camp meetings neglected the fact that so many who made their way to the forest camp ground were unlikely to show up at those local gatherings. Gorham points out that people will often be ready to open their lives to the offer of grace at a camp meeting, simply because of the nature of that event:

> These meetings are perhaps never held without being attended by persons under a painful sense of unforgiven sin, and who go there with an intention, often secret it may be, but firmly fixed nevertheless, to avail themselves of the extraordinary facilities there afforded for seeking salvation.[7]

Camp meetings offered spiritual hospitality, shepherding, and encouragement to anyone who responded to the Word of life.

James Finley reminded those who might undervalue camp meetings: "Many were converted who would not have heard the Gospel; besides, backsliders were reclaimed, and believers were quickened and built up in Christian faith." (W.P. Strickland, ed. Sketches of Western Methodism (etc.). Cincinnati: Methodist Book Concern, 1855.) One pertinent example came at a camp meeting near Lake Erie where an unlikely participant found salvation:

> Many mariners from the port of Erie were there, and some of them became the subjects of awakening grace. I [Finley] heard one say ..., "Mr. B. is down, crying for mercy," [to which a local sheriff responded,] "If the Methodists can make him a better man, it is more than the commonwealth of Pennsylvania can do, for he has been in nearly all the prisons of the state. This called my attention to Mr. B., whom I found in great distress, earnestly seeking the salvation of his soul. I gave him all the instruction I could, and soon the light of heaven broke on him, and the Sun of righteous-

---

[7] B.W. Gorham, *Camp Meeting Manual (etc.)*. Boston: H.V. Degen, 1854, 18.

ness arose with healing in its beams. He was soundly converted, and what fines and imprisonments could not accomplish, the grace of God amply secured. He lived and died a good man.[8]

Camp meetings offered sacred space and time, opportunities to engage with God and with fellow Christians unlike any others in ordinary church life, not as an escape, but as a powerful enrichment for entire churches and communities. "The ambience which enveloped the total camp experience created a level of expectation for Christian worship, fellowship, and spiritual experience which was rarely replicated in other settings."[9]

Camp meetings also provided a venue for countless people who found both faith and a clear call to ministry. Orange Scott, who became one of the founders of the Wesleyan Methodist Connexion in the United States, recalled a camp meeting in Barre, Vermont: "During that meeting I embraced every opportunity to go forward for prayers, up to the last night of the meeting. ... Then I was enabled to submit to God, take Christ without reserve, trust Him with all my ransomed powers, and find peace in believing, and joy in the Holy Ghost." On the foundation of this conversion, "he threw himself into the work of the church and was soon appointed to a circuit even though he had no means of transportation. That means he was more a circuit walker than a circuit rider at first, but somehow he made it work."[10]

Such conversions and vocations could happen in local settings as well, but camp meetings especially lent themselves to this kind of radical commitment.

Fellowship among friends and strangers was a wonderful part of Methodist life, one that continues, whether fully or in attenuated form, even today. The distinctive fellowship of Methodist people transcended local or regional boundaries and connected people even as they connected with the God who brought them together and gave them life. Lester Ruth writes:

> Affectionate Methodist fellowship was both appealing and countercultural. Given a context where honor and status were the building blocks of relationships ... the basing of human relationships on grace that moved the heart was striking, even contagious. Thus the embodying of a community

---

[8] W.P. Strickland, ed. *Autobiography of Rev. James B. Finley (etc.)*. Cincinnati: Methodist Book Concern, 1855, 294; 303.

[9] Wayne E. Caldwell, ed. *Reformers and Revivalists: History of The Wesleyan Church*. Indianapolis: Wesley Press, 1992, 164.

[10] Lucius C. Matlack, *The Life of Rev. Orange Scott (etc.)*. New York: C. Prindle & L.S. Matlack, 1847, 57&58; Robert Black & Keith Drury. *The Story of the Wesleyan Church*. Indianapolis: Wesleyan Publishing House, 2012, 27&28.

of grace was part of the appeal of Methodism. ... A Methodist's experience of this fellowship was often connected directly to her or his experience of God.[11]

Henry Boehm wrote of an 1806 camp meeting on Dover Circuit, in Delaware, at about the time Holy Communion was celebrated: "O how the power and love of God unites the hearts of his people. Glory to my God and Saviour that I have lived to see such times of the outpouring of his Spirit!" Orange Scott included a hymn in his 1830 collection that spoke of this same reality:

> Our souls in love together knit
> Cemented into one,
> One hope, one heart, one mind, one voice,
> 'Tis heaven on earth begun.[12]

Today, even amid strained relationships among groups of Methodists, and within the larger ecumenical context, there remains a significant bond among people, pastors, and churches in the Wesleyan tradition. While this bond has weakened over time, I have experienced it in pan-Methodist gatherings and in traveling to Canada, England, Ireland, Scotland, South Korea, Poland, and the Bahamas. I have known it in our annual Family Bible Camp and in New Room conferences. I have seen it in the collection of artifacts in the World Methodist Museum at Lake Junaluska, North Carolina, and at the restored 1792 Methodist church at Hay Bay, Ontario. While differences of experience and practice remain, I have sensed an overwhelming unity in our common Wesleyan Christianity. This kind of modern experience draws upon an even stronger tie among early Methodists, and in particular those who together made the pilgrimage from seeking and conviction, through conversion and new life, and on toward the transformation Wesley called Christian perfection. All of this happened in camp meetings, those extended times away from distractions when the one Spirit built them into one body.[13] It was in such settings that many realized the truth that "in Christ we, though many, form one body, and each member belongs to all the others."[14]

---

[11] Lester Ruth, *Early Methodist Life and Spirituality: A Reader*. Nashville: Abingdon, 2005, 260.

[12] J.B. Wakeley. *The Patriarch of One Hundred Years ... Henry Boehm*. New York: Nelson & Phillips; Cincinnati: Hitchcock & Walden, 1875, 149; Orange Scott, ed. *The New and Improved Camp Meeting Hymn Book (etc.)*. n.c: Published by the Compiler, 1830, 40.

[13] Ephesians 4:4; I Corinthians 12:13

14 Romans 12:5, NIV.

Camp meetings called for practical cooperation in arranging travel and accommodations, as well as the actual organization and flow of a meeting. This was especially true of the ministers who would lead the formal parts of the experience. Cane Ridge involved the combined efforts of Presbyterian, Methodist, and Baptist preachers. Then Methodists quickly made the camp meeting a key component in their growth and ethos. Methodist preachers, including bishops, worked together to bring the Word, celebrate Holy Communion, shepherd people through spiritual crisis and celebration, and set the tone for the life of a camp ground. Of course, egos, quirks, and annoyances will surface among even the most dedicated disciples, as George Brown found, requiring leadership to keep even the preachers focused on their all-important purpose and calling. Brown carried this kind of responsibility for a time at Methodist Protestant camp meetings. He described his work in this way:

> ... to give a right direction to all the ministerial talent on hand, both local and itinerant, so as to keep down the little, petty jealousies too often found among the preachers on such occasions, and to employ the whole force at his command, both ministerial and lay, in the labors of the altar, so as to bring as many souls as possible to Christ....[15]

Lorenzo Dow

---

[15] George Brown. *Recollections of Itinerant Life: Including Early Reminiscences.* Cincinnati: R.W. Carroll; Springfield, OH: Methodist Protestant Publishing House, 1866, 122.

Charles Giles mentioned the fellowship and anticipation among those making their way to the camp ground. "By the interchange of thoughts on the way our journey was made pleasant and profitable: with bounding hearts we moved along over the rough road, reflecting on the past, and cogitating on the events to come. So the time passed away till we arrived at the place we were so anxious to gain." One part of the anticipation had to do with those who were expected to preach, especially if they were well known or distinctive in some way. As Giles made his way to this particular camp meeting, he could scarcely avoid thinking about Lorenzo Dow, whose powerful preaching and idiosyncratic style were legendary. "He [Dow] evidently studied to be singular in everything; and by the influence of these intentional oddities, he was thrown into an orbit distinct from all others, and left to move alone in his glory. So he became a spectacle for the world to behold."[16]

At Cane Ridge and some of the camp meetings that followed, there could be difficulties in the selection of preachers and control of the events. While I have not encountered many such difficulties, the cases of William Burke and John Johnson come to mind. Burke, a Methodist, preached at Cane Ridge, but was relegated to a secondary role. Johnson, a rough-hewn frontiersman, attended a Virginia camp meeting seeking only a respite after a hard season, yet he felt the rejection of aristocratic preachers who only reluctantly invited him to preach, and then at an inconvenient time. Both these preachers did well in their limited situations. Johnson did so well as to put his aristocratic colleagues to shame.[17]

But most Methodist preachers enjoyed the fellowship of their colleagues and subordinated any rivalries to their common purpose in sharing the gospel. With their lay counterparts, they could sing,

In Jesus' name behold we meet,
far from an evil world retreat,
And all its frantic ways...."[18]

There was a special bond among Methodists, whose theology was foundational to the preaching and spirituality of their own camp meetings. But that fellowship could extend to others who shared the common ap-

---

[16] Charles Giles. *Pioneer* (etc.). New-York: Lane & Sandford, 1844, 95&96.

[17] Paul K. Conkin, *Cane Ridge: America's Pentecost*. Madison, WI: University of Wisconsin Press, 1990, 96; John Berry McFerrin. *History of Methodism in Tennessee, 1818-1840*. Nashville: Southern Methodist Publishing House, 1873, III: 51-53; 55&56.

[18] W. M. McDonald & S. Hubbard, eds. *The Wesleyan Sacred Harp (etc.)*. Boston: John P. Jewett, et al., 1856, 195.

proach to the way of salvation embodied in those meetings. Joseph Hilts saw that Canadian camp meetings could transcend ethnic barriers, especially among those of European stock. These were times when spiritual life in the power of God's presence would also overpower the usual denominational divisions in a given community or region. He said, "at some of these meetings I have seen English, Irish, Scottish, Germans and Canadians all sitting together on the camp-ground – Methodists, Presbyterians, Baptists, Church of England, and in a few instances Roman Catholics have been heard singing the same songs of praise together." Closer to their denominational homes, there was, in Canada as in the States, a special bond between people whose churches shared a common Wesleyan heritage. One example Hilts gives involved members of Methodist and Evangelical Association churches. He describes a camp meeting in Hanvover, Ontario, where people from these groups worked especially well together:

> At the meeting in Hanover there were some members of the Evangelical Association. They enjoyed the services very much, and some of them did all they could to help on with the work. Their strong, manly utterances did good, although their words were broken, and their cheerful, encouraging expressions of faith, and hope, and love, endeared them to our [Methodist] people generally.[19]

George Walker wrote of a local Ohio meeting that took place in two languages, English and German. Speakers alternated in such a way that somehow the mixed audience got the same message and responded accordingly:

> Last night we held a love-feast, composed of Germans and English. Some related their experience in the German language, and others spoke in English. It worked admirably well. We then called forward the mourners, and fifteen presented themselves for prayers. ... I opened the doors of the Church, and seven more were added to the fold. This morning brother Maley preached in English, and Dr. Schmucker is to preach in the German language, and I am to follow him with a sermon in English. We are hoping and praying for a mighty display of the power of God.

Walker was pleased with the results of this unlikely plan, saying "May God continue to shake all nations, till the whole earth shall be filled with his glory!"[20]

---

[19] Joseph H. Hilts. *Experiences of a Backwoods Preacher*. Wiarton, ON: Bruce County Historical Society [Reprint], 1986, 113&114.

[20] Maxwell Pierson Gaddis. *Brief Reflections of the Late Rev George Walker (etc.)*. Cincinnati: Swormstedt & Poe, 1857, 298-300.

The use of camp meetings by German circuit riders was an important way for their churches "to reach and organize German speakers across Pennsylvania, Ohio, and beyond, in the United States and in Canada." One great factor that energized this movement and equipped the German churches to meet this need, was the adoption of the camp meeting. These early gatherings, held by United Brethren and Evangelicals [Evangelical Association], attracted Germans from "sometimes a hundred miles.... These camp meetings [like their English counterparts] came to be considered sacred. For many were converted there. The desire to help win their neighbors to Christ" saw "the children of God greatly edified and advanced in the work of grace." For these German churches and the English Methodists alike, "The number of converts through the camp meetings during the fifty years when they were most popular mounted into the thousands. Many prominent ministers of the church were led to their conversion and call to the ministry through these meetings."[21]

The United Brethren in Christ and their modern counterparts have always remembered the iconic moment in 1767, when two German pastors, representing two different, though parallel denominations, William Otterbein and Martin Boehm, discerned and celebrated their unity while attending a "great meeting" at Isaac Long's Barn in Lancaster County, Pennsylvania. The great meeting joined other tributaries that shaped the American camp meeting. This particular gathering brought people together from several German denominations, people who, like many others at similar meetings, found a deep unity in Christ. It was there at Long's Barn where Otterbein and Boehm greeted each other as Otterbein said, "We are brethren."

That great meeting was followed by many more, into the 19th century – ten in 1800 alone. The spiritual heart of those meetings, as with the camp meetings held by the denomination, was identical to that of the other churches in our tradition. Other signs of unity included Otterbein's presence at Francis Asbury's ordination, and a longstanding recognition of the common theology and purpose shared by United Brethren and Methodists – and, for that matter, by UBs and the Evangelical Association. As it was at Long's Barn, so it continued in years that followed. These outdoor revivals were able to transcend denominational barriers and bring participants to a profound sense of Christian unity.

Great meetings in Virginia in 1800, "were attended with rich effusions of divine power and grace. At some of these, the people fell like mown

---

[21] Raymond W. Albright. *A History of the Evangelical Church*. Harrisburg: Evangelical Press, 1942, 153; 156&157.

grass before the Lord. The cry and distress of soul manifested was great, and great was the succeeding joy." Similar descriptions followed camp meeting after camp meeting, in every part of the Wesleyan family.[22]

Later, William Yost, a preacher of the Evangelical Association, would exemplify the ability of Evangelicals and United Brethren to serve as co-laborers in the Gospel. In this he also demonstrates the importance of these meetings to the overall ministry of his church. One summer, he tells us, he took part in four Evangelical camp meetings in Pennsylvania.

> I also spent a few days at a camp-meeting conducted by the United Brethren, in Millcreek Township, Lebanon County [Pennsylvania], and, upon invitation, assisted in the services. It was a successful meeting. The ministers and people of this denomination possess the same spirit, and work by the same methods that we employ, and we should be one.[23]

William Yost

A powerful example of cross-cultural ministry at camp meetings is the work of indigenous and European Canadian evangelists who ministered among indigenous people, sometimes from several nations.

---

[22] Henry G. Spayth. *United Brethren in Christ*. Circleville, OH: Conference Office of the United Brethren in Christ, 1851, 41&42; 80&81; 84; 89; 94; 142-144.

[23] William Yost. *Reminiscences*. Cleveland: Publishing House of the Evangelical Association, 1911, 98&99.

John Sunday

One camp meeting, held on Snake Island in Lake Simcoe [Upper Canada] in 1828, brought all these people together in common worship in the forest. Among the speakers, John Sunday and Joseph Sawyer were Indian Methodist preachers, while William Case was the leading white Methodist missionary to the Indians. The power of that meeting was evident in the way it ended:

> The Lord's Supper was administered to a deeply affected people. At three o'clock, the preachers and visitors bid farewell to the Simcoe Indians, who followed their friends to the water, and were reluctant to let them go. Like Paul and the elders of Ephesus, they all knelt down on the shore, and commended each other to the care of their Heavenly Father. The sails were set for Holland Landing, the poor Indians were left bathed in tears, and the landing was reached by dark, thus the Gospel continued to spread along the shores and streams of Lake Simcoe, and thus the Gospel commenced on Snake Island, in the lake.[24]

Historian John Carroll preserved much information about camp meetings among the indigenous population of Canada. In the following example, as in some similar events elsewhere, a woman was among the

---

[24] George F. Playter. *The History of Methodism in Canada (etc.)*. Toronto: Anson Green, 1862, Vol. 1, 355&356.

speakers. Peter Jones, a Mississauga Methodist preacher, was part of an 1828 Sydney Camp Meeting, led by William Case, the chief organizer of mission work among native people of Upper Canada. At this meeting several prominent Canadian Methodist preachers participated, including Jones and Case, Egerton Ryerson, who "preached with power," and a Miss Barnes, who "gave a discourse on the incarnation, death, resurrection, and ascension of our Lord and Saviour; she spoke fluently, with a strong voice, and very figuratively." Among the native participants, along with Jones, were members of communities in Rice Lake, Grape Island, and Gananoque. John Sunday and other indigenous preachers also took part. Carroll describes this meeting as "radiant with the glory of salvation," long remembered "as a time of great power and interest." Peter Jones had himself been converted at an 1823 camp meeting at Ancaster, near Hamilton, Upper Canada.[25]

William Case

Jones was back in Ancaster six years after his conversion for another notable camp meeting, where he rejoiced in the variety of participants and reflected on his own conversion "upon the very spot."

---

[25] John Carroll. *Case and His Cotemporaries*. Toronto: Wesleyan Conference Office, 1873, Vol. 3, 184; Scott McLaren. *Pulpit, Press, and Politics: Methodists and the Market for Books in Upper Canada*. Toronto: University of Toronto Press, 2019, 91.

> A Camp meeting which is held about a mile and a half from the Conference, commenced this day. In the afternoon I attended the Camp ground, and was not a little animated to see the white people, the Mohawks, and the Mississaugas, assemble upon the very spot, where I first made the resolution to seek the salvation of my soul six years ago last June. The Camp meeting was then held about 100 yards from where it is now; but during the anguish of my soul, burdened with sin and sorrow, I retired to this sacred spot to form the resolution of becoming a Christian: Little did I think that I should see such a day as this! Little did I think that I should ever see such a company of praying Indians upon this ground. O the peculiar and wonderful dispensations of God to the children of men! Surely his own arm hath brought salvation and deliverance to his chosen people, and himself hath gotten him the victory."

In 1829 Jones and John Sunday preached to Indians and whites in a Yonge Street camp meeting. Jones wrote, "The power of the Spirit rested upon both whites and Indians and several fell to the ground under the power of God, and were obliged to be carried away to their tents." Shared experiences like these were common in Jones' ministry. Their form and spiritual dynamics had become familiar features of Methodist camp meetings across the continent and in very different demographics. For example, Jones, along with John Sunday, William Case, Egerton Ryerson, and others preached at an 1828 camp meeting, in eastern Upper Canada, which brought together Indians from several nearby communities, including Rice Lake, Grape Island, Kingston, and Gananoque. Again, the spiritual dynamics paralleled those in other settings. One example was "a powerful prayer meeting [one] evening, sinners crying for mercy, and professing Christians seeking for sanctification."[26]

In 1835, James Evans described in detail the construction of a camp ground designed for Indian camp meetings. His letter shows the similarity in design with camp grounds in many other places, along with adaptations required for the intended participants.

> The spot selected by the Indian Chiefs and myself for the purpose was on the bank of the St. Clair River, having a gentle inclination toward the water, and admirably adapted by Nature's God to seat a congregation in such a manner as to give to all the best possible opportunity of seeing and hearing in the open air. The Indians were much elated in prospect of this meeting; some of whom, having tasted the joys of salvation at a similar one at Muncey Town, and being instructed from holy writ that God is

---

[26] Peter Jones. *Life and Journals of KAH-KE-WA-QUO-NA-BY: Rev. Peter Jones, Wesleyan Missionary.* Toronto: Anson Green, 1860, 253; 224&235; 156&157.

every where [sic] present, confided in Him for his promised presence on the St. Clair; while several, who had never enjoyed such a privilege, were anxious to taste the blessings of which their converted friends often spoke with ecstacy [sic]. All readily and perseveringly engaged in clearing the ground, which we found in a state of nature, strewed with the trunks of old trees, which had once reared their stately heads and bid defiance for ages to the howling tempest, but which had at length fallen before the unsparing scythe of time. These were cut in pieces and drawn off the ground. The underbrush or small trees were also cut down, and formed into a sort of hedge or fence; while the larger trees were left in all heir majestic grandeur, towering over our heads, forcibly reminding us, while sheltered by their luxuriant foliage, of the promise of Him whom we were met to adore, "The sun shall not smite thee by day, nor the moon by night."

Evans goes on to describe the preacher's stand and congregational seats – made "by splitting large trees into halves or quarters, according to their size." For those who would come without necessary shelter, tents were provided, with suitable arrangements for sleep and cooking.

Far from the obscurity we might well imagine for such a place, this new camp ground attracted Methodist preachers, denominational officials, and others, from as far away as Ohio and Montreal. The meetings attracted Christian Indians and those not a part of the church. A canoe filled with curious non-Christian Indians from the Lake Huron region found themselves unexpectedly caught up in the spirit of the event to the point of experiencing conversion.

The weather included a deluge, but the compelling purpose of the meetings eclipsed any other consideration, so that Evans could write, "As I have heard no complaints from our brethren, I humbly trust they experienced no indisposition from this their camp-meeting excursion; and happy should I be to meet them again on the same spot, even under the same circumstances."[27]

One thing to notice in Evans' description is that, for the Indians present, a camp meeting was not a romantic journey down memory lane. The forest was their natural environment. Yet it was time away from many of their daily activities and customs, devoted to bringing them closer to God, and to each other through God; providing spiritual food for their journey through and beyond this life. The success of these native camp meetings indicates something of the universality of their attraction. And the willingness of European Canadians, including those of standing, to put up with the discomfort of a good soaking on the camp ground, indicates how de-

---

[27] John Carroll. *Case and His Cotemporaries*. Toronto: Wesleyan Conference Office, 1874, Vol. 4, 79-82.

voted they were to their primary purpose in being there. The attraction of the event to a group making its way down the river represents the appeal of these meetings to people who might never enter a church building or attend services in a settled community.

Several African American preachers mention camp and quarterly meetings involving a wide assortment of participants, including black and white preachers and worshipers. David Smith reported that "when it was announced that a colored Elder was to hold a quarterly meeting, the people (white and colored) would come ... from all parts of the country in great crowds." George White was called into ministry at an 1804 camp meeting that attracted "... people of all descriptions," where "many were made the subjects of saving grace, and believers were filled with perfect love." Jarena Lee was part of an African Methodist Episcopal camp meeting in Delaware that drew "immense large congregations." She says, "The people came from all parts, without distinction of sex, size, or color.... There appeared to be as great union with the white friends. ... Right Rev. Bishop Allen was present." After a Maryland camp meeting at which she preached, she said, "all glory to God, for the good done at Camp meetings, though much persecuted, they are a glorious meeting [sic] to me. I pray God to protect the Camp-meetings, while I thank him for the invention."[28]

David Smith recalled an earlier experience, a Methodist Episcopal revival in Pennsylvania, where he "saw the slaves and their masters singing, shouting and praising God together. All seemed to be one in Christ Jesus; there was no distinction as to the rich or poor, bond or free, but all were melted into sweet communion with the spirit [sic] and united in Christian fellowships...." Here was a glimpse, a momentary vision of barriers that could be transcended under the power of the Holy Spirit, yet the rarity of this passing moment shows also the stubborn, tragic persistence of such barriers in everyday life.[29]

Camp meetings were an important part of the experience of African American Methodists from the beginning, even when they involved considerable difficulty and sacrifice. David Smith recorded an Ohio camp meeting at which "Bishop William Paul Quinn was stabbed by some ruffi-

---

[28] David Smith. *Biography of Rev. David Smith, of the A.M.E. Zion Church (etc.)*. n.c: Dodo Press (reprint), orig. 1888; Graham Russell Hodges, ed. *Black Itinerants of the Gospel (etc.)*. New York: Palgrave, 2002, 54; Jarena Lee, *Religious Experience and Journal of Mrs. Jerena Lee* (1848), in Susan Houchins, ed. *Spiritual Narratives*. New York & Oxford: Oxford University Press, 1988, 39.

[29] David Smith. *Biography of Rev. David Smith, of the A.M.E. Church (etc.)*. n.c: Dodo Press (reprint), n.d. (orig. 1888), 10.

an, but we are glad to say it was only a flesh wound." Among Jarena Lee's experiences in ministry was a camp meeting held by the African Methodist Episcopal Church in Denton, Maryland.

> Although in a slave State, we had every thing in order, good preaching, a solemn time, and long to be remembered. Some of the poor slaves came happy in the Lord; walked from 20 to 30, and from that to seventy miles, to worship God. Although through hardships they counted it all joy for the excellency of Christ; and before day, they, or a number of them, had to be at home, ready for work; but some of them came as sinners before God, but went away as new creatures in Christ; and they could not be disputed.

In another Maryland community (Middletown), she describes the experience of transformation at the heart of every such gathering, regardless of ethnicity, demography, or denominational expression within the Wesleyan family: "I next attended and preached several times at a camp meeting which continued five days. We had Pentecostal showers – sinners were pricked to the heart, and cried mightily to god [sic] for succor from impending judgment, and I verily believe the Lord was pleased at our weak endeavors to serve him in the tented grove."

Bishop Daniel Payne recalled,

> The first camp-meeting in our (African Methodist Episcopal) Connection … beginning the 12th of August, 1818, with the following ministers present: Bishop Allen, Jacob Tapsico, James Champion, Dorothy Ripley (a female preacher from England), Rev. John Gloucester (of the Presbyterian Church), Sampson Peters, Edward Jackson, Charles Corr. The Lord was present, and nearly one hundred souls were converted.

William Paul Quinn

This gathering, led by William Paul Quinn, took place only two years after the launching of their new denomination. The number of converts indicates a sizable congregation. The list of preachers included a woman, who was also from another country, and a minister from another tradition, one that had its own place in the history of such meetings.[30]

After such experiences, in all their variety, are thoroughly understood - even admitting their imperfections and excesses – camp meetings offered, and in some places continue to offer, concentrated, extended opportunities for spiritual transformation and renewal, for individual participants and for the larger Church, in ways that have never been duplicated or superseded. Even those ministries that maintain portions of the camp meetings' original purposes – such as Christian camps and conference centers – play an indispensable role in the formation of individuals and their communities.

In order for a camp meeting to be all it can and should be, it must have deep roots in its own past and in the traditions of camp meetings and the whole Church. Stories need to be shared of what God has done in the lives of participants, past and present. The purposes for which camp meetings were originally established cannot be lost, forgotten, or regarded as obsolete or unimportant. There must be continuity among all who have been or will be part of the camp meeting community. Each gathering of that community needs to see itself as part of a larger whole, and each new decision, action, or plan affecting its life and ministry must reflect that continuity with its original purpose. "Camp meetings are a place where the past meets the present day. They are a significant historical and living tradition that continues to unfold, a phenomenon that ... will always be a unique place to worship."

That tradition is represented by the familiar setting of the camp ground, so that entering that sacred space immediately brings back memories of people and events that have been deeply important in participants' lives. For some, this will be the place of their conversion, where Jesus first became personally real and involved in their lives. Some will recall a conversation, a song, or a sermon that suddenly brought clarity to a confused mind or direction in the midst of aimless wandering. For others this is the place where Christian friendships were formed, where someone was willing to really listen to an outpouring of pain and where rejoicing was shared as prayers were answered. This may be the place where your life's direction and calling were first heard and affirmed.

---

[30] Daniel A. Payne. *Recollections of Seventy Years*. Nashville: A.M.E. Sunday School Union, 1888, 81.

In order for a camp ground and its meetings to fulfill all of their purposes and promises, we must return again and again, reliably, so that our experience grows and deepens with every gathering. Even if, as in my case, the first visit is short and exploratory, it soon becomes obvious that it takes time for the blessings of camp to fully sink in and do their spiritual work. The very best way to experience camp meeting is immersion in its life.

Along with the beauty of creation, the peacefulness of the camp ground; the attraction of growing friendships, and the bond of shared memories, there is what Minuette Floyd calls "spiritual integrity," an awareness that what happens here matters enough to command and deserve our time, year after year. Spiritual integrity contrasts with the superficial, frenetic, and often meaningless way we too often live in our everyday world – including our vacations.

> Spiritual integrity is still what draws many thousands of people to camp meetings every year. There is something profound about setting aside that sacred time far in advance. Something profound about being in nature and getting under the oak or pine trees. And something profound about choosing to step back in time.

Each person will have their own set of memories, their own hopes for this year's gathering, and their own connection with God, yet none of these is complete without bringing them together. Here is one person's reflection on a lifetime of camp meetings:

> As for me, I continue to imagine the ancestors who left their footprints there and the hard work, determination, sweat, and tears of thousands of people who made camp meeting what it is today. Many have sung, have laughed, have cried, have repented their sins, and have poured out their testimonies during both good and bad years. Many have left the grounds spiritually fulfilled and have journeyed back home committed to a new level of love, joy, and service in their personal endeavors. I look forward to attending camp meeting. The people that I meet and their stories continue to inspire me. I love the preaching, the singing, reconnecting with old friends, and meeting new ones. My parents introduced me to a unique and heartwarming religious tradition. They thought it was important for us to attend. A few years ago, a preacher at Camp Welfare described my own feelings exactly: "I can feel the spirits of those who were here years ago," she told the congregation. "I can still feel the exhilaration."

There are challenges to reaching and maintaining this kind of profound awareness and participation. Some are new, while others have been around from the beginning. Professor Floyd admits, "Though one of the great joys of the camp meeting is this vivid link to our personal and collective past, it is only fair to mention ways in which modern life can dilute the experience for some who attend."

One of these is a tendency for people to come only for a day, or part of a day, perhaps to renew acquaintances, or to hear a particular speaker, to soak up the sun, or just enjoy a brief moment of peace. These are not bad in themselves, but so much less than they could be when we're not in a hurry to move on. We should even encourage shorter visits for people who have never been to this kind of event. But in time, short stays keep people from enjoying the blessings of full participation, and make it harder to let go of the distractions and preoccupations of life at home or work.

Another is our contemporary world's lack of commitment, which has certainly worked its way into the Church. Such lack of commitment does not lend itself to "the same level of intensity" that was so prevalent in an earlier time.

There are adults who will participate in most campground activities, but manage to stay away from worship, and children who will either fail to attend programs or show their disinterest by their misbehavior. Some will have only a superficial awareness of the tradition and purposes of the camp meeting, so that real Christian fellowship is reduced to chatty conversation, perhaps even gossip. "The question is always: What can we do, individually and collectively, to help camp meetings maintain their spiritual integrity?"[31]

---

[31] Minuette Floyd. *A Place to Worship: African American Camp Meetings in the Carolinas*. Columbia, SC: University of South Carolina Press, 2018, 88-90.

7

Point of Commitment

"Praise be to the God and Father of our Lord Jesus Christ! In his great mercy he has given us new birth into a living hope through the resurrection of Jesus Christ from the dead...."[1]

"On Christ, the Solid Rock, I stand; All other ground is sinking sand, All other ground is sinking sand."[2]

Camp meetings afforded an opportunity or opening for people to begin in Christian life, or to move forward from that beginning toward Christian perfection and an eternal destiny. While the message was essentially the same as that of local churches, this particular instrumentality could reach well beyond those likely to relate to a church. The size of many of these events, their very public nature, and their prolonged intensity, away from the pull of ordinary life, were among the reasons for this. Camp meetings could cast the evangelistic net in ways and in scope unavailable even to local revivals.

W.P. Strickland echoed this theme as he surveyed the camp meeting ministry of Bishop Francis Asbury. Here the example comes from a remote part of the Appalachians:

> Among the mountains of Western Virginia the pioneer Methodist preacher had formed his circuit, and established preaching places in the cabins of the settlers. Camp-meetings were generally held in the valley of the Kanawha during the summer months, where from various and distant parts of the wilderness the people would congregate and pitch their tents. Hundreds and thousands would collect together upon such occasions, and the native

---

[1] I Peter 1:3, NIV.

[2] Edward Mote, "The Solid Rock," *Free Methodist Hymnal*. Winona Lake, IN: Free Methodist Publishing House, 1910. #273.

forests would be made vocal with the praises of the assembled throng. Preachers from adjoining circuits and districts would attend these annual feasts, and with a fervency and zeal characteristic of pioneer preachers, they would pour forth strains of burning eloquence that would find their way to the most impenitent hearts; and multitudes to whom the Gospel would otherwise perhaps never have come, were made the happy subjects of converting grace.[3]

B.W. Gorham argued this point in support of the ongoing need for such gatherings: "Multitudes hear the gospel at camp meetings who rarely or never attend church services elsewhere; and of those attracted to the place as they have been, by the singularity of the occasion, thousands have been converted to God." Gorham believed that the time of their usefulness was far from over. Andrew Carroll echoed the point, saying that, far from rendering camp meetings obsolete, changes in church and society had actually increased their usefulness. Reflecting on the "multitude of people" at an Ohio camp meeting, held in "a densely populated" region, he said:

> At these meetings, many persons attend to the preaching of the word, who but seldom if at all, go to Church. These meetings create an excitement in the mind which no other meetings do. ...there are thousands who never enter a church door. They are blind touching their own interests in this respect. Hence we conclude, that the older the country, and the more meeting-houses we have, the greater the necessity for camp meetings.

Carroll went so far as to call for the multiplication of camp meetings: "You ought to have a camp-meeting at least within every ten square miles."[4]

Peter Cartwright lamented a decline in camp meetings by the 1850s. They had always been a major part of his ministry, and they were particularly useful in attracting those unlikely to get involved in conventional churches. He attributed their decline to the growth and affluence he saw in his own denomination, and at the time he saw no reason to expect their revival that would come in the 1860s.

> I was converted on a camp-ground ... and for many years of my early ministry, after I was appointed presiding elder, lived in the tented grove from two to three months in the year.

---

[3] W.P. Strickland, ed. *The Pioneer Bishop: or, The Life and Times of Francis Asbury*. New-York: Carlton & Porter, 1858, 370.

[4] B.W. Gorham. *Camp Meeting Manual: a Practical Book for the Camp Ground*. Boston: H.V. Degen, 1854, 18; Andrew Carroll. *Moral and Religious Sketches and Collections (etc.)*. Cincinnati: Methodist Book Concern, 1857, 35&36.

I am sorry to say that the Methodist Episcopal Church of late years, since they have become numerous and wealthy, have almost let camp meetings die out. I am very certain that the most successful part of my ministry has been on camp-grounds. There the word of God has reached the hearts of thousands that otherwise, in all probability, never would have been reached by the ordinary means of grace.[5]

Similarly, A.P. Mead offered this challenge:

When we shall have church edifices that will accommodate from four thousand to twenty thousand persons, and when we can get our people to attend a meeting for a week at such a church, in such numbers as attend camp meeting, and when the members of such church will be able and willing to feed and lodge such a host for a week, when the persons attending will hire their board during their stay, and when the preachers can be induced to attend and labor at such meeting as they do now at camp meeting, and when there can be excited in the people at large the same desire to attend a meeting thus held as now moves thousands to the encampment, and when a score of other impossibilities shall stand out of the way, then it will do to propose substituting a meeting in the church for this tremendous engine of spiritual power.[6]

Transformations that took place at camp meetings could be dramatic and even extreme, depending on the spiritual condition of the one being acted upon by the Holy Spirit. But the experience of that person had implications for family, friends, and community and the road was not always easy. John Seybert met with a woman who attacked her husband "because the evening before [,] her husband had been converted." In fact, it often happened that one person's good news of salvation drew opposition and even rejection from others. This particular woman "came into the meeting terribly enraged...."

Just as Seybert was about to offer the prayer in the ordinance of baptism, she came in, picked up a stone and attempted to pound her kneeling spouse, who was one of the candidates for baptism, upon the head. Several brethren interfered and prevented her from executing her brutal purpose, when she began to pound the altar, and screamed like a demoniac, cursing and swearing in a most blasphemous manner, in the midst of solemn worship. Finally, finding that she failed to break up the service in this way, this feminine demon drew from the folds of her clothes, where she had concealed it, a large, murderous butcher knife, wrapped in rags. While she was

---

[5] W.P. Strickland, ed. *Autobiography of Peter Cartwright, The Backwoods Preacher*. New York: Carlton & Porter, 1856, 523.

[6] A.P. Mead. *Manna in the Wilderness; or, the Grove and its Altar (etc.)*. Philadelphia: Perkinpine & Higgins, 1860, 33.

unwrapping it, some one dexterously snatched it out of her hands. This made her fairly wild. She charged that her husband had been seduced from his "faith" by these people, and now the whole family would go to hell! She was going to kill herself. At length the friend succeeded in removing her from the grounds.

Thankfully, there was more to this ghoulish story:

Several years afterwards this woman came to another camp meeting on the same grounds. She came in just as he [Brother Seybert] was preaching. She took a seat, and stared hard at the preacher, while he in turn looked upon her with pity. The Lord blessed his word. The woman fell into great distress of soul, began to plead for pardon, and was saved. The change in her life and manner was remarkable. "The Lord hath done this. Hallelujah!" he exclaimed.[7]

James Finley recorded the story of a husband and wife whose dramatic conversion changed them forever. Of special interest in their story was the role of Mononcue, a Wyandotte Indian preacher, and the context of an Indian camp meeting. Near the site of this meeting lived a couple who had never been part of such an event. Out of curiosity, the woman convinced her husband to let her go to the meeting, while he cared for their children at home. The condition set down by the husband was that if she failed to return that afternoon, he would give her a whipping.

This woman was on the camp ground only a short time when she felt the power of God's presence and ached to find God's mercy. Surrounding her were "prayers from many a sympathizing heart." She knew she had overstayed the time set by her husband, but her need to wrestle in prayer was too great for her to pull away. As night fell, "she embraced the cross with all the fervor of her soul, and her burden, like that of Christian's in Bunyan's *Pilgrim*, rolled away…. It was then that she passed from darkness to light….

When she did return home, her husband rejected all she said about her experience, and carried out his threat to beat her. "He raged like a maniac, and swore that he would take vengeance in firing the encampment that night." Like so many others, he was unprepared for the power he would discover in that meeting. When he reached the camp, the strange "groans of the penitent, and shouts of praise of the converted" filled him with overwhelming fear." Before long, his courage and violent intent had melted away; "his knees trembled, his heart quaked, and he fell prostrate upon the ground, crying for mercy." Surrounded by Indians, praying with and for

---

[7] S.P. Spreng. *The Life and Labors of John Seybert, First Bishop of the Evangelical Association*. Cleveland: Lauer & Matill, 1888, 117&118.

him, he wrestled all night. Early the next morning, in an experience that mirrored his wife's,

> God's mercy came, the long agony was over, and the blasphemer and persecutor was changed into a child of God; the heir of hell was made an heir of heaven. To the astonishment of all, after his first bursts of praise were over, he related his cruel conduct to his wife, and his intention, as a matter of revenge, of setting the encampment on fire."

Word of his story reached Mononcue, whose profound wisdom is seen in this response:

> Mononcue stepped up to him, and taking him by the hand said, "Now, my white brother, God converted your wife, and you whipped her for it, and God has converted you. Go home and tell her what God has done for your soul, and let her take the same whip, if she desires so to do, and whip you in return. It is good that God has converted you both. Go in peace, and sin no more." This couple will never forget the Indian camp meeting.

Mononcue knew, as this couple discovered, that conversion had implications for a change of heart, a change of behavior, and a change of character.[8]

Whatever the circumstances of an individual participant, camp meeting worship could produce profound, life changing results. Those who tried to keep things superficial and under control, like James Finley at Cane Ridge, might soon find those expectations impossible to maintain. Post-camp meeting reports commonly mention one hundred new converts, and often add those who sought, and appeared to receive, the gift of perfect love.

Peter Cartwright saw powerful changes take place in camp meetings he was part of. In one of these, two men who were in love with the same woman, came to the meeting filled with hate for each other and armed for a fight. That night, "there was a visible power more than human rested on the congregation," yet nothing could prepare him for what that power would do in the hearts of these men.

> Both these young men were in the congregation, and the Holy Spirit had convicted each of them; their murderous hearts quailed under the mighty power of God, and with dreadful feelings they made for the altar. One entered on the right, the other on the left. Each was perfectly ignorant of the other being there. I went deliberately to each of them, and took their deadly weapons from their bosoms, and carried them into the preachers' tent, and then returned and labored faithfully with them ... nearly all the

---

[8] W.P. Strickland, ed. *Sketches of Western Methodism ... by Rev. James B. Finley*. Cincinnati: Methodist Book Concern, 1855, 519-522.

afternoon and night. These young men had a sore struggle; but the great deep of their hearts was broken up, and they cried hard for mercy....

Within a few minutes of each other, both men rose victorious from the altar. When they saw each other, they walked toward each other "and instantly clasped each other in their arms," causing a great shout from those gathered around. "There were a great many more who were converted that night; and, indeed, it was a night long to be remembered for the clear conversion of souls."[9]

Cartwright once saw a hostile "rowdy" go from making threats to crying out for mercy at the altar. In another case, a woman who had sought the blessing of perfect love found her way blocked by her family's ownership of slaves.

> She could almost lay hold, and claim the promise, but she said her slaves would seem to step right in between her and her Savior, and prevent its reception; but while she was on her knees, and struggling as in an agony for a clean heart, she then and there covenanted with the Lord, if he would give her the blessing, she would give up her slaves and set them free. She said the covenant had hardly been made one moment, when God filled her soul with such an overwhelming sense of Divine love, that she did not really know if she was in or out of the body. She rose from her knees, and proclaimed to listening hundreds that she had obtained the blessing, and also the terms on which she had obtained it. She went through the vast crowd with holy shouts of joy, and exhorting all to taste and see that the Lord was gracious, and such a power attended her words that hundreds fell to the ground, and scores more were happily born into the kingdom of God that afternoon and during the night. Shortly after this they set their slaves free, and the end of that family was peace.[10]

Clearly the experiences of conversion and sanctification lived out in camp meetings were expected to be deep, real, thorough, and effective. The Word of God was never meant to "return ... empty (Isaiah 55:11)." The power of God could make a radical, often unexpected difference in people's lives and in their treatment of others. Convincing rhetoric alone would not have transformed a rowdy into a convert, or inspired a family to free their slaves. At a camp meeting, the power of God could reach "the great deep of their hearts," to change their thoughts, feelings, and intended actions. At these events,

---

[9] W.P. Strickland. Autobiography of Peter Cartwright (etc.). New York: Phillips & Hunt, 1856, 238&239.

[10] W.P. Strickland, ed. *Autobiography of Peter Cartwright, the Backwoods Preacher*, New York: Carlton & Porter, 1856, 143-145; 130.

The foundations of human sympathy were broken up, and what no appeals of truth or power or persuasion could accomplish was effected by the exhibition of converting power. The conversion of a soul is an omnipotent moral power pervading an entire congregation; it touches the hearts of angels and excites joy in heaven.[11]

Such changes, and the dramatic ways they often took place, fascinated and attracted people, even when they did not understand or appreciate what was happening. Thus it is no wonder that people were drawn, for every kind of reason, to enter these camp grounds, and, in many cases – often by surprise - to find their lives changed forever. Whether in eastern cities or western forests, there was a need to break through barriers erected by everything from lawlessness to intellectual skepticism and "infidelity" – something beyond what most local churches could manage.

> Something of an extraordinary nature was necessary to arrest the attention of skeptical people who were ready to conclude that Christianity was a fable and futurity a dream. This great work of God did it. It confounded infidelity ["Disbelief in the inspiration of the Scriptures, or the divine original of Christianity...."] and vice into silence, and brought numbers beyond calculation under the influence of experimental ["having personal experience"] religion and practical piety.[12]

This kind of transformation required an encounter with God that reached into the depths of hearts and minds. While this encounter could only be initiated and delivered by God's powerful grace, there were components of the experience that sought and welcomed that grace. One of them was preaching, which generally took place several times each day, and sometimes in more than one location on the camp ground. The preachers who gathered for such events knew how important their preaching could be in opening the floodgates of heaven. Benjamin Paddock left this account of an 1826 camp meeting, held in conjunction with his annual conference, just outside Palmyra, New York:

> A great camp-meeting was held in connection with [the conference]. The ground was only about a mile from the village, so that members of the Conference not immediately and specially employed could take part in its

---

[11] W.P. Strickland, ed. *Autobiography of Peter Cartwright, the Backwoods Preacher*. New York: Carlton & Porter, 1856, 238; W.P. Strickland, ed. *The Life of Jacob Gruber*. New York: Carlton & Porter, 1860, 64.

[12] A.P. Mead. *Manna in the Wilderness, or, the Grove and its Altar (etc.)*. Philadelphia: Perkinpine & Higgins, 1860, 25; Noah Webster. *An American Dictionary of the English Language (etc.)*. Springfield, MA: George & Charles Merriam, 1848, 602; 424.

services. At that early day, and previously, meetings of this kind were not unfrequently held in the neighborhood of our Annual Conferences; but the present one was exceptionally large. There were more than one hundred tents on the ground, and these were occupied by our people from almost all parts of the country, many of them coming from a distance of one hundred miles or more. The spirit of the meeting was admirable. Conversions were numerous and powerful; while ministers and people seemed to vie with each other in their efforts to promote the work of God. But the Sabbath was the great day of the feast. Beginning in the morning at eight o'clock, *five* sermons were preached before the services closed in the evening. Bishop Hedding and Dr. [Nathan] Bangs took the two appointments nearest the meridian of the day, and preached with even more than their ordinary freedom and power. At about five in the afternoon the stand was assigned to the Rev. Glezen Fillmore, then in the vigor of mature manhood, now trembling on the extreme verge of time. The sermon was in his best style – more carefully prepared and more effectively delivered than were his discourses generally. The latter part of it contemplated the whole process of personal salvation, from its incipiency to its consummation in the world of light. Having traced the track of the believer, all along from the dawn of spiritual life till he had entered the land of Beulah, and was about to plume himself for his flight to the celestial city, the speaker paused as if struggling with irrepressible emotion, and, looking upward, exclaimed, 'O God, hold thy servant together while for a moment he looks through the gates ajar into the New Jerusalem!' To describe the effect would be quite impossible. A tide of emotions swept over the congregation that seemed to carry all before it. I was seated near Bishop Hedding, who, from fatigue, was reclining upon a bed under and a little in the rear of the stand. It had been noticed before that he was much affected by the sermon; but when the sentence given above was uttered, the tears almost literally spurted from his eyes, and his noble form shook as if under the resistless control of a galvanic battery. The Rev. Goodwin Stoddard exhorted, and invited seekers within the circle of prayer in front of the stand. Hundreds came forward; some said nearly every unconverted person on the ground.[13]

Evangelical preacher and bishop John Seybert described a similar experience, this one in 1835, near Lebanon, Pennsylvania. His biographer, S.P. Spreng, wrote, "Brother Seybert preached the first sermon on Monday evening, and the Lord so blessed his people during the preaching of the Word, that to the right and left, there arose a great demonstration of shouting and weeping for joy. This became so general and so loud, that he finally ceased preaching and sat himself down, quite oppressed with the

---

[13] Zechariah Paddock. *Memoir of Rev. Benjamin G Paddock (etc.)*. New York: Mason & Lane, 1i839, 179-181.

weight of glory." In another camp meeting, we read more about people's response to Seybert's preaching:

> ...the cries of the penitent became so tumultuous that the sermon was interrupted, and they began to labor with seekers. Finally there was a general 'breaking through into eternal life', which occasioned such rejoicing among God's children, that their shouts and songs were heard afar.... Many were so utterly filled with the eternal love of God', that they fell overwhelmed with an exceeding weight of glory, as though they had been dead men.[14]

Benjamin Paddock described the powerful impact of George Cary's preaching:

> When fully aroused, as he was apt to be at camp-meetings and on other such like occasions, he carried all before him. At such times his whole soul was thrown into his theme, while every glance of his eye, every utterance of his lips, every action of his body, gave force to the Divine message he was delivering. God and man seemed to meet. The whole assembly was moved, as if in the presence of the Divine itself. He himself melted and wept, and so did the people.[15]

Preaching was essential in other settings, as well. Nathan Bangs, who helped organize Canada's first camp meeting, said, "I endeavor ... in every sermon I preach, to deliver it as if it were my last." As he thought about Bishop Asbury, "who spent the last shred of his valuable life in the service of his great Master," Bangs said, "I wish to do good, to be greatly taken up in my blessed Master's work, that my last may be my best days"[16]

One of the most compelling preachers was Henry Bascom, of whom James Finley wrote, "...the grand, sublime roar of the lion-like Bascom, as with the majestic sweep of a hurricane it leveled the forests of men at immense camp meetings...."

Finley said of Michael Ellis, "his heart was full of the love of God, and when he would pour out that heart, it was refreshing and fructifying as the dews of heaven that descended upon the mountains of Zion, where the Lord commanded his blessing, even life for evermore.

John Collins brought many distinctive gifts to his preaching ministry, from an outstanding voice to his ability to choose and apply Scriptures and

---

[14] S.P. Spreng. *The Life and Labor of John Seybert (etc.).* Cleveland: Lauer & Mattill, 1888, 153; 165.

[15] *Zechariah Paddock. Memoir of Rev. Benjamin Paddock (etc.).* New York: Nelson & Phillips; Cincinnati: Hitchcock & Walden, 1875, 310.

[16] Nathan Bangs. *The Life of the Rev. Freeborn Garrettson (etc.).* New York: Mason & Lane, 1839.

illustrations to fit an audience. Finley described Collins as "a profound student of human nature" whose messages could break through any barriers people or situations might put in the way. He spoke to people as Jesus did, with examples taken from the frontier life they all shared, in a way that connected his heart with theirs. There were times when he could not finish a sermon because "his voice, clear, shrill, and powerful as it was, was drowned, in the louder, clearer, shriller cries for mercy, which rent the heavens, mingled with the loftiest shouts of praise."[17]

Nicholas Snethen

William Yost's ministry included participation in many camp meetings. One summer he attended four of them conducted among Evangelicals and was invited to preach at each one. "They were all seasons of quickening, converting and sanctifying grace." That same summer he assisted with a United Brethren camp meeting and found they had so much in common that "we should be one."[18]

---

[17] W.P. Strickland, ed. *Sketches of Western Methodism ... by Rev. James Finley*. Cincinnati: Methodist Book Concern, 1855, 479; 99; 327.

[18] William Yost. *Reminiscenses*. Cleveland: Publishing House of the Evangelical Association, 98&99.

Schuyler Stewart saw that God's radical power, exhibited and experienced in camp meetings, radiated outward and "scattered in all the surrounding country," where the work of conversion continued. He described the closing worship at a camp meeting near Watertown, New York. "The greatest manifestation of God's power was the closing sermon on Sunday evening, ... The Word, quick and powerful, took such effect that scores were seen dropping down like men shot in battle. The preacher had to pause several times and lean on the stand to keep from falling himself." Stewart recalled two camp meetings in New York State, where people who were hostile to Methodism were stopped in their tracks, struck down by the Spirit, and brought to conversion and Christian fellowship. This kind of radical change occurred in camp meetings across the continent, giving some indication of the power involved in these encounters. In both incidents, the prayers of nearby worshipers helped turn these opposers around.[19]

Minuette Floyd gives us this powerful testimony to the effect an outstanding camp meeting preacher can have on an audience *even today*: "To hear an orator such as Rev. [David] Rice is to experience the essence of the camp meeting tradition. Preaching of this caliber can ignite in listeners a spiritual flame that consumes all sense of ego, allowing them to experience oneness with God and oneness with each other as well."[20]

The holy fire of God's presence, conveyed through the amazing variety of preachers and congregants, surrounded by God's inspiring, renewing creation, would often generate intense interest from camp meeting attendees. An example came at an 1830 camp meeting that featured two well-known Methodist Protestant preachers. "During this meeting, these two eminent men delivered each a memorable discourse from the same text." Asa Shinn and Nicholas Snethen had decided, independently of each other, to base their sermons on John 3:16&17. Each spoke in his own way the Wesleyan message of universally available, freely chosen grace. Rather than burden or bore their audience with unfortunate repetition, each presentation came at the subject from a different but complementary angle, and in ways that reflected the distinctive personalities and gifts of the speakers. Historian Ancell Bassett explains:

> In representing the fullness and freeness of the great salvation, he [Shinn] called attention to the manner in which the word "*world*" is reiterated and

---

[19] Schuyler Stewart. *The Life of Rev. Schuyler Stewart (etc.)*. Hamilton, ON: Methodist Episcopal Book Room, 16; 44&45.

[20] Minuette Floyd. *A Place to Worship; African American Camp Meetings in the Carolinas*. Columbia, SC: University of South Carolina Press, 2018, 66.

emphasized in the text. "God so loved the *world*, that He gave His only begotten Son; He sent not His Son into the *world*, to condemn the WORLD, but that the WORLD through Him might be saved." Thus, divine love took the broadest possible scope. Shinn emphasized the universality of God's love, but also the responsibility of each person to respond, and the consequences of rejecting or neglecting that love:

> If, after all, any man if found persistently to slight such dying love, and trample underfoot mercies so large and free, such a one, the speaker [Shinn] declared, with awful solemnity, in the light of the text, absolutely ought to be *damned*, and God would be unjust to bring him to the holy place assigned to His obedient care. This overwhelming utterance was given but as an emphasizing and reiteration of the divine anathema. It was uttered as no man but Shinn could utter it....

The next day, Snethen spoke on the same passage, but emphasizing the role of grace and faith in making salvation possible to the person – "whosoever"– being rescued from perishing. The power of God, universally accessible, achieves the otherwise impossible feat of turning people around, which Snethen compared to overcoming the power of gravity that would normally drag us downward. The grace needed to be saved is offered not to just an elect few, but "whosoever" believes. Thus in different ways, both speakers were preaching the Wesleyan Arminian gospel so essential to these camp meetings. Nothing external to members of the audience could prevent them from being saved, but only their own apathy or stubborn refusal. As Ancell Bassett, who heard both sermons, put it, "The tide of sin and worldliness would bear us all away, but we may seek and have the overwhelming power" by which God was "reconciling the world unto Himself."[21]

What may at first have seemed a needless repetition, actually succeeded in growing and deepening their understanding and application of the text. Thus, the nature of Scripture is such that it speaks in different ways, and different times, to the constantly changing circumstances of our lives, through the rich variety of preachers who seek to communicate its meaning.

These are a few examples from the tremendous variety of preachers' gifts, personalities, experiences, and styles, all of which contributed to a similar variety in the needs, personalities, situations, and transformation which attendees brought to and took from these gatherings. A.P. Mead rec-

---

[21] Ancell H. Bassett. *A Concise History of the Methodist Protestant Church (etc.)*. Pittsburgh: James Robison; Baltimore: W.J.C. Dulaney, 1882, 352-354; 356.

ognized this principle, saying: "God loves variety. ... The same wisdom that gave variety to the inspired page, has ordained equal diversity in the instruments that proclaim the truth. This meets the necessity arising from the diversity of those to whom the truth is addressed." Thus the rich variety among preachers with its necessary correspondence to a like variety among lay people is part of God's purpose and plan for ministry. "...God has chosen his ministers from the *people*, having all the diversity of intellect and manner peculiar to the multitude they serve."[22]

Those who told the stories of camp meetings often made note of the variety of preachers they saw and heard. One example is John L. Smith's account of an Indiana camp meeting in 1840:

> Among the ministers in attendance were Robert Burns, the presiding elder; Joseph Ockerman, Hardin H. Bradbury, Seth Smith, Hezekiah Smith, John S. Donaldson, and the two circuit preachers. Burns was modest, amiable, and tender. – a capital preacher, and a powerful exhorter. Bruce [not included in his list] was of Teutonic mould, strong in argument, and somewhat pugilistic. Ockerman was delicate in person, feminine in voice, and a sweet singer. Bradbury was mighty in prayer, mighty in the Scriptures, a sound theologian, and an able preacher. Seth Smith was a chaste speaker, a Christian gentleman, and a pious, lovable minister. Hezekiah Smith was a great worker, and excellent pastor, a persuasive exhorter, and a most successful minister. Donaldson was of Hibernian extraction – eccentric, ready witted, an expert at repartee, a good exhorter, and a good preacher.

George Coles was so impressed with the distinctive character and gifts of each preacher at a Connecticut camp meeting, that he wrote a song mentioning each one. He began the song with these words, thanking God for this gathering of his servants, "Who shine upon us with a borrowed lustre."

> Adorable Saviour, who, in thy right hand,
> Hold'st the stars, and they shine at thy gracious command;
> We thank thee that Canaan [the camp ground's name] is blessed with a cluster, Who shine upon us with a borrowed lustre.

Along with the credentialed preachers, whether traveling or local, were others who came to known for their powerful preaching, singing, and exhorting. In another setting, Smith mentions a little girl who witnessed from the speakers' stand and whose message brought many to God. "As the result of her talk more than fifty souls were there and then so convicted

---

[22] A.P. Mead. *Manna in the Wilderness, or, The Grove and its Altar (etc.)*. Philadelphia: Perkinpine & Higgins, 1860, 319&320.

of sin that they came rushing to the alter [sic], to find peace and pardon in believing."[23]

At other times, there might be a seemingly spontaneous outburst of prayer and song that would grow and spread through the camp ground until it moved people in ways much like their responses to preaching. Joseph Hilts witnessed such a time:

> ... one evening, some young girls got together on an elevated place, and commenced to sing some of the old-time camp meeting hymns. At first not much notice was taken of them; but one and another joined with them until there were some twenty-five or thirty young women and girls in the group. The singing became louder and more animated, as the number of singers increased. Others, and older ones, now began to join them, and in a short time the company had so added to its numbers that it contained not less than a hundred persons. Men, women and children were mingling their voices in holy song.

The result was much like that which would follow a moving sermon. "Some were weeping, some were laughing, and some were singing; others were lying on the ground as if they had been stricken down by an electric shock; many of them were insensible."[24] Hilts' description echoes many others in detailing certain observable effects of the power of God in worship. Rimi Xhemajli has rightly focused on the powerful presence of God in worship, including specific effects among worshipers, in a well-argued attempt to restore these realities to their original place in early Methodism in America, and to better explain spiritual transformation and numerical growth in that movement. Xhemajli sees neglect in this area as a reason for Methodist decline, and restoration as essential to renewed vitality.[25]

Hilts also relates the story of an Ontario camp meeting, where a lay person was given the opportunity to preach. Lay people more often sang, prayed, and gave their own testimony, but in this case a farmer was invited to hold forth from the preacher's stand for the main afternoon service. His sermon was met with initial skepticism, which was soon transformed "from the lowest degree of appreciation to the highest point of admira-

---

[23] Elbert Osborn. *Passages in the Life and Ministry of Elbert Osborn (etc.)*. New-York: Conference Office, 1847, 102-104; John L. Smith. *Indiana Methodism (etc.)*. Valparaiso, IN: John L. Smith, 1892, 40.

[24] Joseph H. Hilts. *Experiences of a Backwoods Preacher*. Wiarton, ON: Bruce County Historical Society [Reprint]. 1986, 109&110.

[25] Rimi Xhemajli. *The Supernatural and the Circuit Riders: The Rise of Early American Methodism*. Eugene, OR: Pickwick, 2021.

tion and enthusiasm." Hilts described the crescendo as Thomas Moore preached:

> He had only uttered a few sentences when it became evident that he knew what he was doing. ... As the speaker became more at home in the anomalous position in which he was placed, he seemed to catch an inspiration that carried him away above himself, and beyond anything that his most intimate friends had ever thought him capable of doing. I had so often heard him preach, and preach well, but in his effort that day I was completely taken by surprise – so was everyone else. Before he got done speaking that was one of the noisiest audiences that I have been in. Some were shouting, some were weeping, and other praying. The sermon was talked about more than all the other discourses delivered at that camp-meeting.[26]

Several African American women, often formerly enslaved, were swept into service at camp meetings and other revivals, even among largely white attendees. One of them was Julia A.J. Foote, whose testimony and passion for holiness made her a regular presence at holiness camp meetings across the states. After an agonizing struggle over whether she should accept a call to preach, and amid extreme discouragement from some, including her mother, Julia found ample foundation in Scripture, and inspiration in the Lord, to go forth and proclaim the message God had entrusted to her. When her minister tried to dissuade her, saying 'You don't know anything," she answered, "My gifts are very small, I know, but I can no longer be shaken by what you or anyone else may think or say."

Julia Foote had a painfully hard time dealing with her mother's rejection, yet her mother eventually came to accept what her daughter plainly did so well.

> As my mother embraced me, she exclaimed: "So you are a preacher, are you? I replied, "So they say." "Well, Julia," said she, "when I first heard that you were a preacher, I said that I would rather hear you were dead." These words, coming so unexpectedly from my mother, filled me with anguish. Was I to meet opposition here, too? But my mother, with streaming eyes, continued: "My dear daughter, it is all past now. I have heard from those who have attended your meetings what the Lord has done for you, and I am satisfied."

In his introduction to her autobiography, Thomas K. Doty wrote that he had heard her preach at a revival "where she held the almost breathless attention of five thousand people, by the eloquence of the Holy Ghost...." She wrote to other women who labored under a similar call: "Dear sisters,

---

[26] Joseph H. Hilts. *Experiences of a Backwoods Preacher*. Wiarton, ON: Bruce County Historical Society [reprint], 1986, 102-105.

who are in the evangelistic work now, you may think you have hard times, let me tell you, I feel that the lion and the lamb are lying down together, as compared with twenty-five or thirty years ago. Yes, yes; our God is marching on. Glory to his name!" In a hymn she wrote, Sister Foote included a verse saying, "Sometimes I am in doubting, And think I have no grace; Sometimes I am a'shouting, And camp-meeting is the place." Clearly the camp meeting venue provided nurture, encouragement, and fulfillment for her ministry.[27]

Julia Foote became the first woman ordained a Deacon in the African Methodist Episcopal Zion Church, in 1894, by Bishop James Walker Hood, followed in 1900 by her ordination as an Elder.[28]

James Walker Hood

Especially in the days of slavery, African American preachers – men and women – experienced within themselves, and conveyed to their African American hearers, personal and social blessings beyond those we might categorize as spiritual. Albert Raboteau writes:

---

[27] Julia A.J. Foote. *A Brand Plucked from the Fire: Autobiographical Sketch.* Cleveland: Lauer & Yost, 1881, 65-67; 78-80; 72; 84&85; 7; 89; 123.

[28] Larry G. Murphy, J. Gordon Melton, & Gary L. Ward, eds. *Encyclopedia of African-American Religions.* New York & London: Garland, 1993, 274.

In the role of preacher, slaves achieved respect, authority, and power. The conversion experience equipped the slave with a sense of importance that counteracted the dehumanizing force of slavery. In their prayer meetings, slaves enjoyed community and fellowship, which transformed their individual sorrows into moments of joy. In the midst of slavery, they treasured these and other ways in which religion brought meaning, hope, and inner freedom to their lives.[29]

Some preachers had a wealth of illustrations, analogies, and practical applications at their beck and call. James Finley said of the western pioneer preacher John Collins,

> No man was ever more thoroughly stored with incident than was brother Collins. He possessed the faculty, in an eminent degree, of weaving into his discourses the every-day incidents of life, and of applying them with the most admirable judgement to his hearers. He was a profound student of human nature; and possessing the keenest perceptive faculties, united with his knowledge of the secret springs of the human heart, he was enabled to discriminate so nicely that every sinner felt under his preaching as David under the pointed personal reproof of the prophet Nathan.

Henry Bascom was one of the most sought after preachers of his time. Finley recalled "…the grand, sublime roar of the lion-like Bascom, as with the majestic sweep of a hurricane it leveled the forests of men at immense camp meetings." Of Michael Ellis, Finley wrote: "His heart was full of the love of God, and when he would pour out that heart, it was refreshing and fructifying as the 'dews of heaven that descended upon the mountains of Zion, where the Lord commanded his blessing, even life for evermore." And it was Finley who portrayed for the whole Church the larger than life character and impact of the Wyandotte preacher Mononcue.[30]

Camp Meetings have thrived on good preaching, and also from the active involvement of those who attended or assisted in various ways. Elbert Osborn, who noted and appreciated the gifts and idiosyncrasies of camp meeting preachers, also "recalled Elvira Stillman, - with whom, and her amiable companion, I formed an acquaintance. Her simplicity in witnessing for God, her fervor in prayer and praise, her courageous yet prudent manner of warning the lukewarm professor and the careless sinner, have left an indelible impression on my mind." Osborn also met

> "Elisha West and his pious wife…. They seemed to take a deep interest

---

[29] Albert J. Raboteau. *African-American Religion.* New York & Oxford: Oxford University Press, 1999, 62&63.

[30] W.P. Strickland, ed. *Sketches of Western Methodism … Rev. James B. Finley.* Cincinnati: Methodist Book Concern, 1855, 327; 479; 99; 519-522.

in the temporal welfare of the preachers, and were still more solicitous for their spiritual prosperity. To lead the younger ministers nearer to God, and to encourage them to plunge into the divine fullness, was the delight of their hearts. But they have gone to their eternal home; and 'they, being dead, yet speak.'"[31]

One dimension of camp meetings in the Methodist tradition is that while these were distinctly Wesleyan in theology and leadership, there was often room for a larger fellowship, Alfred Cookman, one of the leaders and preachers in the holiness camp meetings of the late 19th century, noted, "There is a great catholicity of feeling prevailing – Baptist and Methodist, Quaker and Episcopalian, Congregationalist and Presbyterian, sitting together 'in heavenly places in Christ Jesus,' without any friction of sectarianism." While even this is less ecumenical than we would like to see today, in an era of great religious competition, it was quite an accomplishment.[32]

Camp meetings aimed not so much to entertain or impress, but to invite, encourage, and facilitate commitment. God poured out his Holy Spirit, and people responded, often in life and world changing ways.

---

[31] Elbert Osborn. *Passages in the Life and Ministry of Elbert Osborn (etc.)*. New-York: Conference Office, 1847, 23&24.

[32] Henry B. Ridgaway. *The Life of the Rev. Alfred Cookman (etc.)*. New York: Nelson & Phillips; Cincinnati: Hitchcock & Walden, 1874, 415.

8

Growing in Grace toward an Eternal Destiny

"…that you may know the hope to which he has called you, the riches of his glorious inheritance in his holy people, and his incomparably great power for us who believe."[1]

"With all thy great salvation bless,
And make me all like thee."[2]

One woman who took part in the 1890 Douglas Camp Meeting in Massachusetts said, "This is a hallowed spot to my soul." That same year Rev. J.A. Wood said, "This is about the dearest spot on earth to me. It is worth a trip across the continent to mingle with the saints on this ground." Another said, "Here God called me by name and here God spoke perfect peace to my soul. I always go home with a thankful heart. It is a Pentecost to my soul." One anonymous participant said, "Surely Douglas [Camp Meeting] is the next place to heaven itself!" Each of these illuminates the core of the camp meeting experience. Whatever may have taken place along the road to Douglas; whatever meals may have been served; the style of the "tents" people lived in; the particulars of weather and the words that were sung or spoken, all of these were necessary background or details around that essential core.[3]

---

[1] Ephesians 1:18&19, NIV.
[2] Charles Wesley, in W. McDonald & S. Hubbard, eds. *The Wesleyan Sacred Harp, (etc.).* Boston: John P. Jewett; Cleveland: Jewett, Proctor & Worthington; New York: Sheldon, Lamport & Blakeman, 94.
[3] Edward E. Davies. *Illustrated History of Douglas Camp Meeting.* Wilmore, KY: First Fruits, 2016 (orig. 1890), 70; 96.

The sacredness of a camp ground was and is that it facilitates an encounter with God, a preview and even an experience of heaven, and the company of fellow pilgrims on the road to glory. Here participants can see and feel the intimate presence of God. Here they share the bread of life as food for the journey to a heavenly destination. Here they meet with those they would meet again in glory, even if their paths might not cross again in this life. All of this happens in an atmosphere of love, "the essence of all religion, and the mightiest influence in the universe."[4]

In 1888,

> B.W. Gorham was on the [Douglas] camp ground for the last time, and was quite feeble, but still full of divine energy. I remember he had charge of the first afternoon meeting before the opening service. ...while we were singing the fire of God fell upon us, till before we got through there was a heavenly conflagration. He was a blessed, holy man, never to be forgotten....

One of the speakers at Gorham's 1890 funeral said: "He would pray a camp meeting out of the mud into the third heaven." Gorham's vision of heaven was much like that of Adam Clarke, a vision of grace-empowered sanctification in this life, transitioning to "endless progress afterwards [in eternity]." It was a journey he [Gorham] wanted for everyone, but which only some would take. "Thus it is, that he who would walk the path to heaven must consent to walk with the few, instead of the many. Have we the courage to do it? I wish we all had: I fear we have not." Yet his whole life as a pastor and revivalist pointed, with great effect, to the glory of that narrow way.[5]

A "divine energy" that could lift such a gathering "out of the mud into the third heaven" points again to the essence of the camp meeting experience. Powered by grace and leading into the realms of glory, speakers and worshipers availed themselves of these precious gifts, gifts that were far greater than mere vacation or escape. Glorious as they were in themselves, these gifts propelled people into their true identity and purpose, in this world and beyond.

One preacher at Douglas related our destiny in Christ to the Transfiguration. That spectacular, mysterious event revealed Jesus' "1. Immaculate

---

[4] B.W. Gorham, in Edward E. Davies. *Illustrated History of Douglas Camp Meeting.* Wilmore, KY: First Fruits, 2016 (orig. 1890), 37; 56.

[5] Edward E. Davies. *Illustrated History of Douglas Camp Meeting.* Wilmore, KY: First Fruits, 2016 (orig. 1890), 56; 64; B.W. Gorham. *God's Method with Man, or, Sacred Scenes Along the Path to Heaven.* Cincinnati: Hitchcock & Walden, 1879, 157; 267&268; Adam Clarke. *Christian Theology.* Salem, OH: Convention Book Store, 1967 (reprint), 376-380.

purity; 2. Translucent love;" and "3. Superlative light. It was as Christ prayed that the fashion of his countenance was changed. So it may be with us." Still another, William McDonald, said that "heaven is in the distance, but we that believe do now enter into this blessed rest." Always there was the awareness that Christians could participate in that transfigured reality in times of worship, such as they experienced in camp meetings.[6]

Lester Ruth writes: "Seeking terms strong enough to describe their wonderful experiences in worship, Methodists often spoke of these times as an experience of heaven now." At camp meetings there was both a "longing for heaven," and a realization of that longing.[7]

The road to glory was one of spiritual transformation, in which people got a glimpse and foretaste of their destiny in Christ. Grace was the power to move along that road. The goal was holiness or Christian perfection. In the New Testament, sanctification, transformation, or transfiguration described the way to that goal. We see it in II Corinthians, where Paul says "we all ... are being transformed into his (Jesus' or God's) image with ever-increasing glory, which comes from the Lord, who is the Spirit." The astonishing goal of this transformation, made possible only by grace, is given in I John, where out of the "great love the Father has lavished on us," we become children on God, and ultimately we grow "like him" (Christ). We are commanded and empowered to "be holy in all [we] do," as we "participate in the divine nature."[8] This was the essence of the Wesleyan message, though shared, often in different terms, by other traditions.[9]

Melvin Dieter explains the rival perspectives and the misperception among some in the Methodist Episcopal Church that the holiness movement was somehow "un-Wesleyan:"

> ...many Methodists looked upon the holiness revival within its ranks as Methodism's best hope for preserving the primitive piety and vital spirit of the Church. The holiness party claimed to be fostering renewal of the one biblical truth which had distinguished Methodism among other Christian movements. Critics often charged that the preaching of Christian perfec-

---

[6] Edward E. Davies. *Illustrated History of Douglas Camp Meeting*, Wilmore, KY: First Fruits, 2016 (orig. 1890), 47.

[7] Lester Ruth, *Early Methodist Life and Spirituality: A Reader*. Nashville: Abingdon, 2005, 144; 139.

[8] II Corinthians 3:18; I John 3:1&2; I Peter 1:15&16; II Peter 1:4, NIV.

[9] See Joseph Coleson, ed. *Be Holy (etc.)*. Indianapolis: Wesleyan Publishing House, 2008; D. Gregory Van Dussen. *Transfiguration and Hope: A Conversation Across Time and Space*. Eugene, OR: Wipf & Stock, 2018; Andreas Andreopoulos. *This Is My Beloved Son: The Transfiguration of Christ*. Brewster, MA: Paraclete, 2012.

tion which became characteristic of the revival was un-Wesleyan because the context of American revivalism tended to create variations in the presentation and emphasis of the doctrine; but that judgment never won the day. When the conflict over the place of the holiness movement in Methodism came to a head towards the end of the century, it was not, tragically, that Methodism freed itself from a radically deviant Wesleyanism, but rather that Methodism largely was willing to leave Wesley behind for the greener pastures of more contemporary theologies and cultural relationships.[10]

Holiness was both the central teaching of Wesley and his movement, and a focus of controversy intertwined with the history of Methodist camp meetings. In his own time, John Wesley found it necessary and important to clarify what holiness or Christian perfection meant and did not mean. Methodists in North America differed with other denominations over the extent to which such transformation was possible in this life. By the latter half of the nineteenth-century, Methodists were debating among themselves concerning both the meaning and the importance of holiness theology in camp meetings and in the churches. The first National Camp Meeting for the Promotion of Holiness, held in Vineland, NJ in 1867, sought to confirm and strengthen the teaching and experience of Christian perfection in the life of the Church. It is interesting to note that several Methodist leaders, including bishops, preached at these meetings amid the controversy over which direction the Methodist Episcopal Church (and others) would take.

Alfred Cookman, one of the leaders of these holiness meetings, appreciated the encouragement their efforts received from many denominational leaders. Henry Ridgaway, Cookman's biographer, made the point clearly:

> In no respect have the bishops of the Methodist Episcopal Church shown more wisdom than in their promptness to countenance all movements in the Church looking to the advancement either of the moral purity or the more thorough and efficient working of its ecclesiastical polity. Bishop Simpson, in this instance and in others, did not stand aloof because of the possible dangers which might be suggested to calm criticism; but, seeing good and true men honestly engaged in an enterprise which in his opinion was at variance neither with the doctrines not the usages of Methodism, he

---

[10] Melvin Dieter, in Wayne E. Caldwell, ed. *Reformers and Revivalists: History of The Wesleyan Church*. Indianapolis: Wesley Press, 1992, 165.

gave them his presence and cooperation.[11]

It was Cookman's view that the holiness movement was simply affirming and implementing the Wesleyan theology that had been the common heritage of Methodism from the beginning. He lifted up the vows taken by those being ordained as elders as an official articulation of this enduring standard. Cookman was wholeheartedly involved in the first National Association camp meeting "(1867, Vineland)", as a powerful supplement, not a replacement, for the older, regional gatherings. Thus he expressed, in a letter to his wife, his enthusiasm for another camp meeting he attended that same summer, this one on the eastern shore of Maryland, part of which read: "My soul was in heaven. Oh, what precious experiences God vouchsafed to me in that consecrate grove, and how wonderfully, how unusually he used me! This week I think surely I have been in the order of God."[12]

Charles C. McCabe

---

[11] Henry B. Ridgaway. *The Life of the Rev. Alfred Cookman (etc.)*. New York: Nelson & Phillips; Cincinnati: Hitchcock & Walden, 1873, 317. But see Kevin M. Watson. *Old or New School Methodism? The Fragmentation of a Theological Tradition*. New York: Oxford University Press, 2019, which details Bishop Simpson's differences with B.T. Roberts and Free Methodism, but also his larger views of the doctrine of Christian perfection.

[12] Henry B. Ridgaway. *The Life of the Rev. Alfred Cookman (etc.)*. New York: Nelson & Phillips; Cincinnati: Hitchcock & Walden, 1873, 320; 325-327.

Bishop Charles McCabe, one of the most popular bishops of the late 19th century, saw traditional Wesleyan theology as both the key to Methodist growth up to his time, and to its ongoing prosperity:

> The theology of the Wesleys, so far from being obsolete, was never so vigorous and so triumphant as it is to-day. In the Methodist Church of the United States, taking all branches, North and South, there are 5,800,000 communicants. We have 11,600,000 people who believe the theology of John Wesley and sing the hymns of Charles Wesley.

Yet his statement implies that there were some within the movement who did in fact see Wesley's theology, or at least parts of it, as obsolete. The holiness movement with its massive camp meetings was a reaffirmation of its perennial vitality.[13]

This movement included a reaffirmation of holiness by many in Canadian Methodism. One leader in Canada's movement was Ralph C. Horner, a Methodist evangelist whose troubled relationship with his denomination ended in the establishment of the Standard Church, later (2004) part of the Wesleyan Church. Horner believed that "by 1875, Methodists were becoming a middle class church and began to enjoy political influence." Horner blamed much of the problem on Methodist seminaries, where, in his view, "Younger faculty knew little of John Wesley and became enamored with German higher criticism and English Darwinism." Thus, in

Ralph C. Horner

---

[13] Frank Milton Bristol. *The Life of Chaplain McCabe: Bishop of the Methodist Episcopal Church.* New York, et al: Fleming H. Revell, 1908, 373.

the training of new ministers, there was a break with, or at least a moving away from, the tradional, Wesleyan stheological/spiritual content of faith and ministry.[14]

Horner was converted at a Methodist camp meeting in Quebec. Camp meetings were a major part of his ministry, but in the view of his movement,

> ...the 1850s saw a subtle change in the nature of camp meetings, one of the traditional venues for the highly emotional, religious experiences associated with Methodist conversion and entire sanctification. Although camp meetings reached the height of their success in the early part of the decade, during the same period there were calls to establish permanent campsites in order to make them more respectable. Within twenty years, a transition had occurred and permanent sites were developed, some with large tabernacle – auditoriums surrounded by clusters of summer cottages. The nature of the camp meeting began to shift from a place of revival preaching to that of a vacation in the country. ... By the 1870s the nature of the camp meeting had shifted to where the benefits were more social and recreational than religious. ... This shift in values and emphasis caused great concern among conservative, orthodox Methodists.[15]

Horner's position was complicated by his desire to stay clear of pastoral appointments and work entirely as a traveling evangelist and camp meeting speaker. The old fashioned style of his meetings drew fire from church leaders, even as others appreciated his advocacy and leadership of "old-time" revivals. Horner "became a leading voice" against "what the conservative wing viewed as the threat of modernism and liberalism." He would continue his leadership in holiness ministry, eventually outside mainstream Methodism. His camp meetings would continue earlier traditions and methods, but in a church environment far less friendly than that of older times.[16]

Among the United Brethren were those who shared a yearning for real holiness. William Hanby describes an intense period in 1845 when that longing seemed especially strong, but of course rather than being something new and foreign to their thinking and spiritual life, it was the culmination of a growing awareness, rooted in doctrine and experience inherent in their tradition.

---

[14] Laurence Crowell & Mark Crowell. *Lift Up a Standard: The Life and Legacy of Ralph C. Horner.* n.c.: Wesleyan Publishing House, 2012, 30&31.

[15] Laurence Crowell & Mark Crowell. *Lift Up a Standard: The Life and Legacy of Ralph C. Horner.* n.c: Wesleyan Publishing House, 2012, 31&32.

[16] Laurence Crowell & Mark Crowell. *Lift Up a Standard: The Life and Legacy of Ralph C. Horner.* n.c: Wesleyan Publishing House, 2012, 49; 77-82.

Many prominent members and ministers, had felt for years, the necessity of higher attainments in a divine life. They longed for a perfect deliverance from the carnal mind – a perfect victory through the merits of Christ, over a naturally selfish and corrupt heart. True, all prayed for the perfection of their natures, to be cleansed from all unrighteousness; but while they thus prayed, they did not have definite faith to believe, that God was just as ready to give them the great blessings *now*, as at any future period. They prayed to be sanctified – but that work was to be performed gradually – perhaps just before death, God would come and complete the work. But few really enjoyed a glorious fullness, in an entire consecration to the will of God.

This understanding of holiness as the fruit of grace, Hanby "traced back to the early fathers of the Church," and lifted up the words of Christian Newcomer to give that understanding full expression. After some time relegating holiness to a future time, perhaps to come only "through severe trials and manifold tribulations," he [Newcomer] came to a place where he saw this wonderful experience as a gift to be sought now. Hanby says, "Father Newcomer ... longed and prayed for a deeper – more thorough and glorious work of grace in his heart. He reached forward with anxious faith for the prize of perfect love." Then he breaks off his account of Newcomer to offer "his own testimony" to the quest for holiness and its realization:

> For some fourteen years of the early part of his Christian experience, this path was rough and very thorny. Some times [sic] up, and sometimes down; sometimes miserable, and sometimes very happy; sometimes very willing to preach and suffer all the will of God, and sometimes very unwilling to do either; sometimes felt as though he could preach pretty well, and at other times so discouraged in view of his feeble efforts, that he would be tempted never to try to preach again. In the fall of 1844, after about three months hard struggling with head and heart, (being hitherto a disbeliever in the doctrine of sanctification,) he by simple, naked, living, child-like faith, consecrated his *all* to God. Since that time, he has enjoyed a constant peace, a sea of glory unknown before. May all who love the Lord Jesus, enter into this *rest*: Amen.[17]

The renewed emphasis on Christian perfection and the road to glory was not an aberration or side road leading away from the Wesleyan main-

---

[17]William Hanby. History of the Church of the United Brethren in Christ. Circleville, OH: Conference Office of the United Brethren in Christ, 1851, 295-298 (bound with Henry G. Spayth. *United Brethren in Christ*. Circleville, OH: Conference Office of the United Brethren in Christ, 1851. Hanby was an abolitionist and active participant in the Underground Railroad. He served as a bishop in the U.B. Church from 1845-1849 and was cofounder of Otterbein University.

stream. Rather, it sprang from a deep appreciation for Wesley's theology and a realization that developments in 19th century North America – especially within churches of the Wesleyan movement – were moving Methodism away from its original purpose. Leaders in the world of holiness theology and practice represented neither a curious backwater nor a departure from what had been mainstream teaching and experience. Holiness was, in the words of Daniel Steele, "a great Gospel truth struggling to reveal itself to the Church." Steele and many others felt that by their time, too many Christians and churches had settled for a form of religion with too little power; a manageable way of life that fell far short of what people need and God is able and willing to give. "We must be satisfied with nothing less than the bright shining of the Divine presence upon our individual soul. We must believe it attainable, and resolve to attain it at whatever cost."[18]

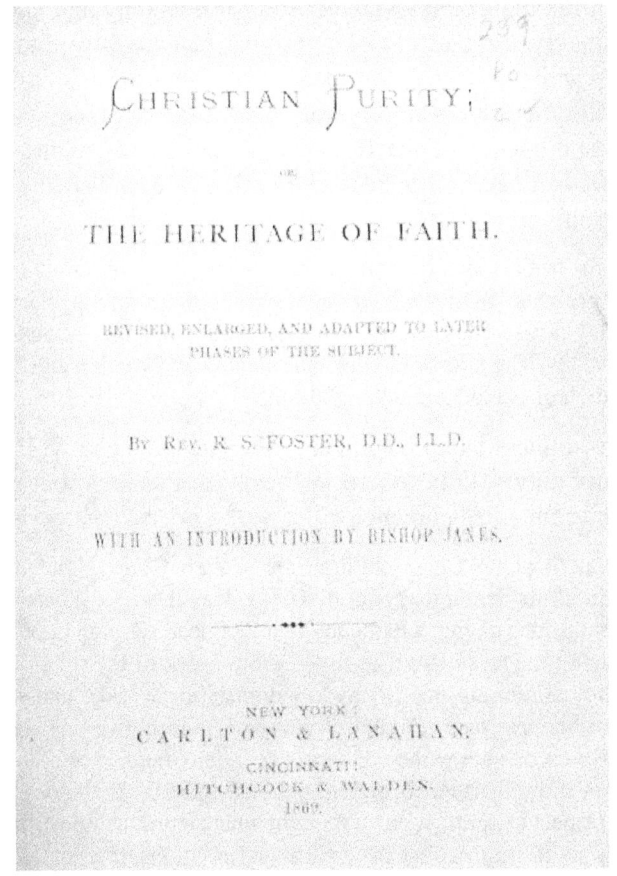

---

[18] Daniel Steele. *Love Enthroned: Essays on Evangelical Perfection*. New York: Phillips & Hunt; Cincinnati: Hitchcock & Walden, 1880, 3; 188.

In his introduction to Randolph Foster's *Christian Purity*, a respected and popular expression of holiness theology, Bishop Edmund S. Janes states clearly that Foster's work is consistent with the theology of Wesley and other early Methodist writers on Christian perfection. In Janes' view, Foster seeks to be non-sectarian, yet genuinely Methodist.

> In executing this important work, the author has not set himself forth as a theological reformer. He has given us no new and novel theory. He has set up no rivalry with other writers on the subject. He has made no assaults upon standard Wesleyan authorities. He has not attempted to modify the long and generally received and cherished doctrines of the Methodist Church on this question; nor has he, as a sectarian, labored to contravert, the opinions of other Churches.

Janes further argues that a prominent focus on sanctification is no more than a reaffirmation of the vision of God for humanity and the reason for Christ's ministry. "Foster has shown most conclusively that this is the great object and aim of the Gospel economy; that for this purpose Christ died, the Holy Scriptures were given, the means of grace instituted, and the offices and agency of the Holy Ghost furnished." At the same time, there is always a need for a fresh expression of established teaching. As Foster himself wrote,

> Though the truth is ever the same, circumstances are constantly changing, and that presentation of it which met the want of a former age or a certain place, may not so completely fill the demand of another period and different locality. The altered circumstances, now and yonder, call for a new presentation of the old and unaltered truth.[19]

Like the holiness camp meetings of the late 19th century, Foster's purpose was not only solidly rooted in Wesleyan theology, but designed to embrace an ecumenical audience:

> ...remembering that God's children are scattered throughout the entire Church in all its denominational divisions, it will be his [Foster's] effort to avoid allusions having a tendency to inflict needless pain upon any, and at the same time to assist all in the glorious work of their common mission – the building up of Christ's kingdom in the world, "and spreading Scriptural holiness *over all* lands." We shall, indeed give our views fully and undisguisedly, but without entering at all into merely sectarian contentions, or attempting to secure denominational ends. We write for Christians without respect to *name*, with no thought whatever to their peculiar badge, and with no desire to affect their particular relations, but purely to assist

---

[19] Randolph S. Foster. *Christian Purity (etc.)*. New York: Eaton & Mains; Cincinnati: Jennings & Pye, 1897 (revised edition), 10, 12, 15&16, 37.

them in the great matter of Christian experience. Here we have a common interest, and may, without infringing personal or denominational rights, be coworkers together....

We are, indeed, and we think properly and profitably, under existing circumstances, distinguished by various appellatives and diversified usages and symbols; but our foundation, our faith, our experience, our hope, our heaven, is one. Children of one heavenly Father – ransomed by one Saviour – renewed by one Holy Spirit – and going forward to one everlasting home, we can but feel a fraternal sympathy; and, overlooking all petty distinctions, must delight to recognize the invisible bond of a glorious and divine brotherhood – the union and fellowship of hearts![20]

Bishop Charles McCabe, one of the most popular and powerful voices in mainstream, late 19th century Methodism, said, "Randolph Foster's name is like a household word to me. His work on 'Christian Purity' I regard as one of the most beneficial I have ever read. I met it years ago, and have read it often since." Concerning his own spiritual life, McCabe once said, "I want hereafter to spend the first Friday of each month as a day of fasting and prayer for the continued evidence of my pardon, and the permanent indwelling of the Holy Spirit."[21]

Like Foster, other important leaders and authors in this movement articulated the original Wesleyan vision and purpose for a new generation. Among these were Daniel Steel, B.W, Gorham, Gilbert Haven, Phoebe Palmer, John Inskip, J. A. Wood, and, in Canada, James Caughey. Others prominent in the 19th century tradition were George Peck and Nathan Bangs. Respected within their own denomination, the Methodist Episcopal Church, and recognized throughout the larger movement, these people

---

[20] Randolph S. Foster. *Christian Purity (etc.)*. New York: Eaton & Mains; Cincinnati: Jennings & Pye, 1897 (revised edition), 39-41.

[21] Frank Milton Bristol. *The Life of Chaplain McCabe: Bishop of the Methodist Episcopal Church*. New York, et al: Fleming H. Revell, 1908, 166; 222.

knew, taught, and lived essential, traditional Methodism.[22] Kevin Watson's recent study of the conflict between Free Methodism and the Methodist Episcopal Church highlights different theological and spiritual approaches of leaders trying to relate to a changing culture.[23]

Clearly the Holiness Movement flourished both inside and outside the mainstream bodies of American and Canadian Methodism. I would argue that the movement's restatement of Wesley's sanctification theology, rather than taking Methodism in a new direction, seemed to provoke and intensify the efforts of some key leaders away from what they saw as outdated and irrelevant. Leaders such as B.T. Roberts and Ralph C. Horner saw the need to organize and minister outside the changing denominations they had served. Others, such as Bishops Gilbert Haven and Randolph Foster, chose to work within the mainstream. Still others with classic Wesleyan theology and historical connections, like the Wesleyan Methodists, took nourishment from the holiness revival and sought to embody its spirituality. They were joined by the Church of the Nazarene and the Church of God, Anderson, Indiana.[24]

---

[22] Daniel Steele, *Love Enthroned: Essays on Evangelical Perfection.* New York: Phillips & Hunt; Cincinnati: Hitchcock & Walden, 1880; B.W. Gorham. *God's Method with Man, or, Sacred Scenes along the Path to Heaven.* Cincinnati: Hitchcock & Walden, 1879; Gilbert Haven, Introduction, George Hughes. *Days of Power in the Forest Temple.* Boston: John Bent, 1873; Charles Edward White. The Beauty of Holiness: *Phoebe Palmer as Theologian, Revivalist, Feminist, and Humanitarian.* Grand Rapids, MI: Francis Asbury, 1986; W, McDonald & John E. Searles. *The Life of Rev. John Inskip.* Boston: McDonald & Gill, 1885; J.A. Wood. *Perfect Love (etc.).* Chicago: Christian Witness, 191; Daniel Wise. Earnest Christianity (etc.). Toronto: G.R. Sanderson, 1855; George Peck. *The Scripture Doctrine of Christian Perfection (etc.).* New-York: Carlton & Phillips, 1854; Nathan Bangs. *The Necessity, Nature, and Fruits of Sanctification (etc.).* New-York: Lane & Scott, 1851; Timothy Merritt. *The Christian's Manual: a Treatise on Christian Perfection*,etc.) New-York: Mason & Lane,1836.

[23] Kevin M. Watson. *Old or New School Methodism?: The Fragmentation of a Theological Tradition.* Oxford, UK & New York: Oxford University Press, 2019.) Watson's *Perfect Love* restates Wesleyan teaching on entire sanctification for 21st century Methodism. (Kevin M. Watson. *Perfect Love: Recovering Entire Sanctification – the Lost Power of the Methodist Movement.* Franklin, TN: Seedbed, 2021.

[24] Melvin Dieter, in Wayne E. Caldwell, ed. *Reformers and Revivalists: History of The Wesleyan Church.* Indianapolis: Wesley Press, 1992, 168&169; John W.V. Smith. *The Quest for Holiness and Unity: A Centennial History of the Church of God (Anderson, Indiana).* Anderson, IN: Warner, 1980.

Camp Meetings for the Wesleyan Methodist Connexion symbolized a renewed emphasis on holiness after the Civil War. Wesleyans saw the National Camp Meeting Association for the Promotion of Holiness as the leading force for camp meetings and the major expression of holiness theology and practice. Leaders like Methodist preacher John Inskip and massive camp meeting revivals across the United States symbolized a Methodist movement far greater than any single denomination. This new leadership and renewed camp meeting movement provided encouragement for people in smaller, Wesleyan tradition denominations.[25]

John Inskip

Holiness camp meetings, in the late 19th century and beyond, kept Wesley's sanctification theology alive and influential in the Methodist movement. They were not unaware of changes in the surrounding society, but they were, or tried to be, selective in what changes they might accept and integrate with the revivals they had known. The issue of relevance sometimes led to proposals to change the doctrine, culture, and ministries of the churches in order, sometimes only ostensibly, to speak to the new realities of their world. The churches and the Holiness Movement had to look criti-

---

[25] Robert Black & Keith Drury. *The Story of the Wesleyan Church*. Indianapolis: Wesleyan Publishing House, 2012, 78&79; Wayne E. Caldwell. *Reformers and Revivalists: The History of the Wesleyan Church*. Indianapolis: Wesley, 1992, 162-164.

cally at these things in order to maintain Scriptural authority and continuity with Wesleyan theology.

Holiness camp meetings were "designed to summon the Church herself to a reconsecration" whose goal was "the replenishing of the Church with grace," Bishop Haven knew the world's power to "push[] its earthly and corrupting influences upon the Church," Haven saw the world offering to Christians its secular, material goods as replacements for their love for God. That corrupting world "invades the Church at every pore, and weakens and destroys her: so she has fallen again and again in her past long history; so will she fall again and again, unless power divine continually inspires, upraises, sanctifies." To meet this challenge, "these forest meetings have been held."[26]

The grace-empowered goal of sanctification is for each person to become what God created us to be. The setting forth and encouragement of that goal is, and always has been, essential to the Methodist movement, and, in fact, to Scriptural Christianity. Whenever there has been a revival of this gospel of holiness, it has signaled not a foreign, divisive departure from normal Methodist doctrine and practice, but a return to our original identity and purpose.

---

[26] Gilbert Haven, Introduction, George Hughes. *Days of Power in the Forest Temple (etc.)*. Boston: John Bent, 1873, 5.

9

Inspiration for Mission

"But you will receive power when the Holy Spirit comes on you; and you will be my witnesses in Jerusalem, and in all Judea and Samaria, and to the ends of the earth."[1]

"Fly abroad, thou mighty Gospel, Win and conquer, never cease;
May thy lasting, wide dominions / Multiply and still increase;
Sway thy scepter, Saviour, all the world around."[2]

When the National Association for the Promotion of Holiness held its massive camp meeting at Round Lake, NY, in 1869, Methodist preachers from across North America, representing several denominations, held forth the message of salvation and sanctification common to their Wesleyan tradition. One of them was AME Zion Bishop Singleton T. Jones, who, toward the end of that gathering, urged his listeners not to keep the experience of that meeting to themselves, but instead "go home and tell them how great things the Lord has done for you," and enlist them in telling others.

> Thus shall we be instrumental in carrying the blessed benefits of this Round Lake meeting wherever we go. Our friends, many of them, could not be here. Some of them are invalids; others are attending to business; others are too poor to come. We have been here, blessed by God! and we have enjoyed these heavenly influences. Let us carry them home, then, to

---

[1] Acts 1:8, NIV.

[2] William Williams, "O'er the gloomy hills of darkness," v. 3, quoted in Alexander Clark, "Prayer Entreated for the Spread of the Gospel," in *Fraternal Camp-Meeting Sermons, Preached by Minister of the Various Branches of Methodism at the Round Lake Camp-Meeting, New York, July,1874*. New York: Nelson & Phillips; Cincinnati: Hitchcock & Walden, 1875, 389.

others.³

Beginning with family, friends, and neighbors, people should take the message from the mountain top of camp meeting to their world, with ripple effects that could reach even farther. In another sermon, M.E. Bishop Jesse Peck urged his hearers to live out the Great Commission by the promised presence of Jesus for this work:

> ...Do not give up the idea of making disciples of all nations; the Gospel of the kingdom is to be preached to all nations, "beginning at Jerusalem." Let us go on with it. O why linger! Rouse ye, brethren, in the name of the Lord! Teach men the knowledge of the true God, of the only Saviour... the way to escape hell and find a home in heaven. Rouse ye! Millions of men are under guilt and moving rapidly on to endless ruin. Rouse ye, servants of God! the world languishes and dies for want of the Gospel! Rouse ye! O rouse ye! The blood of perishing millions will be required at your hands.
>
> Christian ministers, see the power of your Divine Master, and the authority passed on to you. Hear the command, "Go into all the world and disciple all nations," and do not disobey. Go out and teach the nations, bring them to Jesus, baptizing them in the name of the holy Trinity. Teach them, O teach *the world*, all things whatsoever Jesus has commanded, and take courage as you hear him say, "Lo, I am with you always, even unto the end of the world."

To Bishop Peck's message we can add that of the Canadian Wesleyan preacher George Douglass, who said "The Power of the Gospel," is "unbounded benevolence" invading a world of "universal selfishness."⁴

Camp meetings were never intended for their immediate participants *only*, but as centers of inspiration that would transform families, churches, communities, regions, nations, and ultimately the world itself. Bishop Peck's ringing presentation of the Great Commission was a forceful reminder of this. The blessings of Round Lake and every such gathering were meant to be widely shared and productive, for God's redeeming love was not, and is not, a weak or trivial thing.

> As the rain and the snow come down from heaven, and do not return to it without watering the earth and making it bud and flourish, so that it yields

---

³ Singleton T. Jones, "Duty of Working for Christ," in *Fraternal Camp-Meeting Sermons (etc.)*. New York: Nelson & Phillips; Cincinnati: Hitchcock & Walden, 1875, 406.

⁴ Jesse Peck, "The Great Commission, and George Douglass, "The Power of the Gospel," in *Fraternal Camp-Meeting Sermons (etc.)*. New York: Nelson & Phillips; Cincinnati: Hitchcock & Walden, 1875, 345&346; 249-259.

seed for the sower and bread for the eater, so is my word that goes out from my mouth: it will not return to me empty, but will accomplish what I desire and achieve the purpose for which I sent it.[5]

Like the early apostles, those leaving camp meetings went forth fired up, equipped, and ready to take what F.F. Bruce called "the spreading flame" to a world in desperate need.[6] When some felt unequal to this task, their preachers would remind them of the Source and seriousness of the call, and the power available to carry it out. The world might present formidable obstacles to this mission, but "the transforming power of grace," working through God's people, could break through them all.[7]

Early on, Douglas Camp Meeting in Massachusetts devoted time and energy to missions, hearing from prominent missionaries, and raising funds for their cause. "Indeed, this may be called a missionary camp meeting; for many have been called of God to the mission field on these grounds." Commitments made and priorities rearranged on the camp ground made a difference wherever people went – and in decisions about where they would go. Douglas attracted well-known preachers like B.W. Gorham, John Inskip, Daniel Steele, William McDonald and Amanda Berry Smith. While Douglas proclaimed itself happily "undenominational," it embodied a thoroughly Wesleyan holiness message and was an important part of the National Camp Meeting Association for the Promotion of Holiness. In the words of one of its preachers, Rev. A. Lowrey, "Holiness is the very heart of Christianity itself."[8]

Douglas was not unique in this regard. Ohio's Camp Sychar has also made missions an important part of its camp meeting, influenced by the work of Methodist Episcopal Bishop William Taylor and others.[9] Two classic studies show the connection between revival spirituality and practical, even political action based on Christian ethics and the Holy Spirit's inspiration and motivation. These are Timothy L. Smith. *Revivalism and Social Reform* (etc.). New York: Harper & Row, 1957, and Gilbert

---

[5] Isaiah 55:10&11, NIV.

[6] F.F. Bruce, *The Spreading Flame (etc.)*. Eugene, OR: Wipf & Stock, 2004.

[7] Thomas C. Oden, *The Transforming Power of Grace*. Nashville: Abingdon, 1993.

[8] Edward E. Davies, *Illustrated History of Douglas Camp Meeting*. Wilmore, KY: First Fruits, 2016 (orig. 1890), 9; 15-17; 19; 23; 43.

[9] Edward E. Davies. *Illustrated History of the Douglas Camp Meeting*. Wilmore, KY: First Fruits, 2016 (orig. Boston: McDonald, Gill, 1890), 21; Kenneth O. Brown. *A History of Camp Sychar (etc.)*. Hazleton, PA: Holiness Archives, 2000, 111-114; 128.

Hobbs Barnes. *The Antislavery Impulse, 1830-1845*. Gloucester, MA: Peter Smith, 1973. Both demonstrate linkages in thought and action between evangelical religion and social issues of the time. Phoebe Palmer illustrates the specific connection between holiness theology and social involvement in her outreach to the Four Points neighborhood in New York City. An excellent example in England is the career of William Wilberforce, in which his evangelical faith and values motivated his tireless campaign to abolish slavery.[10]

Phoebe Palmer

The balance between piety and action is captured in a camp meeting hymn, which says,

"Betwixt the mount and multitude;
Our day is spent in doing good,
Our night in praise and prayer."[11]

---

[10] Charles Edward White. The Beauty of Holiness: Phoebe Palmer as Theologian, Revivalist, Feminist, and Humanitarian. Grand Rapids, MI: Francis Asbury, 1986; Mark O. Hatfield, Foreword, William Wilberforce. *Real Christianity (etc.)*. Portland, OR: Multnomah, 1982, xv-xxix.

[11] W. McDonald & S. Hubbard, eds. *The Wesleyan Sacred Harp (etc.)*. Boston: John P. Jewett; Cleveland: Jewett, Proctor & Worthington; New York: Sheldon, Lamport & Blakeman, 1856, 155.

Gilbert Haven, widely known as an abolitionist, scholar, and later a Methodist Episcopal bishop, was a participant in, and advocate for, the holiness camp meetings of his day. Clearly he saw the connection between the way of salvation and Christian involvement in social issues. One example was his appreciative introduction to the biography Maggie Newton Van Cott, an accomplished evangelist and the first woman to receive a license to preach in the M.E. Church. In that introduction he argued forcefully for the complete legitimacy of woman acting upon God's call to ministry, and said that women active in Methodist ministry are fully in line with the view of John Wesley and the relevant Biblical interpretation of Adam Clarke. While Clarke believed there were ministries other than preaching "of which men only, and men called of God, are capable," he said this about women as preachers in his commentary on Romans 16:12:

> ...Christian *women*, as well as *men*, laboured in the ministry of the word. In those times of simplicity, all persons, whether men or women, who had received the knowledge of the truth, believed it to be their duty to propagate it to the uttermost of their power. Many have spent much useless labour in attempting to prove that these women did not *preach*. That there were some *prophetesses*, as well as *prophets*, in the Christian church, we learn, and that a woman might *pray* or *prophesy*, provided she had her *head covered*, we know: and that whoever *prophesied*, spoke unto others to *edification, exhortation*, and *comfort*, St. Paul declares in I Cor. Xiv. 3. And that no preacher can do *more*, every person must acknowledge; because to *edify, exhort*, and *comfort*, are the prime ends of the Gospel ministry. If women thus *prophesied*, then women *preached*.[12]

Like Bishop Haven, John Inskip was both a revival preacher and "a thorough abolitionist." His first priority was to his work as a pastor and camp meeting preacher and organizer, and it is in this role he is most remembered. He joined the Union army and believed the Civil War would put an end to slavery. He showed great pastoral compassion for the soldiers he served, yet "with no animosity towards the South." He explained in a letter to his New York City church, "My business is to preach the Gospel of peace to mankind, and to induce men to love each other and to do good even to their enemies."[13]

---

[12] Gilbert Haven, Introduction to John O. Foster. *Life and Labors of Maggie Newton Van Cott, The first Lady Licensed to Preach in the Methodist Episcopal Church in the United States.* Cincinnati: Hitchcock & Walden, 1872, xxi; xxiii; xxvi; Adam Clarke. *The New Testament ... with a Commentary and Critical Notes (etc.).* Baltimore: John J. Harrod, Methodist Protestant Church, 1838, ii: 169.

[13] W. McDonald & John E. Searles. The Life of Rev. John S. Inskip (etc.). Boston: McDonald & Gill, 1885. 133; 135; 137.

Maggie Newton Van Cott

Nathan Bangs, who started his involvement in camp meetings while a young preacher in Canada, was able to raise support for the cause of missions at later such gatherings. Both camp meetings and denominational missionary outreach were expressions of Methodism's foundational purpose, "to reform the continent, and spread Scripture-holiness over these lands."[14]

In Canada, Mississauga preacher Peter Jones was converted at a camp meeting (1823) where he "was led to believe that the Supreme Being was in the midst of the people who were now engaged in worshipping him." Jones worked with William Case and many others to bring Indians into the Methodist fold, often through camp meetings. Case led the camp

---

[14] S.M. Stiles & J.G. Patterson, eds. *Fraternal Camp-Meeting Sermon, Preached by Ministers of the Various Branches of Methodism at the Round Lake Camp-Meeting (etc.)*. New York: Nelson & Phillips; Cincinnati: Hitchcock & Walden, 1875, 398-407; 326-346;249-266; Jared Maddox, *Nathan Bangs and the Methodist Episcopal Church (etc.)*. Nashville: New Room, 2018, 76; *The Doctrines and Discipline of the Methodist Episcopal Church (etc.)*. Philadelphia: Henry Tuckniss, 1797, iii.

meeting in Ancaster, Upper Canada, where Jones found his new life with God. In response, Case said, "... now is the door opened for the work of conversion among his nation." Peter Jones became a renowned preacher, interpreter, author, and diplomat within Canadian Methodism. The connection between camp meetings and mission could not have been clearer. He wrote, "Oh that the Lord would carry on his work until all the nations of the earth are brought to the knowledge of the truth."

Jones described camp meetings attended by Indians and whites together, where he felt the presence of God in the midst of the people. At a meeting in 1826 at Twelve Mile Creek, he wrote, "my native brethren rejoiced greatly in that Great Being who is no respecter of persons, but disperses His heavenly blessings on all who call on His name." At one point Upper Canada's Governor Peregrine Maitland tried to shut down any further camp meetings, but after a respectful, though temporary compliance, indigenous Methodists resumed their gatherings. At one camp meeting near present day Toronto, Jones spoke to Indians who had come from Lake Simcoe, and to Europeans who were also present, focusing on the blessings of eternal life and the prospects of Indian missions moving farther West. At this gathering, thirty-six Indians were baptized following their "change of heart."

In still another (1828) camp meeting, Peter Jones and his native colleague Peter Jacobs took part and interpreted for a large audience that included two to three hundred Indians. Jones' includes a fascinating description of the tent where the meeting was held, an adaptation of what had become the expected arrangements everywhere:

> The Camp ground enclosed about two acres, which was surrounded with board tents, having one large gate for teams to go in and out, and three smaller ones. The Indians occupied one large tent, which was 240 feet long and 15 feet broad. It was covered over head with boards, and the sides were made tight with bushes, to make it secure from any encroachments. It had four doors fronting the Camp ground. In this long house, the Indians arranged themselves in families, as is their custom....

Another meeting that same year saw people from several communities across Upper Canada join in a common effort, with native preachers Jones, Peter Jacobs, and John Sunday working alongside missionary William Case. "We had a very powerful prayer meeting in the evening, sinners crying for mercy, and professing christians (sic) seeking for sanctification." The departure at the end of this meeting reflected the experiences of many others across the continent. Jones pictures the scene following the closing Communion:

At 3, P.M. we bade our Indian brethren farewell, who followed us to the water, and seemed reluctant to let us go. We all knelt down by the shore of the lake, and again commended each other to the protection of Almighty God in prayer, and then set sail for the Holland Landing. We left our Indian friends bathed in tears.

In still another gathering, "the following languages were used in praising and praying to the Great Spirit, viz. English, Mohawk, Oneida, Seneca, Tuscarora, Cayuga, Onondaga, and Chippaway – eight in all. God heard and understood all these tongues, and so blessed them all." Whatever adaptations were made in order to connect with indigenous people, maintained the same faith and spiritual experience as other such meetings. The ethnic barriers, while significant, did not prevent powerful, often shared experiences of the power of God.[15]

When Alfred Cookman spoke to the 50th Anniversary celebration of the Mission Society of the M.E. Church in Washington, DC, in 1869, he affirmed the necessary connection between spiritual motivation and missionary action. He did this so effectively that a *Christian Advocate* writer could say: "The address was pervaded with the blessed Spirit of the Master, and at times in rapt delight the audience wept and rejoiced; and when the speaker closed his remarks, all present must have felt that they had been with him at the feet of Jesus receiving instruction and comfort for further effort."

Alfred Cookman

---

[15] Peter Jones, *Life and Journals of Kah-Ke-Wah-Quo-Na-By (etc.)*. Toronto: Anson Green, 1860, 9&10; 14; 34; 70; 74&75; 90; 149; 172-176; 391.

In the course of his speech, Cookman asked,

> What is the missionary spirit? Is it an ordinary interest in, or a kind of general concern for, the heathen abroad and the heathen at home? – a cold and calculating love for those millions that have so long, too long, lingered in the shadow of sin and of death? Nay, sir, such a spirit as that would never convert the world – has never illustrated itself as the secret spring or motive power of self-sacrificing and successful endeavor in this world. There must be love, it is true, but then let us remember it must be love on fire; it must be love in a paroxysm; it must be love intensified, absorbing, all-controlling. Observe, if you please, the missionary quitting his home, kindred, native land, and accustomed comforts. He is willing to abide in the ends of the earth, encompassed by heart-sickening idolatrous superstition and crime. Wherefore? Is it because of a simple concern respecting the temporal, or even the spiritual, welfare of those by whom he may be encompassed? Nay, I insist it is rather because of the Christ-given and Christ-like love that burns in his heart and literally consumes his life. Oh, sir! it is the missionary spirit that crosses broad seas, that clambers cloud-crowned mountains, that traverses far-distant regions, that sails around the world if it may save but a single soul. It is the missionary spirit that breathes miasmas, that bears heavy burdens, that challenges adversaries, that imperils precious life, that laughs at impossibilities, and cries, "This must, and this shall be done." It is the missionary spirit that gives and bears sacrifices, and dies, if it were necessary, and if it were possible, a hundred thousand deaths, if, like its divine Exemplar, it might be going about doing good. Now, as I have said, there may be liberality, but there can not be the missionary spirit where there is not a conscientious, Christ-like liberality.[16]

More recently, in holiness camp meetings in the Wesleyan/Pilgrim Holiness portion of the movement, the ties between camp meeting revival and mission grew especially strong. However, mission generally equated with evangelism, flowing from the Great Commission.[17] In more liberal, mainstream circles, mission on the one hand, and evangelism and holiness on the other, were redefined so as to create an unnecessary gap between piety and practical, compassionate outreach.[18]

Mission, when it is deep and genuine, flows from a loving heart and spiritual energy reflecting the love and power of God. These are fruits of the kind of transformation at the heart of the camp meeting experience. Beyond anything secular altruism can produce, this grace-empowered,

---

[16] Henry B. Ridgaway. *The Life of the Rev. Alfred Cookman (etc.)*. New York: Nelson & Phillips; Cincinnati: Hitchcock & Walden, 1874, 354-356.

[17] Matthew 28:16-20.

[18] Leon O Hinson, in Wayne E. Caldwell, ed. Reformers and Revivalists: *History of the Wesleyan Church*. Indianapolis: Wesley Press, 1992, 236-239.

outward-flowing love and energy is found in people who see the world and its people differently in Christ. "We love because he first loved us."[19]

---

[19] I John 4:19, NIV.

10

Decline, Renewal, and Hope I

"...it is God who works in you to will and to act in order to fulfill his good purpose."[1]

"Jesus, Saviour, great Example, Pattern of all purity,
I would follow in Thy footseps [sic], Daily growing more like Thee."[2]

From time to time, people have voiced concerns about the future of camp meetings. At such times, it has been important to revisit the original purpose of these meetings, to ask whether that purpose remains God's purpose, and if so, to see how that purpose can be carried out in a new day. It is possible that any instrumentality may run its course. Camp meetings have always functioned as an extraordinary means of grace, so it might be time for something else, perhaps even the ordinary means of grace, to take their place. But if, with prayer and reflection - even under adverse, discouraging circumstances - it is clear that camp meetings remain "his good purpose," we can forge ahead with confidence, not based on our own limited vision and resources, but the limitless vision and resources of the One who works in us.

The camp grounds chosen for this study represent many more. While it would be impossible to cover the entirety of their journeys, their histories illustrate the various directions they have taken since they began, and the decisions or circumstances that took them one way or another. All of them have, or once had, a place in the Methodist or Methodist Holiness tradition

---

[1] Philippians 2:13, NIV.
[2] W.J. Kirkpatrick, "More Like Thee," in J.S. Inskip, ed. *Songs of Triumph: Adapted to Prayer Meetings, Camp Meetings, and All Other Seasons of Religious Worship*. Philadelphia: National Publishing Association for the Promotion of Holiness, 1882, 27.

in North America. Many of them have tried to balance, or choose between, their original, spiritual purposes, and newer opportunities to diversify, so as to become summer resorts. Some replaced revival with some form of cultural enrichment in a religious atmosphere. In other cases, leaders and governing boards were able to maintain the purposes of their founders, while still others saw a growing need to provide an enjoyable vacation experience with a spiritual center and environment. Of this last group, there are some that, quickly or over time, essentially gave up their original purpose and became secular resorts. Some were/are associated with one of the many denominations in the Methodist family, while others are genuinely Wesleyan without those institutional ties.

As Kenneth O. Brown has shown us, there are also many places and programs that address one or more of the needs that have been met by camp meeting grounds. Church camps, Bible conferences, Christian music festivals, and Christian retreat centers would fit in this category, and even some thoroughly secular institutions provide elements of the experience offered by camp meetings, such as time away from work or a place to enjoy the outdoors.[3]

Dan Young expressed a common concern that camp meetings were morphing into something different, something that could take them away from their original purpose and simplicity. In his 1860 autobiography, Young says, "Camp-meetings have been a source of great good; but I have fears that the introduction of luxury, as in the keeping of a sumptuous table, will in some measure destroy their usefulness. Persons should go to these meetings to feast their souls and not their bodies."[4]

John Collins saw camp meetings change in order to relate to a changing society. He was sure that "wherever there shall be a departure from the primitive modes of Methodism, there will be a decline in the spirituality of the Church and in its growth." He could only see dimly, from afar, just how prophetic his observations would prove to be.[5]

---

[3] Kenneth O. Brown. *Holy Ground, Too*. Hazleton, PA: Holiness Archives, 1997. See also Samuel Avery Quinn. *Cities of Zion: The Holiness Movement and Methodist Camp Meeting Towns in America*. Lanham, MD: Lexington Books, 2019.

[4] W.P. Strickland, ed. *Autobiography of Dan Young (etc.)*. New York: Carlton & Porter, 1860, 204.

[5] *A Sketch of the Life of Rev. John Collins (etc.)*. Cincinnati: Swormstedt & Power, 1850, 117.

Others envisioned a kind of prosperity in the spiritual impact of camp meetings, commensurate with the growing prosperity of the Church and its capacity for service.

> When we compare the present state of the Church with its wealth and means of doing good, we should be humble and thankful. Our camp-grounds are not ... without seats, or preacher's stand, or tents [as in some of the earliest experiences]. Now all these are made ready, with beautiful cottages, and other accommodations. In view of all this, we, with hearts filled with love to God and man, should go to save souls by thousands. Then will these meetings be crowned with Pentecostal fire.[6]

Nathan Bangs' long ministry coincided with the first decades of the camp meeting, beginning with his involvement at Canada's first such gathering in 1805. There he witnessed both transformational power and the fact that emotional responses could devolve into "wild excesses." Throughout his career he attended and preached at many camp meetings, even after his retirement. He saw a need for participants to "distinguish between divinely inspired emotions and depraved passions," not only to avoid the latter, but because he had seen how genuine emotions "draw people closer to God." Because he knew their blessings so well from his own observation and experience, "he advocated for and preached at camp meetings and revivals his entire life."

Bangs was also one of the voices explaining and defending Wesleyan sanctification theology. He noticed that as his denomination (Methodist Episcopal) grew stronger and more "respectable," it also compromised important parts of its identity and purpose. Jared Maddox writes: "In order to attain respectability, itinerants and laity surrendered fundamental beliefs and practices, including their attendance at camp meetings, adherence to the 'General Rules,' and belief in the immediate presence and power of the Holy Spirit." After working effectively to strengthen his church's support for its ministers, its educational opportunities, and its missionary outreach, as integral parts of its overall growth, one of the unintended consequences was a weakening of its spiritual foundation.

Bangs also recognized a need to maintain original Wesleyan sanctification theology amid newer elaborations, such as some elements in Phoebe Palmer's outline of steps to holiness (though his long friendship with Palmer remained intact.) Whatever else was happening, he continued participating in camp meetings, and held on to other perspectives he considered essential to the movement, especially his opposition to Slavery and to

---

[6] Gilbert Haven & Thomas Russell. *Incidents and Anecdotes of Rev. Edward T. Taylor (etc.)*. Boston: B.B. Russell, 1872, 228.

Calvinism. His many books, from his four-volume history, to his biography of Freeborn Garrettson, to those addressing specific issues, remain as testimony to his faithfulness in the Wesleyan cause.[7]

After a period of decline, traditional hopes soared with the opening of holiness camp meetings, beginning in 1867. But concerns remained that something of the original life and purpose of such meetings had been compromised or replaced in the Victorian age. George Hughes alluded to a larger context of change within much of the Wesleyan movement. For example, he said, "In some places, class meetings have been totally abandoned; in others, they exist only in name; and there is almost universally a growing neglect." Hughes asks, "Has there not been a great overshadowing of vital piety by that which is merely formal and external in its character? In a word, has there not been everywhere a fearful inundation of worldliness?"

Given the many benefits of camp meetings, including the way these events embodied the original purpose of the Wesleyan movement, it is no wonder that many would do all they could, not only to save their form, but recover their essence, restore their effectiveness, and expand their influence. By the late 19th century, camp meetings were under fire from some quarters, and some had lost the vitality they had once known. In some, their original energy had waned and was in need of recharging. Some were changing from what they had been. Some had died, though a new burst of spiritual energy was already surfacing. George Brown, late in his life, reflected on the meaning of camp meetings for his own pilgrimage, for people he had known and churches he had served. He looked back with sadness, and wished those times could return. "Most gladly now, in my old age, would I attend another such meeting; but I suppose I never shall, for our people have no more camp meetings." We can hear the sorrow in his voice, and rejoice that his statement was far from universal.[8]

George Hughes saw this pattern flowing from a decline, weakening, and dilution of teaching on sanctification, an essential part of Wesleyan theology and central to the mission of the Methodist movement in all its denominational expressions. Some camp meetings shared, as he saw it, in this general malaise, which necessitated the work of the National Camp

---

[7] Jared Maddox. *Nathan Bangs and the Methodist Episcopal Church: The Spread of Scriptural Holiness in Nineteenth-Century America*. Nashville: New Room, 2018, xv; 16&17; 98, n.25; 107; 104; 108; 112&113; 118; 124.

[8] George Brown. *Recollections of Itinerant Life: Including Early Reminiscences*. Cincinnati: R.W. Carroll; Springfield (OH): Methodist Protestant Publishing House, 1866, 341.

Meetings for the Promotion of Holiness. Too many camp meetings were operating without their original focus and power.

> They had become, to a large extent, places of recreation and pleasant social intercourse. Families secured their tenting-ground, put up swings for their children, arranged for their favorite croquet-game, and, in short, prepared for a week or ten days' relaxation in the grove. All this was very agreeable in its social and recreative features; but giving it the name of a camp-meeting was a misnomer.

Hughes goes on to speak of small business ventures, misuse of the Sabbath, and sermons designed more to impress than convert. "Here and there were honorable examples of camp-meetings being run on different principles, where a good degree of saving work was done, but they were the exceptions." There were many who felt that the day of camp meetings was over, either because they were no longer effective, or no longer needed. But Hughes and many others believed "there was a remnant with undefiled garments standing by the old doctrine, and keeping it alive amid tears and prayers and hard struggling." Faithful to "the blessed gospel truth of full salvation, they believed it would come up again before the church with fresh interest." To this end, the National Camp Meeting Association for the Promotion of Holiness began operating massive camp meetings in 1867. Those who organized and led these meetings were mostly prominent ministers in the Methodist movement, but participants included preachers and attendees from several non-Methodist denominations as well.[9]

John Inskip is best known for his leadership of the Association. He had earlier been an apologist for Methodist teaching and practice, while having some reticence about Christian perfection. After years of ministry in the Methodist Episcopal Church, he came to a point where he recognized [in theory] the blessings of perfect love, while remaining a skeptic. "He did his best to encourage the people to go on, but, as he often said, he did not know where they were going." The day came when he could no longer preach about this without seeking it for himself.

> The culminating point [in a sermon] was reached, and in the most vehement manner he exclaimed: "Brethren, lay aside every weight! Do it now. You can do it now, and therefore should do it. It is your privilege, and therefore your duty at this moment to make a consecration of your all to God, and declare that you will henceforth be wholly and forever the Lord's!" He sought to make this point very clear, and emphasized it with increased earnestness. "Let us *now* lay aside every weight," he said, "and

---

[9] George Hughes. *Days of Power in the Forest Temple (etc.)*. Boston: John Bent, 1873, 12; 13; 19; 26&27; 29-31.

the sin which doth so easily beset us." He dwelt upon the thought; and as he continued to urge the admonition, a voice within said, "Do it yourself." He paused a moment, and the admonition was repeated, "Do it yourself, and do it now." Must he turn away from his own teaching, and urge others to do what he would not do himself? He could, consistently, do nothing but obey. He believed most fully in the correctness of the views he had presented, and urged his people to adopt. As an honest man he could not do otherwise than lead in their practical observance. He was not long in deciding what course to pursue. In the same earnest manner he said: "Come, brethren, follow your pastor. I call Heaven and earth to witness that I now declare I will be henceforth wholly and forever the Lord's."

Inskip found that his ministry from that point on was stronger and more effective. "Everywhere he proclaimed the great salvation. It soon became impressed upon his mind that God had called him to special work, in the spread of scriptural holiness." He was convinced that "its spread in the churches meant the salvation of the world." Looking over the journey of Methodism since the beginning, he concluded that, instead of progressing, "we have retrograded." His hope was "that we will seek to restore the 'old land-marks.' We must revive the old doctrine of Christian holiness." Whether in local congregations or in what would become the National Camp Meeting Association for the Promotion of Holiness, his ministry would be dedicated to this cause.

The renewal of spiritual vitality, harnessed to the proven, traditional instrumentality of the camp meeting, would drive the movement forward into a new era of revivalism. As with earlier wars, following the Civil War "the churches were weakened spiritually in every part of the land." Camp meetings had gone through their own doldrums and were regarded by some as outmoded, if not useless in energizing the churches. Yet the holiness movement brought a revitalized vision of what camp meetings could yet become. With their initial effort at Vineland in 1867, and for many years after that in many places, Inskip and his fellow leaders in the movement more than proved their point. Starting with their initial camp meeting, John Inskip would be President of the Association, supported by the Methodist Episcopal Church.

Ironically, critics of the movement saw its leaders as divisive, even "schismatic." The camp meeting, long a successful platform for evangelism and spiritual growth based on Wesleyan theology, had been a source of unity around shared principles. It is ironic that those breaking away from this unity saw traditionalists as the cause of division. Moreover, the new National meetings included a warm invitation to people of other denominations to join in a common evangelical witness. While some thought of these new gatherings as "the first holiness camp meetings ever held since Pentecost," in reality they were reconnecting with earlier camp meetings in a purpose they all shared. The presence of Inskip, B.W. Gorham, and others, connected the movement with that earlier history. Indeed there is impressive common ground from Wesley's time through the holiness movement. Along with shared theology, and typical of the first camp meetings, and the Presbyterian Communion occasions before them, the Lord's Supper would remain an important part of these holiness events. Acclamations and expressions of appreciation came from one community after another.[10]

Nor was the Association alone in recognizing this need. The bishops of the Methodist Episcopal Church, in their address to the 1864 General Conference, said, "A gracious revival of religion, deep, pervading, and permanent, is the great demand of our time." For this reason, they said, "Let God, our heavenly Father, behold in us tears and confidence before his throne, pleading night and day, through the Redeemer, for the outpouring of the Holy Ghost upon the church, the nation, and the world. This is our only hope: let our faith command it, and it shall be."[11]

Elijah Hedding

---

[10] John S. Inskip. *Methodism Explained and Defended*. Cincinnati: H. S. & J. Applegate, 1851; W. McDonald & John Searles. *The Life of Rev. John S. Inskip (etc.)*. Boston: McDonald & Gill, 1885, 125; 150-152; 186-188; 190-192; 196-198; 250&251.

[11] George Hughes, *Days of Power in the Forest Temple (etc.)*. Boston: John Bent, 1873, 34.

When camp grounds were established for National Association camp meetings, they included streets named for key figures in the Methodist movement. At Manheim, PA, where "B.W. Gorham was commissioned to superintend the preparation of the ground," streets named for John Wesley, Francis Asbury, Bishops Hedding and Hamline, and others, reminded those who walked on them of the long heritage of sanctification theology leading up to that moment (1868). Other camp grounds would do the same, including one at Silver Lake, NY, where even today, with camp meeting worship only a distant memory, people walk and drive on streets named Wesley, Hamline, Haven, and Hedding. Other holiness meetings would follow, scattered across the states. Canadian Methodists would share this resurgence in their own camp meetings. The selection of preachers and topics, the form and symbols used, and experience lived at these holiness camp grounds demonstrated the continuity of this renewed and renewing movement with the tradition and purpose of Wesleyan Christianity. In Hughes words, "The enterprise was inherently loyal, loyal in doctrine and disciplinary aspects, loyal to the entire history of the Church, to the cardinal ideas of its founder, and the whole genius of the system of Christianity." Melvin Dieter confirmed this in his history of the holiness movement:

> The Methodist pastors who formed the National Camp Meeting Association for the Promotion of Holiness were as ardent Methodists as they were holiness advocates. They were completely honest in their consistent denial that there was anything schismatic in their adoption of the Methodist camp meeting for their own special purpose. They were sure that here was the most suitable platform for the sounding of the call to bring the church back to its central message and the only insurance of its continued blessing and usefulness. What they were really accomplishing, was to transplant a revivalistic doctrine and way of life with strong roots and vigorous new shoots into the structure of the only established institution congenial enough to the doctrine to nurture and preserve it through the tumultuous late nineteenth century.

The active involvement and public support of bishops and other prominent leaders gave legitimacy to these camp meetings: Dieter says, "The participation of bishops, presiding elders, and large numbers of Methodist laymen in the National Camp Meetings testified to a growing acceptance of the methods by the organized church." Another factor was that while the theological and spiritual substance of these meetings built upon the older camp meeting tradition, some of the more bizarre and widely criticized elements of the early gatherings were no longer encouraged and seldom seen.[12]

Within holiness circles, J.V. Watson recognized a problem that he believed was causing unnecessary disunity by focusing on differences in presentation of holiness theology and practice among those who articulated them for a new generation. Even more important was agreement on the basic meaning and importance of Christian perfection. Thus the need to shift perspective to this agreed upon center of the holiness message.

> Certain definitions, however, have been set up, occasioning among us much dispute, such as the difference between regeneration and sanctification, where and when the latter begins, and what is implied in its completion. These and other distinctions have led to as many definitions as definers, and it is seldom that two writers agree on the subject of Christian holiness, where the *mode* of the thing's progress, rather than the thing itself, has been the subject of discussion. Disputes have waxed warm, and even parties and sectional organizations have been temporarily created. Perhaps all will agree with us, that very little has been done by these discussions to harmonize the views of the Church, while, in some instances, the Christian's spirituality has been endangered. May it not be possible that we err in attempting to map out the process by which the justified sinner is advanced from incipient grace to perfect holiness in the fear of the Lord?

The acts of the Holy Spirit in transforming a person's life must be approached with humility, with an appreciation for the mystery involved. Watson could see little to be gained in putting too fine a point on the matter. "Rather let us speak of the *thing*, and abandon disputation on the *mode*. Who ever knew a sharp controversialist on the subject of the mode of Christian holiness, that did not give evidence before he got through, that he wrote far less from experience than from theory?"

Watson wanted to cut through schedules and "modes" to a renewed clarity on essence. To get at this, he offered the Great Commandment as the content and measure of holiness. "Theories and speculations aside, let us seek to know that God is supremely loved, and then are we supremely blessed." Even if we cannot explain to everyone's satisfaction the details or timetable of sanctification, "we nevertheless believe in giving it promi-

---

[12] George Hughes. *Days of Power in the Forest Temple (etc.)*. Boston: John Bent, 1873, 66&67; 425); Melvin Easterday Dieter. *The Holiness Movement of the Nineteenth Century*. Metuchen, NJ & London, UK: Scarecrow, 1980, 118; 125; Some of the sermons from the National Camp Meetings are available in *The Double Cure: or Echoes from National Camp-Meetings*. Wilmore, KY: First Fruits, 2016, and *Fraternal Camp-Meeting Sermons ... Round Lake Camp-Meeting ... 1874.*) New York: Nelson & Phillips, 1874.

nence in all our worship and religious teachings" – especially for Methodists. "If the doctrine be not peculiar to Methodists, we have always held it peculiarly." Among Biblical examples of its importance, Watson cites Paul's blessing: "The very God of peace sanctify you wholly; and I pray God your whole spirit, soul, and body, be preserved blameless unto the coming of our Lord Jesus Christ." Anyone reading this might well go on to verse 24: "The one who calls you is faithful and he will do it," clearly identifying the source and power of sanctification.[13]

In a similar vein, Darius Salter writes: "The Wesleyan Holiness Movement has been characterized by a robust theology of the Holy Spirit. We need to get beyond the arguments as to whether our pneumatology is Wesleyan, Palmerian, Finneyan, Mahanan, and Keswickian, or most representative of the 19th century Association for the Promotion of Holiness. ... We need to again confess that our only hope is to be found in the power and presence of the Holy Spirit."[14] Mark R. Quanstrom's history of holiness theology in the Church of the Nazarene shows how approaches to entire sanctification went through change and conflict in that denomination in its first century, even though the doctrine itself remains central to Nazarene identity. John W.V. Smith shows that another Wesleyan denomination, The Church of God (Anderson, Indiana), has wrestled with issues raised by holiness theology, while holiness itself maintained its importance for all concerned.[15]

At the same time, the larger Methodist movement was increasingly divided over Wesleyan sanctification theology and practice. Many were moving away from these, and from the chief engine of holiness preaching, the camp meeting. The great revival of camp meetings under the National Camp Meeting Association for the Promotion of Holiness put this area of teaching and experience back on center stage (without losing a strong emphasis on conversion). This was happening as many others thought the time for emphasizing such theology and practice – and for camp meetings themselves – had come to an end or was inevitably in decline.

---

[13] J.V. Watson. *Helps to the Promotion of Revivals*. New-York: Carlton & Porter, 1856, 219-221; 223, including his quote from I Thessalonians 5:23. The present author's quote is I Thessalonians 5:24, NIV.

[14] Darius L. Salter. *The Demise of the American Holiness Movement (etc.)*. Wilmore, KY: First Fruits, 2020, 383.

[15] Mark R. Quanstrom. *A Century of Holiness Theology (etc.)*. Kansas City, MO: Beacon Hill, 2004; John W.V. Smith. *The Quest for Holiness and Unity: A Centennial History of the Church of God (Anderson, Indiana)*. Anderson: IN: Warner, 1980.

Meanwhile, there was a divergence of camp meetings in the Methodist tradition into factions, with one group redoubling its efforts to maintain evangelical worship, including holiness, as their foundational and permanent purpose, while others were adding various forms of recreational and/or cultural programming, which often eclipsed or sublimated the original purpose.

Some camp meetings have tried to preserve the original purpose and "feel" of their annual events. Minuette Floyd, who has attended camp meetings for many years, expresses the value of continuity in these words:

> Spiritual integrity is still what draws many thousands of people to camp meetings each year. There is something profound about setting aside that sacred time far in advance. Something profound about being in nature and gathering under the oak or pine trees. And something profound about choosing to step back in time – to minimal plumbing, worn or mismatched furniture, and no way to avoid the ubiquitous dirt and dust.[16]

Professor Floyd is writing about camp meetings that continue into the present with relatively minimal changes. Other camp meetings have adapted more extensively to needs and interests in their changing world. Ocean Grove, New Jersey, for example, began, in many respects, as a classic Methodist gathering, founded by the well-known holiness preacher William B. Osborn and incorporated in 1870. Its primary purpose was to continue and strengthen the preaching of central Wesleyan teachings and involved many of the leading figures in the National Camp Meeting Association, including John Inskip, the Association's first President. But there were changes, some of them immediate. Ocean Grove was designed as a permanent site for annual camp meetings. That permanence was itself seen as a problem by some who thought a kind of transience was needed to preserve and continue earlier traditions. But over time, permanence has not been the difference maker its cautioners had feared. The camp meetings described and experienced by Minuette Floyd are also permanent, as are others that have successfully maintained their purpose and simplicity from an earlier time.

When the largest Methodist Churches in Canada or the United States went through conflict over their theological and spiritual identity and purpose, groups that left to form their own denominations often organized their own camp meetings, as did such earlier denominations as the Wesleyan Methodists and Free Methodists.

---

[16] Minuette Floyd. *A Place to Worship (etc.).* Columbia, SC: University of South Carolina Press, 2018, 89.

Howard Snyder notes that those who eventually became Free Methodists played an active role in Methodist Episcopal camp meetings and operated their own after they left. Speakers at these meetings were committed to Wesley's theology of conversion and Christian holiness. Some who were specifically and approvingly mentioned were Phoebe Palmer, Stephen Olin, Nathan Bangs, L.L. Hamline, B.W. Gorham, and John Wesley Redfield. "Redfield was converted in a Methodist camp meeting" and then found these meetings ideal for sharing the Wesleyan message and experience with great numbers of people. Both Benjamin Titus Roberts and his wife Ellen Stowe Roberts came from within the heart of Methodism's doctrine and practice with regard to holiness. Their struggles over, and living encounter with, sanctification developed and grew at camp meetings. Roberts once wrote about a camp meeting held in Portville, New York, calling it "the best he'd experienced." He said, "The conversions were very marked and clear. Many were sanctified, and the members generally were very much quickened." In an article for the *Northern Christian Advocate*, he wrote, "The meeting commenced in the spirit [sic], progressed in power, and closed in triumph." As he went on, the picture he drew fit very well the kind of camp meeting that followed Cane Ridge. He closed with "Long live camp meetings!" Roberts read with satisfaction reports of James Caughey's revival ministry in Canada. Once Free Methodism was on its own, camp meetings continued as a regular and important part of the new church's life.[17]

John Wesley Redfield

---

[17] Howard A. Snyder. *Populist Saints: B.T. and Ellen Roberts and the first Free Methodists*. Grand Rapids, MI & Cambridge, UK: William B. Eerdmans, 2006, 75-77; 91;94; 123; 127; 179&180; 211&212; 283-285; 297-301; 350; 397; 581; 691.

Of all the camp meetings associated with those who were to become Free Methodists, the one that held its first session in 1854, in **Bergen, New York**, was preeminent. A contested relationship to the (Methodist Episcopal) Genesee Conference would eventually end its short but illustrious life as a camp ground. Howard Snyder wrote, "Over the next few years the Bergen camp meeting played an increasingly important role in the events that led to Roberts' eventual expulsion from the Methodist Episcopal Church. At the same time, it was virtually the prototype of the many camp meetings that marked the early days of Free Methodism."

The camp ground itself consisted of "twenty-five acres of heavily forested land," not far from the Erie Canal village of Brockport, where Roberts had been appointed pastor. Other leaders in this venture held appointments in nearby communities. Speakers and participants would come from near and far and would include B.W. Gorham, author of the *Camp Meeting Manual*, who was a preacher and organizer at many holiness camp meetings.

The second annual Bergen camp meeting (1855) drew large crowds, who traveled by horse and wagon, or on the Erie Canal, or on the nearby New York Central Railroad. Those who guided these camp meetings were also key figures in the growing movement seeking to reform the Genesee Conference and the larger denomination. Among the issues bringing them together were their rejection of slavery, opposition to secret societies, and resistance to using pew rents to finance expensive, elaborate new churches. Behind these and other important matters was their desire to return to an older, simpler way of church life, one that would not lose sight of the poor in the rush for affluence and respectability. They were committed to the theology of sanctification and a way of living that held full salvation as its ultimate goal. To accomplish this, "Roberts wanted the Bergen camp meeting to be decidedly Methodist, but with its own organization, distinct and semi-independent from the conference. For this purpose he organized the Genesee Camp-Ground Association." To further assure and maintain its purpose and independence, the camp ground gave "Laymen's Conventions" a role in its management and in charting its future course. A long and contentious series of accusations and trials heightened tensions in the conference. Roberts and others would be expelled or, in solidarity with those who were expelled, would join their new denomination.

> By this time [the 1858 meeting] the Bergen camp meeting itself had gotten caught up in conference politics. Was the camp, and especially the Genesee Camp-Ground Association that sponsored it, an instrument of the Genesee Conference? Or was it independent, possibly schismatic? ... The ensuing struggle for the control of the camp meeting led to its demise.

Even so, the larger conflict did not keep participants from experiencing at Bergen the essence of traditional camp meetings. Ellen Roberts said of the same event, "While Bro. [Loren] Stiles was preaching the power of God came down all over the ground – I felt while here at one time as if in the suburbs of glory...."

It was still possible to hold the annual camp meeting in 1859. One participant, Ann Chesbrough, made it clear that the basic purpose of the meeting had not been overtaken by controversy. After describing the camp ground, she wrote, "Such a sense of holiness as pervaded the grounds I never felt before. It was heaven below. ... Many were saved and sanctified, the work went on in glorious power and spread in every direction."[18]

The two groups sought control over the camp ground for a few years, with both groups holding their meetings on the site. The M.E. Conference tried to discourage visitors from attending unauthorized (Free Methodist) gatherings at Bergen. Free Methodist (later Bishop) Edward Payson Hart wrote that 1862 was to be "the last meeting held by our people on the old Bergen camp-ground." New York State decided the ownership and control issue in favor of the M.E. Conference. Reports vary on the conference's success in holding approved camp meetings on the Bergen site, something they continued until 1872. The next year conference meetings moved to Silver Lake, New York. In a sad and apparently spiteful ending, the conference had the property (a neighbor, University of Chicago professor Galusha Anderson, had described it as a "beautiful primeval forest") lumbered, and in that unusable condition, sold it as a farm. By that time the Free Methodists had moved their camp meetings elsewhere.

The official M.E. view of the situation lauds "as a grand success" a Conference sponsored camp meeting at Bergen, in which Bishops Simpson and Ames took part. According to F.W. Conable's account,

> ...the happy results of the meeting in the quickening of the membership and the fresh anointing of the ministers for their work, rendered the meeting creditable to the Conference and to Methodism, and retrieved the time-honored and efficient means of grace "from the disgrace and odium which had been made to attach to it for many years, by its association with Nazaritical folly and fanaticism in the minds of our people."

Once ensconced in its new location, "Silver Lake camp ground," the camp meetings were seen by the M.E. Conference "as an instrumentality for good to the Church and for the salvation of the people." The 1876 ses-

---

[18] Howard A. Snyder. *Populist Saints: B.T. and Ellen Roberts and the First Free Methodists.* Grand Rapids, MI & Cambridge, UK: William B. Eerdmans, 2006, 283; 285; 299; 349&350; 420&421; 489.

sion of Conference committed itself to "seek to interest our people in the enterprise there initiated, and to secure their attendance upon the annual meetings, hoping and praying that this institution may become not only a bond of union to the whole Conference, but also a source of great spiritual power." These efforts continued and included some of the adaptations that occurred in other camp grounds, including Chautauqua-like cultural activities. The eventual results would be the Silver Lake Institute, with ties to the Conference until very recently, and a summer church camp named for Francis Asbury and continuing under Conference auspices to this day.[19] "Nazarite," which in the Old Testament designated someone who had voluntarily assumed an especially strict way of life, became a term of derision used against the reformers who became Free Methodists.

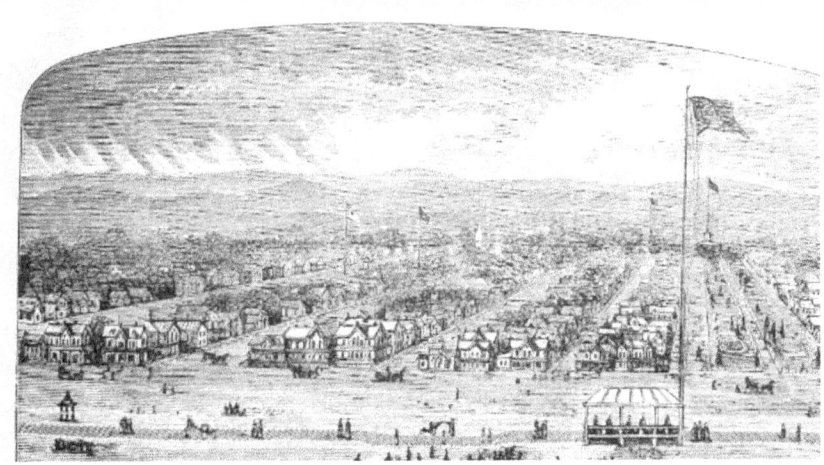

Ocean Grove Camp Ground

Ocean Grove, New Jersey, attempted to preserve the original purpose of Methodist camp meetings, while adding new levels of organization and elements of "a seaside summer resort." Founder W.B. Osborn established, or helped establish, camp meetings in India and Australia as well as North

---

[19] D. Gregory Van Dussen. "The Bergen Camp Meeting in the American Holiness Movement," *Methodist History*, XXL, 2 (January, 1983), 77-81; Joseph Goodwin Terrill. *The Life of Rev. John Wesley Redfield, M.D.* Chicago: Free Methodist Publishing House, 1889, 295; F.W. Conable. *History of the Genesee Annual Conference of the Methodist Episcopal Church (etc.)*. New York: Phillips & Hunt, 1885, 683; 741.

America. He was one of the organizers for the National Camp Meeting Association for the Promotion of Holiness, with its first camp meeting held at Vineland, New Jersey. Osborn envisioned and promoted "a seaside summer resort for ministers and the long-cherished idea of a camp-meeting by the sea." As different as Ocean Grove would be from earlier camp meetings, it was propelled, especially in its early years, by classic Wesleyan sanctification theology.

Although the location he chose appeared far from promising, Osborn knew the advantages of its two lakes and proximity to the ocean, and forged ahead with his plan.

> Strange to say we had not gone far [in looking over the site] before the conviction seized every mind, that dismal and destitute as it was, it possessed capabilities of being made to bloom and blossom as the rose. Especially as we stood in the sand drifts south of Main Avenue and looked out over the sea, it seemed as if a more magnificent site for cottage could not be found.

Ellwood H. Stokes, first president of the Ocean Grove Camp Meeting Association, said in 1869, "'God is here,' here in the beginning, and he trusted would be in the continuance – and to the end." Later, with the project well underway and growing, Stokes restated his conviction that God would always be the heart of Ocean Grove: "So long as we rigidly adhere to the principles of our organization and keep our eyes single to the Divine glory, the future of Ocean Grove cannot be otherwise than secure."[20]

Ocean Grove sought to offer improvements in housing, transportation, and entertainment, without losing its reason for being. Nearby Asbury Park chose a very different path, and that difference has grown over time. But at Ocean Grove, the centrality of worship, control of alcohol, and respect for the Sabbath all signaled the intention that this be a Christian camp ground, modified to meet genuine needs of a changing society without surrendering its founding purpose. Osborn and the other founders had been serious about creating a "Christian resort," to which world-weary people and families could go for a comprehensive Christian environment; "a permanent Christian Camp Meeting community," an enjoyable refuge, "where spiritual and physical health could be renewed."

One example of building on an early model, was the recognition that some form of policing would often be needed in order to keep "rowdies" at bay and insure that services and prayer meetings could proceed without

---

[20] Mrs. W.B. Osborn. *Pioneer Days at Ocean Grove*. New York: Methodist Book Concern, n.d. [1918], 4; 6-8; 11&12; 15; 21; 27&28; Troy Messenger. *Holy Leisure: Recreation and Religion in God's Square Mile*. Philadelphia: Temple University Press, 1999, 14, Fig. 3.

unwanted interruption. This had originally been accomplished through local leaders, magistrates, or unofficial deputies, sometimes recruited from among the rowdies themselves. Ocean Grove and others developed that provision to meet the needs of large, permanent communities by establishing designated police, who were to enforce rules against such things as alcohol consumption or disruptive noise.

To the camp's spiritual programs they added the attractions of ocean front scenery and recreation, a healthful environment, and increasingly enhanced housing. Soon there were boats on the campground's two lakes, stores to fully and reliably supply the needs of attendees, and Victorian summer homes to replace many of the original tents, though a significant number of prominent tents would remain.

Gardens and attractive walkways replaced a more rustic surrounding, transportation to and from the camp was greatly improved, and the time people spent on the ground increased to allow proper care and maintenance of buildings and grounds. Noted speakers such as Ulysses S. Grant would add to the presence of well-known preachers. This expanded and diversified facility "would allow desired rest and great salvation to be secured at the same time." Patriotic observances were held alongside religious services. An enlarged speakers' stand held seventy-five preachers and a vast pavilion seated 9,600 people. An enormous pipe organ symbolized how far worship had evolved and professionalized. Hotels and gathering places for specific groups added to the appearance and convenience of the place. Campground historian Wayne T. Bell sees all this in a positive light: "This is Ocean Grove, now a year-round community where neighbors help and care about each other, a place where one can find rest, recreation, religious riches, and personal renewal. Ocean Grove, created in the 19th century, is truly a model for the 21st century." What some would see as a decline from religious camp meeting to religious vacation spot, others would applaud as adaptation to a more modern, comfortable way of life. The critical distinction is that, at Ocean Grove, the foundation did not collapse under the adaptations.[21]

An 1879 report said "that the great central fact of Ocean Grove is *Salvation*. This is the foundation, superstructure, and capstone. When salvation ceases to be her fundamental and crowning work she will lose her strength and her glory will depart." This clarity and determination would enable Ocean Grove to make the religion/recreation balance work.

The same report restated W.B. Osborn's vision for Ocean Grove:

---

[21] Wayne T. Bell. *Ocean Grove*. Charleston, SC: Arcadia, 2000, 6-10; 15; 42; 46-48; 62-88.

...to maintain a place where those who would spend a few days or weeks at the seashore, can do so at moderate cost, and maintain for the members and friends of the Methodist Episcopal Church a proper, convenient, and desirable camp-meeting ground and seaside resort, free from the temptations and dissipations usually attendant upon fashionable watering places. This was our original declaration and this we propose in good faith to carry out unto the end.[22]

Did/does Ocean Grove accomplish, to a significant degree, the purpose of its founder and the purposes of a camp meeting? Troy Messenger says that for worshipers who came early in its history, "a stay at Ocean Grove was indeed a visit to the Holy. A summer lived in community with fellow pilgrims was time out of time – a sacred, festival time – when the routines of daily life were put aside for the pursuit of perfection." Specific practices might change over the years, but great effort was put into maintaining the essential vision. Ocean Grove was certainly not like the gatherings of the early 19th century. The Christian resort by the sea was far different from the older meetings in the wilderness. Yet it managed to join the basic teachings of Methodism with the needs of a new generation in ways that kept both remarkably intact. It began as a resurgence of the impulse that created the older camp meetings, but with a strategy designed for the future. Messenger says,

Ocean Grove was founded by members of the National Camp Meeting Association for the Promotion of Holiness. Today, two centuries after the explosive growth of camp meetings in America, thousands still make their pilgrimage to Ocean Grove every summer for a week-long camp meeting revival by the sea. Camp meeting, the ubiquitous religious and social gathering ground of nineteenth-century frontier America, may sound like an anachronism as America begins the twenty-first century.... Yet throughout America, camp meetings remain an enduring phenomenon.

Far from being nostalgic re-enactments, "for many participants, they remain an essential ritual of summer - a means of defining self and community."[23]

At the time Ocean Grove was established, those who were directing their energies toward holiness revival understood themselves not as creators of theological novelty, but inheritors of John Wesley's teaching

---

[22] Mrs. W.B. Osborn. *Pioneer Days at Ocean Grove*. New York: Methodist Book Concern, n.d. [1918], 36&37; See also Morris S. Daniels. *The Story of Ocean Grove (etc.)*. New York & Cincinnati: Methodist Book Concern, 1919.

[23] Troy Messenger. *Holy Leisure: Recreation and Religion in God's Square Mile*. Philadelphia; Temple University Press, 1999, 3; 5.

on Christian perfection, which itself reached back to the earliest days of Christianity, and outward to other branches of the Church. Wesley himself made it clear that sanctification or Christian perfection is far more than a peripheral, let alone optional aspect of Methodism. Wesley called it "the grand depositum which God has lodged with the people called Methodists; and it is for the sake of propagating this chiefly He appeared to have raised us up."[24]

When Ocean Grove and other holiness camp meetings were launched, "they appealed particularly to the urban Methodist middle class, who were attracted to the holiness movement and who had the recently acquired resources and time to enjoy a measure of leisure." The way of life developing in urban areas cried out for times of rest and relaxation as well as the universal need for spiritual growth and renewal – "outside the corrupting influences of urban industrialism and close to God's creation." Both concerns were genuine causes for Christian concern and action. Ocean Grove sought to build the kind of alternative community that should result from sanctifying grace at work in people's lives.

Alfred Cookman was one who bought property at Ocean Grove, and from his standpoint as one of the foremost holiness preachers of the late 19th century, approved and personally enjoyed its two-fold ministry. "The modern innovation of combining the social element of the family life and the devotional element of religious worship in the camp-meeting was pleasing to him, as meeting not only his own want, but also a want which he believed to be quite generally felt among Christian people." Here he believed "people can be practically taught the union which should always subsist between social and spiritual enjoyments."[25]

This community would soon look very different from its rough-hewn, frontier ancestors, yet, in its own way, it would still embody the essential purpose those ancestors tried to achieve. Elegant streets of Victorian cottages, along with hotels and other changes to accommodate middle class visitors, might well shock someone accustomed to older camp meetings, yet serious efforts were made to make Ocean Grove a distinctly Christian community. In time, changes in the familiar ban on Sunday recreation and sales would symbolize a move away from Methodist governing authority,

---

[24] John Wesley, Letter to Robert Carr Brackenbury, September 15, 1790, quoted in Kevin Watson, *Perfect Love (etc.)*. Franklin, TN: Seedbed, 2021, n.p; D. Gregory Van Dussen. *Transfiguration and Hope: A Conversation across Time and Space*. Eugene, OR: Wipf & Stock, 2018.

[25] Henry B. Ridgaway. The Life of the Rev. Alfred Cookman (etc.). New York: Nelson & Phillips; Cincinnati: Hitchcock & Walden, 1874, 412 & 413.

yet Ocean Grove remains true to its original identity. "Ocean Grove is most definitely not Asbury Park," as we will see, and the difference is both substantial and instructive.

While some of its activities are new, with visible changes designed to accommodate huge numbers and to balance "recreation and religion," Ocean Grove continues to see itself as "a city that is at once an earthly and a heavenly home, a bridge between the everyday world of the city and the millennial new Jerusalem." Its culture and ethos have created an atmosphere in which Christian experience and values remain welcome and influential. Even the new arrangements of orderly, dignified, organized structures convey this reality. "From the ethereal glow of tents to the perfect grid of avenues, the architecture of holiness presented a powerful model of the divine city of God lifted above the disorderly confusion and corrupting influences of the city."[26]

The onslaught of change did not end in 1980 with relaxing Sabbath restrictions or with any other modification or adjustment to its way of life. Each generation has had to forge its own balance, decide which battles to fight, and define itself vis-s-vis surrounding and neighboring cultures. Proximity to Asbury Park has helped clarify that process, though new challenges are likely to come from many directions. One of these is the lack of clarity within many denominations as to the beliefs and values that once defined their purpose and gave shape and content to an alternative community. Included here is a shared vision of what holiness looks like as well as a coherent strategy for attaining it. It has become difficult for many to identify where Methodism, or Christianity in general, stands among the options available to a pluralistic society, or to point clearly to what God asks or requires us to be amid countless permutations in what salvation and sanctification are meant to accomplish in a person, a church, or a community. What institution or set of teachings can serve as the bedrock upon which to live and around which to gather? Some of the questions Christians ask and debate are so basic they seem to preclude the certainty of earlier generations. These are questions we will have to consider if the varied experience of Wesleyan tradition camp meetings is to fulfill any of its purposes on the road ahead.

Located across Wesley Lake from Ocean Grove is **Asbury Park**, which began as a Methodist camp ground, then became more and more a resort until its religious identity had been effectively replaced. Like Ocean Grove, Asbury Park was a response to the social dislocation and distrac-

---

[26] Troy Messenger. *Holy Leisure: Recreation and Religion in God's Square Mile*. Philadelphia: Temple University Press, 1999, 11; 16; 23; 43; 51.

tions of nearby eastern cities. Asbury Park began as the vision of James A. Bradley, a Methodist who sought to build a Christian vacation spot, "a buffer between Long Branch [entirely secular – "the Jersey Shore sin capital"] and Ocean Grove." In their book on Asbury Park's history, Joseph Bilby and Harry Ziegler write, "If people do indeed spin in graves, the old Methodist prohibitionist James Allen Bradley is no doubt rotating rapidly. It is safe to say that Asbury Park … did not turn out the way that Bradley hoped it would…." Francis Asbury, for whom the park was named, might well be spinning with Bradley. As Troy Messenger puts it, "Asbury Park … soon provided many of the activities that Ocean Grove sought to eliminate." In fact, "Asbury Park had no pretenses about providing a retreat for religious renewal. Its summer guests were there to enjoy themselves, in a wholesome Christian environment, yes, but without any obligation to seek moral perfection." The question would be how to build and maintain "a healthy Christian environment" with little definition as to what this might entail. The difference between the institutions on either side of Wesley Lake has long been symbolized by a large sign on an Asbury Park hotel, which advertises to those in Ocean Grove the ready availability of a product (liquor) long forbidden by the more conservative community. Thus, "Asbury Park and Ocean Grove presented two competing visions of Christian America's perfect leisure community."

Bradley's goal was a vacation spot that would "be attractive to and demonstrative of the values of middle-class white Protestant America but without the theological intensity of Ocean Grove." Originally, no alcoholic beverages could be sold in Asbury Park. The design called for a pleasant summer alternative both to nearby cities and to the purely secular resorts like Long Branch. This was Asbury Park in the 1870s, but soon it would become a city itself, with hundreds of thousands of summer visitors and entertainment that would not always meet with Bradley's approval. People found ways to access alcohol. In spite of his efforts, Asbury Park soon "appeared to have a higher per capita alcohol consumption rate than Long Branch, where 'the saloons were wide open.'" Bradley tried unsuccessfully to bring the situation under control.

This was only a symbol of the breakdown of Bradley's purpose. Other problems associated with large, urban communities plagued Asbury Park, from gambling, to racial conflict, to political corruption. Entertainment and commercial projects overcame any religious motivations. Though a statue was erected of the founder; Bradley and the park's origins were "eulogized, but disregarded." Sadly, "In the end, he [Bradley] said, 'I would have been much happier in my old age had I never heard of the place.'" Soon, "Methodist hopes to the contrary, Asbury Park had, in fact, turned into a pretty tough town, where you could find trouble If you were looking for it, and you didn't have to look too far."[27]

Ocean City, New Jersey, offers another example of attempting to blend or balance the spirit of a camp ground with that of a summer resort. On line publicity for Ocean City, "America's Favorite Family Resort," identifies it as a dry town, with much to attract families to its recreational options, but does not lift up religion or worship as a prominent part of its life. Harold Lee writes, "Ocean City is a city founded on religious principles, but which has changed its character over more than a century so that it could keep in step with changes in pubic customs and perceptions." Because of these changes, "Anyone who was here at or about the tune of the [19th to 20th] century would not even recognize the place today." Lee says that since most of the older buildings are gone, "we have become an island of lost landmarks."[28]

Ocean City began as the vision of "Methodist ministers who dreamed of establishing a Christian colony at the shore," but also of "real estate developers who dreamed of making their fortunes here. It is about quiet Sundays amidst the hustle and bustle of a resort town." It was 1850 before Ocean City, under its earlier name of "Peck's Beach," had its first permanent settler. Two Methodist preachers, Wesley Lake and William Wood, envisioned a seaside community something like Ocean Grove. Others, including Robert Fisher, a new arrival from Ireland, came seeking seclusion and peace, only to help develop and lead the town that would become the resort. Methodist preachers James Lake and Ezra Lake began in 1879 to create the new community, still patterned after Ocean Grove, to be an alternative to New Jersey's secular resorts, Long Branch and Atlantic City. Their new venture would, like Ocean Grove, host camp meeting revivals and feature laws that would carry out Christian values as they were understood and practiced by the Methodists of that day, particularly concerning Sabbath observance, modest dress, and an absence of alcoholic beverages.

The Ocean City Association held its first camp meeting in 1880, and quickly built a tabernacle to house future worship. The attraction for visitors was immediate. The Association set aside land for people to set up

---

[27] Joseph Bilby & Harry Ziegler. *Asbury Park: A Brief History*. Charleston, SC: History Press, 2009, 17; 13; 21&22; 52; 62; Troy Messenger. *Holy Leisure: Recreation and Religion in God's Square Mile*. Philadelphia: Temple University Press, 1999, 20&21; 22, fig. 3.

[28] www.ocnj.us; http://oceancityvacation.com; Harold Lee, Foreword to Tim Cain. *Peck's Beach: A Pictorial History of Ocean City, NJ*. West Creek, NJ: Down the Shore & The SandPaper, 2016.

tents, and sought to provide "every possible facility that will contribute to their comfort." Beside the annual camp meeting, the grounds would host other events consistent with Methodist principles. Soon more permanent buildings would begin replacing the tents.

While leadership has gone from firm Methodist control to "a fully secular City Council," a growing number of churches would continue to shape the ethos of the community. "More than 100 years ... after its founding as a Christian resort, Ocean City is a city of churches."

William Wood believed that Ocean City's location as an island would facilitate an "exemption from various annoyances; and especially Sabbath desecration," but it wasn't long before that exemption would be challenged. Not all who came would see the place through Methodist eyes. Even so, Sabbath restrictions would remain for a very long time. As this principle continued to clash with changing social expectations, the city found it necessary, or at least expedient, to allow exceptions, which made the rules confusing and hard to enforce. Finally, the community voted in a referendum to do away with all blue laws, which "ended a tradition that, for better or worse, had been a part of Ocean City's history since its founding." The beach lent itself to more problematic issues and behavior. Should men and women use the same areas? What kind of clothing would be appropriate? How should rules be enforced? Should beaches be open or closed on Sundays? While "attitudes and customs have changed to accommodate a more pluralistic society in Ocean City ... though no longer legislated, quiet Sundays remain a treasured tradition."[29]

Like other ocean camp ground/resorts, its attractions are many and the possibility of a single, powerful, overarching spiritual purpose has proven impossible. Ocean City has grown and diversified tremendously, though Christianity and its churches continue to hold an important place in the city and among its visitors. Christians, including Methodists, still sense a hospitable environment for times of renewal and recreation that respect and even encourage their life and values. Thus Ocean City occupies a precarious place on a continuum between Ocean Grove and Asbury Park.

Methodist Camp meetings in New England included **Wesleyan Grove at Martha's Vineyard, Massachusetts**, founded in 1835. While it began as a simple, traditional camp meeting, its location on an island near Cape Cod made its evolution almost inevitable. We can see how this unfolded early in the camp ground's history as it was documented year by year. Its

---

[29] Tim Cain. *Peck's Beach: A Pictorial History of Ocean City, NJ*. West Creek, NJ: Down the Shore & the Sand Paper, 2016, 11; 25-33; 35-45.

Methodist character was a matter of shared commitment, rather than institutional control.

The earliest camp meetings at Wesleyan Grove, like others at that time, used a basic layout and schedule to accommodate worship and rest. "At these camp meetings it was customary to have, at some time, a Love Feast and the Sacrament." By 1859, the camp ground had become more permanent, with wooden sheds replacing some of the tents, a headquarters building, store room, office, equipment, a better source for water, and a large meeting space. Already the residential area could be described as "village like." There were streets and a park, named for important figures in Methodist history, as well as a large bell to gather people for worship. A Boston newspaper reported an attendance of "probably, twenty thousand persons," many of them "elegantly dressed." If the reporter was correct, he was seeing a change with ominous implications for the identity and purpose of the place: "Many thousand persons visited the camp-meeting merely to enjoy a day's pleasure, and seemed to take not the slightest interest in the religious services...." This article did say that no one tried to intrude in the services, and, "There was a sacred circle of Christians within the great outside crowd, from whence went up to the great God fervent prayers from the heart, and great and ever-living biblical truths."[30]

Over the next years of operation, Wesleyan Grove continued to add to its facilities, program offerings, and accessibility in ways that required careful consideration. Regarding the state of things in 1860, we read,

> Some good people had come to think that the religious character of our gathering here had very much changed of late years, and that the rustic and social antepast had much to do with the wanings of spirituality at our camp-meetings. There was therefore this year an earnest effort put forth by many, both of the ministry and laity, who had the vital interests at heart, to revive the old standards of effectiveness of other years.

Leaders took steps during bad weather, to offer preaching in several locations on the ground, and discussed the possibility that these alternative venues could help reach the growing number of people at camp meeting in future years.

A summary of the 1860 session expressed this encouraging conclusion:

> The general religious character of this meeting was decidedly better than for several years. The object for which many had preached, prayed, and labored, that the religious element might predominate, had been realized.

---

[30] H. Vincent. *History of the Camp-meeting and Grounds at Wesleyan Grove (etc.)*. Boston: Lee & Shepard, 1870,15; 18; 30-34; 42.

There had been quite a number of conversions.

For the 1861 season, there was a new preaching stand and new, more comfortable seating for congregations, along with a large food tent to accommodate the needs of attendees. The official summary for the year rejoiced at the way camp meetings created and strengthened friendships among the laity and clergy who attended, and also wondered whether the social aspect of the meetings might overtake their religious purpose. "We have evidently great need of watchfulness on this score, lest the benefits which should be made secondary, be allowed to supersede the original, primary object to be sought here." Even so, the summary concluded that, given renewed efforts to focus on the main purpose, "the glory of other years seemed to be returning."[31]

During these years of Civil War, the progress of the war and concern for its outcome was part of the backdrop for camp meeting conversations. Leaders were concerned about possible reductions in attendance for 1862, and were relieved to find that participation remained high, even if not as high as had once been the case. The report for 1863 gave extended space to the attractiveness of the island as a summer refuge from the heat and cramped quarters of nearby cities. More and more people were coming to "this island oasis" for longer stays.

During 1864 and '65, there was once again concern about changes in the camp meeting experience and the possibility that its original purpose would be eroded or eclipsed.

> It is true that other things were attended to besides religious worship by many gathered here; for it cannot be denied that very many came, as on other occasions, for purposes of pleasure and recreation, rather than for any higher object.... Promenading ["Walking for amusement or exercise."] was followed no less than in former years, and sea-bathing was more extensively practiced than ever before. Well as these things are in their places, they should not engross too much of precious time. Nor were they allowed to do so by all.

The report for 1864 assures its readers that in spite of the way all this may look to those critical of camp meetings,

> ...hundreds and thousands of Christians, ministers and laymen, came for the same holy purposes and in the same devout spirit as in by-gone days. It does not follow that because we do not live all together in large tents, and sleep in the straw, that therefore our religion has died out. Having some-

---

[31] H. Vincent. *History of the Camp Meeting and Grounds at Wesleyan Grove, Martha's Vineyard (etc.)*. Boston: Lee & Shepard, 1870, 45; 47; 50; 71&72; 82.

what more of conveniences for the comfort of our bodies may not render our gratitude to the great Giver any the less, certainly.

In 1865 there was extended notice taken of impressive improvements on the ground.

> But while so much was being done for the comfort of the physical man, there was a growing solicitude, on the part of many, lest the plenitude of these provisions should greatly detract from the degree of spirituality manifest on these occasions in by-gone years. Hence there was an earnest endeavor to have all the means at hand to contribute to the spiritual good of the people.

One concern was that, "whatever might be the disposition of people to rusticate ["To dwell or reside in the country."] here before and after the camp-meeting, the week of camp meeting was sacredly set apart for religious work; and it was not desirable than any persons, especially Christians, should visit the place during that week with any different understanding."

The report was careful to distinguish between this camp ground and purely secular resorts, as well as to express hope that some who may visit Martha's Vineyard for less than spiritual reasons, "will sometimes listen to a gospel sermon, who seldom, if ever, do so in the church of God at home."[32]

In the same report, we find a Christian rationale for the recreational dimension of the camp, one which Martha's Vineyard shared with other seaside camp meetings.

> At the present time even Christian people – many of them, at least – visit the place for other and somewhat different purposes than the primary one, yet highly justifiable objects. Relaxation from business cares, health, friendly greetings, - all are consistent with the Christian character – nay, of themselves, are Christian duties.

The 1866 report expanded on the purposes for coming to the camp ground.

> Formerly we came here for the benefit of the soul only; now we come for the improvement of the casket of the soul, and for the cultivation of the social elements, as well. ... The means of recuperation and the boon of health were here. We had not the luxuries, not the "congress water;" ["a saline

---

[32] H. Vincent. *History of the Camp-meeting and Grounds at Martha's Vineyard (etc.)*. Boston: Lee & Shepard, 1870, 40; 103-105; 119&120; 127-130; 134; 137; 143; Noah Webster. *American Dictionary of the English Language (etc.)*. Springfield, MA: George & Charles Merriam, 1848, 876; 972.

mineral water from the Congress Spring at Saratoga, in the State of New York."] but we had what was quite as useful as the furnishings at Saratoga, and at far less rates; and then we were under better influences.

Very many come but for a few hours, or perhaps a day or two. Some come, doubtless, from motives of sheer curiosity; others, who have heard of the fame of the place, visit it to see for themselves what these Christians are doing here, and perhaps with the thought of taking up a temporary residence with them.

For some, of course, the camp became an attractive holiday destination and that was enough. Soon the demand for land at Martha's Vineyard presented another difficulty. Investors became rivals for land needed for housing camp meeting attendees. Another complication came from clergy who would come for a few days and then return to their congregations on Sunday. By 1867, there were radical contrasts made between those who had come long ago, and those attending today. "Instead of the few hundreds of poor, humble followers of the Master, who came here to worship, dwelling in rough tents, we have now, it is true, a remnant, a sprinkling of these, but mostly those of fashion, and many of large wealth."

Visitors were certainly impressed by the beauty of the place. William Perrine, a preacher and professor from Albion College in Michigan, declared in 1867 that "there is nothing like it, nor equal to it, of the camp meeting kind, in all the world." The same year, the Association governing the camp ground reaffirmed its original purpose, which was "strictly religious, and that this design should be paramount to all others.... The blessings of life on the grounds," they said, "have arisen from the distinctive religious influence that has characterized it." Back and forth went the observations and advocacy, as the spiritual purpose of the camp meeting vied with, or cooperated with, that of the summer resort. The worship in 1869 included many conversions, which must have been reassuring to those wanting to regain the emphasis from the past, but the report from that year acknowledged, "There had been no such meeting as this here for very many years." The report then balances this statement by saying that the religious success of that year…fully proved that neither comfortable cottages, ample provisions for comfortable living, nor yet coming here for weeks of relaxation from business and for the improvement of health, prevent the original objects of a camp meeting from being attained, if we come here trusting in God, and if ministers and people enter into Christian labors as the fathers did, and as we should do." The 1869 report ended with another assurance that the camp meeting and resort could in fact coexist;

that in fact the large number and variety of visitors to the island presented an evangelistic opportunity to the camp meeting.[33]

1867 brought the neighboring community of **Oak Bluffs**. Increasingly, these communities, and others like them, developed a distinctive Victorian architecture, with each house located "cheek by jowl on lots so tiny that there is no room for private outdoor space other than front porches." Ellen Weiss describes and illustrates the

> ...urbanlike density of people and buildings hidden in untrammeled nature, 'a city in the woods.' They took the pervasive American event, the camp-meeting revival in the woods, and brought it to a spectacular conclusion in a form that has something to do with that pervasive American residential habit, the suburb. Both, after all, were intended as societies of the like-minded, with strong family ideology, living in nature.

Wesleyan Grove remained a retreat from the urban world. Where some communities emphasized entertainment and religion, or education and religion, in this camp ground, "Fashion and religion seemed in balance, and the creative tensions between the two would persist for decades...." Fashion would take many forms, in such things as dress, socializing, or recreation, and now architecture. No longer would the residential arrangements of camp meeting be simply matters of practicality for those whose primary activity was worship; these summer residences were ends in themselves, the result of creativity, attention, and investment. Here was an ideal city, free of many of the problems and distractions of ordinary cities. Here the idea of Christian perfection took visible shape, but in a way that could itself prove distracting from the theological and spiritual essence from which they had, indirectly, emerged. Weiss concludes:

> Wesleyan Grove became a special residential environment which, growing out of nature-immersion and spatial orientation of the early camp meeting, continued the sense of otherworldly dislocation necessary for religious experience, and thereby created a form that was almost the American romantic suburb as it would later develop.[34]

The result held, and still holds, such a powerful attraction itself, that it can function quite well without the spiritual experience that brought

---

[33] H. Vincent. *History of the Camp-meeting and Grounds a Wesleyan Grove, Martha's Vineyard (etc.)*. Boston: Lee & Shepard, 1870, 142 &143; 156; 170-176-179; 185&186; 195; 242&243; 248; https.//www.webster-dictionary.org.

[34] Ellen Weiss. *City in the Woods: The Life and Design of an American Camp Meeting on Martha's Vineyard*. Boston: Northeastern University Press, 1998, xv; xvii&xviii; 34; 38.

it into being. As in so many parallel situations, well-intentioned balance would prove difficult, and eventually, impossible. The mission of today's Martha's Vineyard Camp Meeting Association expresses a vague connection between the camp ground as a monument, and the spiritual dynamism that once gave it life: "To perpetuate our religious and historical heritage, engaging all in education and spiritual growth in a welcoming faith community."[35]

The development of **Chautauqua**, in the **State of New York**, and its extensive family of assemblies [such as Mt. Gretna, Pennsylvania and Big Stone Lake, South Dakota, "The Great Chautauqua of the West."] and "traveling Chautauquas" was quite different from that of Ocean Grove or the other camp meetings mentioned above. Bishop John H. Vincent, one of Chautauqua's founders, made it clear that while Chautauqua Assembly met on the former Fair Point Camp Ground on Chautauqua Lake, "the Assembly was totally unlike the camp-meeting. We did our best to make it so." Fair Point had been recently (1871) chartered as a camp meeting ground of the Erie Conference of the Methodist Episcopal Church. Those responsible for this new venue must have seen the purpose of Bishop Vincent and his associates as sufficiently close to their own that they were willing to assign the ground to the new assembly in 1873. Vincent and Lewis Miller, "during the camp-meeting of 1873 ... visited 'Fair Point,' and selected it as the place for our 'Assembly." Miller wrote: "The Chautauqua Camp-meeting Managers gave the Assembly movement a most hearty welcome, and, when permanence was assured, deeded over their charter with its privileges and all their property to the Management of the Sunday-school Assembly." So Chautauqua did not evolve organically from the camp meeting, but rather substituted a program of Christian education, especially the training of Sunday School teachers, that seemed to share the larger purposes of the Methodist Episcopal Church.[36]

The Assembly did gather and train Sunday School teachers, but the vision of its leaders was larger and somewhat different. First, they sought participants from a wide variety of churches. Methodist camp meetings had long included other denominations among their audiences and even occasionally among speakers, but it was always clear who was in charge and what theology would come from the speakers' stand. Methodist Holiness camp meetings embraced several denominations, while organizers nearly

---

[35] https://www.mvcma.org>history-narrative.html.

[36] Matthew D. Smith, et al. Circuit Riders of the Middle Border (etc.). n.c: south Dakota Conference of the Methodist Church, 1965, 57; John H. Vincent. *The Chautauqua Movement*. Boston: Chautauqua, 1886, 16&17; viii.

always came from the Methodist Episcopal Church, or another Methodist body sponsoring the event. Chautauqua intentionally sought to broaden its constituency, believing that the churches held enough in common to cooperate in this new venture. It was generally understood that "all-denominations" meant all Protestants. In more recent years the constituency has broadened greatly, within and even beyond Christianity. Miller envisioned Chautauqua as "a place where each denomination or organization brings its best contribution which the particular order would develop as a consecrated offering for magnifying God's word and work...." Vincent recalled the history of cooperation between Methodists and Presbyterians early in the camp meeting movement and called for the same kind of cooperation in this new venture. His vision was even more expansive:

> The original intension was to make Chautauqua an international centre, - a place where the highest officials in all spheres of life should come to give the Book that recognition which would magnify it in the eyes of all the people, so that every citizen throughout the land should have a higher appreciation of the church and church-school in their midst.

The classes, speakers, and reading provided or encouraged by Chautauqua would extend well beyond the training of Sunday School teachers, though they would long hold a special place in Vincent's program. Other topics and areas of interest would multiply. Prestigious national leaders, such as Ulysses Grant and James Garfield, took their place in Chautauqua programing . Garfield told Chautauquans, "It has been the struggle of the world to get more leisure but it was left for Chautauqua to show how to use it.[37]

Among the principles of this movement was a democratization of education resting on a commitment to the equality and capacity of all. Each person and family offered, or could offer, something profoundly important to the whole of society. Undergirding this principle was the idea "that life is one, and that religion belongs everywhere." The right kind of education would connect "divine motive" with every part of life, "touching with its sanctifying power every hour of every day." Vincent wrote, "We need an alliance and a hearty cooperation of Home, Pulpit, School, and Shop – an alliance consecrated to universal culture for young and old." Chautauqua's outreach would be comprehensive, constituting "a splendid university in which people of all ages and conditions may be enrolled as students."[38]

---

[37] John H. Vincent. *The Chautauqua Movement*. Boston: Chautauqua,1886, v-vii; 22&23.

[38] John H. Vincent. *The Chautauqua Movement*. Boston: Chautauqua, 1886, vii; 2; 4&5.

For Vincent, religion, education, and culture were compatible and mutually beneficial, since "all realms of knowledge, past and present, are flooded with the light of God." The wisdom he hoped to encourage and facilitate was rooted in God. He saw "harmony with the Divine character as the ideal of life for time and eternity." There were no limits of age or social class that would ultimately prevent anyone from growing in wisdom, especially under the encouragement and direction of Chautauqua.[39]

Vincent said that "It was called by some a 'camp-meeting'. But a 'camp meeting' it was not, in any sense, except that the most of us lived in tents. There were few sermons preached, and no so-called evangelistic services held. It was simply a Sunday-school institute, a protracted institute in the woods." Vincent did not intend that the training at Chautauqua was a departure from Christianity or Scripture, for "The mission of Chautauqua has been to 'study the Word ... of God." Scripture would be studied within the broadest possible context, paying "attention to His manifold 'works' in nature, in history, in mind...." Co-founder Lewis Miller saw this approach as an improvement over the more narrowly focused, evangelistic program of the camp meeting, "one that should enlarge the outlook of the already consecrated church member."

The initial effort to deepen and broaden the education of Sunday School teachers quickly expanded. Founded with the approval of Methodist Episcopal Sunday School Union, the institute welcomed participation from Baptists, Presbyterians, and the American Sunday School Union, among others, until, in Vincent's words, "the denominational lines were almost entirely obliterated...." The point was to serve all participating churches and leaders, and to better understand the distinctives of each body, while cooperating in every way possible.[40]

In some ways, Vincent's *The Revival and After the Revival* paralleled the concerns and dream behind Chautauqua, this time for new converts and their churches, In it he addressed what he saw as a superficial form of Methodism that focused too much on the moment and setting of conversion, and lacked comprehensive growth in discipleship. While he did not denigrate revival, he believed that revival by itself must be part of a larger picture. He wanted pastors and churches to shepherd the faith and life of converts, bringing all of life to the cross and equipping growing Christians for change within themselves and their world. He urged pastors to take

---

[39] John H. Vincent. *The Chautauqua Movement*. Boston: Chautauqua, 1886, 5; 8; 12&13.

[40] John H. Vincent, *The Chautauqua Movement*. Boston, Chautauqua, 1886, 16-18; 27.

each convert's six month probation seriously, as a time for solid education on the basic teachings of the faith and church they were joining. He wanted churches to surround each new and growing Christian with a full array of positive experiences, much like those embodied in the original Chautauqua idea. The central question was, "How shall we promote the growth of souls in the life of God?" To this end he prayed, "God of all grace, give thy ministers wisdom to watch over these new-born energies, and direct them into channels of activity and usefulness." Worldly preoccupations must be replaced by a thoroughgoing transformation, so that transformed Christians would influence every aspect of life. Revival could not be an end in itself, but the beginning of a great journey.[41]

A pattern of diversification quickly took Chautauqua into new disciplines, "departments," and regions. Bishop Vincent continued to express a high view of Scripture and its place in the movement, but insisted on a complete program, including recreation and a variety of subject matter, that would attract and hold his audience. Such a diversified program would meet significant needs and address the whole of life's experiences and issues with the Bible's wisdom. He assumed that while the offerings of Chautauqua were broadening, the centrality and foundation found in God and his Word would remain paramount and would infuse all of life, learning, and culture. He saw the goodness of God's gifts across the panorama of creation, never realizing how quickly those gifts could be detached from the One who created them. The great abolitionist and camp meeting bishop, Gilbert Haven, saw that same era as one of "supersecularization, this elevating of man above his Creator." Though Haven knew that such detachment of creation from its Creator, even when unintentional, must ultimately be temporary, he also saw its temporary power. The Chautauqua idea, with all its pros and cons, was indeed powerful – even explosive. There quickly emerged a long list of "other Chautauquas" across the United States and even beyond.[42]

One contributor to Vincent's thinking and Chautauqua's outward trajectory was the bishop's recognition both of the value and limitations of the camp meeting. From his vantage point in the late nineteenth-century, he could see the tremendous growth in his own church and others, coming from the camp ground experience and from revivalism generally. He saw

---

[41] John Heyl Vincent. *The Revival and After the Revival.* New York: Phillips & Hunt; Cincinnati: Cranston & Stowe, 1882, 50; 61; 63&4; 72-74.

[42] John H. Vincent, *The Chautauqua Movement.* Boston: Chautauqua, 1886, 29&30; 41-43; Gilbert Haven. Christus Consolator (etc.). New York: Hunt & Eaton; Cincinnati: Cranston & Curts, 1893, 82&83.

the need for lifelong growth and discipleship that would build upon conversion and infiltrate all of life. He sought Christian maturity, not only in narrowly defined sanctification, but in the sanctification of families, communities, peoples, and the myriad pursuits of a complete way of life. He wanted very much to deepen and enrich the Christian experience of church members. He paid great respect to the camp meeting tradition, yet the path of his movement would lead well beyond the spirituality of evangelical Christianity. While this is not the place for a complete history of Chautauqua, it is clear that its development over time, on a trajectory begun by its founders, has resulted in an institution light years away from the old Fair Point Campground, or even the Sunday School Institute. Perhaps he *assumed* the underlying faith which the revivalists sought with such clarity and emotion. Perhaps he had grown weary of the denunciations of sin and the "the world."[43] Andrew Reiser notes that "a dechristianization process is clearly in evidence by the turn of the century." The reigning theology is, more than a century later, generally progressive, and ecumenism has been stretched to include non-Christian religions. There remains a great reverence for learning, reflection, and cultural excellence, but the movement away from its origins is now a commonplace for conversation, on and off the grounds.[44]

Ohio's Lakeside, on the shore of Lake Erie, followed a similar pattern to that of the original Chautauqua. Comparing Lakeside with revival predecessors, James Allen Kestle writes: "While much of America was immersed in the camp meeting hysteria, a quiet study of religion was being followed by consecrated and often 'longing' spirits." The study he had in mind included, as at Chautauqua, a serious look at America's "expanding society and the stirring of events in the world beyond America." Lakeside would offer an accessible liberal arts curriculum that brought Christianity and culture closer together. Kestle's reference to "the camp meeting hysteria" indicates the distance separating what had become parallel, contrasting institutions.[45]

The vision behind Lakeside began at the same time – the late 1860s - when Holiness camp meetings were beginning a major new era and

---

[43] I John 15, NIV.

[44] James R. Schultz. *The Romance of Small-Town Chautauquas*. Columbia, MO: University of Missouri Press, 2002; Andrew C. Rieser. *The Chautauqua Moment: Protestants, Progressives, and the Culture of Modern Liberalism*. New York: Columbia University Press, 2003.

[45] James Allen Kestle. *This Is Lakeside, 1873-1973: The Centennial History*. Lakeside, OH (privately published), 1973,17.

drawing enormous crowds. What began as the Lakeside Camp Meeting Association would eventually drop its "Camp Meeting" designation, as the former sold its property to the Lakeside Association for a dollar in 1920. The original vision included evangelism. A more recent summary of its purpose describes Lakeside in this way: "(a) Lakeside is a conference center; (b) Lakeside is a religious center; (c) Lakeside is a cultural center; and (d) Lakeside is an entertainment center," corresponding to "four basic desires of individuals and families who have been looking for 'the something more' in life than the meeting of its physical and basic needs." Lakeside became a "Vacation with a purpose." It moved toward ecumenism and pluralism, including the featuring of speakers with "widely divergent theological expressions." Speakers would range from holiness preacher and singer Amanda Berry Smith to aviator Amelia Earhart; from William Jennings Bryan to Ralph Sockman and Billy Sunday. Methodist bishops have often appeared. Secular entertainers like "Doc" Severinsen and Al Hirt performed there. The articles of incorporation saw the new Association's role as "the promotion and expansion of its programs carried on for religious, scientific, literary and educational purposes." Launched under the auspices of the Methodist Episcopal Church, it continued as a denominational resource, especially to its Ohio conferences. It moved from a summer gathering to a year-round community, with a more elaborate structure. Always there was the desire to model society as it should be. Lakeside has never lost its religious component, though it moved in a direction far different from its camp meeting roots.[46]

The late 19th century saw many attempts to extend and expand the camp meeting phenomenon, as well as efforts to reshape or even replace camp meetings. The result was an abundance of large and small gatherings, moving in disparate directions, all across the continent. Some became vacation resorts, refuges from increasingly unlivable cities, built around worship and ministry. They sought to accomplish more than one purpose by adding various forms of entertainment. Others focused on educational and cultural programming designed to augment spiritual growth with intellectual and artistic elements. While some were determined to build in a way that was consistent with their original identity and purpose, others moved in new directions.

Mainstream Methodist bodies came under the influence of modern, often European theological ideas and emphases, as well as a growing desire to keep pace with a rapidly changing society. Neil Semple's exploration

---

[46] James Allen Kestle. *This Is Lakeside, 1873-1973: The Centennnial History.* Lakeside, OH (privately published), 1973, 17-20; 25&26; 49; 56; 57; 59&60; 66.

of these new directions in the Canadian context, reflects similar patterns operating across North America. While these patterns were not limited to the Methodist tradition, they had a dramatic effect on the ways Methodist camp meetings lived out and often modified their mandate.

"During the late nineteenth and early twentieth centuries, all the Christian churches of Canada were buffeted by new and threatening intellectual and social forces." Some new approaches were designed "to elaborate, not abandon" Wesleyan emphases on conversion and holiness. Others reflected a growing desire for more radical change.

> Typical of the transformation occurring in all the social means of grace [such as class and camp meetings] was a shift away from dramatic revival as the basis for spiritual growth leading to conversion and sanctification. Revival certainly remained vital and popular, but Canadian Methodists demanded broader and more enlightened patterns of religious fellowship.[47]

Of course, the terms "broader and more enlightened" carry assumptions others would see as camp meetings veering off course, losing their way, or winning the world at the cost of their soul. B.W. Gorham saw the waning of support for camp meetings from some quarters arising from "the growing worldliness of the church." This viewpoint would be the thrust of B.T. Roberts and Free Methodism.

While liberal and conservative Methodists advanced their increasingly disparate visions for the church and its message, camp meetings lived out those competing visions. Some sought to rekindle the old Wesleyan message and the tradition of the earlier movement, while others evolved into very different institutions. Those that were moving away from the tradition did so in many cases by adding to or modifying their purpose in ways that reflected changes in Canadian and American societies. Semple notes that "they became institutionalized annual gatherings for general religious fellowship. Social refreshment, which came with a vacation from life's daily routine, kept them popular, but they bore little resemblance to the revivals of old." There certainly was a need for people to break away from the routine and preoccupations of what was becoming a fast-paced, pressurized, urban society. Thus the idea of worshiping God in creation morphed into simple enjoyment of the outdoors, and Victorian villages offered an alternative to ordinary urban communities. Entertainment in a variety of forms offered diversion from an unhealthy urban lifestyle, but also an enticing alternative to the original focus on one's journey with God. Each day, with

---

[47] Neil Semple. *The Lord's Dominion: The History of Canadian Methodism*. Montreal, et al: McGill-Queens University Press, 1996, 211.

the possible exception of the Sabbath, offered entertainment, education, socialization, and much more – a seemingly endless array of distractions from the impulse that once drew people to the camp ground. Yet we will continue to see that earlier impulse live on in camp meetings that refused to be distracted; that would not let go of the divine reality that remained eternally relevant to people in every time and place.

Canadian camp grounds like **Wesley Park (Niagara Falls, ON)**, **Big Bay Point (Lake Simcoe, ON)**, and **Thousand Island Park** on the St. Lawrence became resort communities, offering a variety of amusements along with religious services with lower temperatures than the white hot revivals of the past. This occurred even when the initial impetus for a given camp meeting, as in the case of Wesley Park, arose from the holiness movement and one of its most productive and successful organizers, William B. Osborn. Wesley Park, as it turns out, was unable to function long as a camp ground.

> In 1884, the Niagara Falls International Camp Meeting Association opened Wesley Park. It was to be a huge camp ground and summer resort and covered 200 acres. The land was laid out in circles, crescents and streets. Within the large circle called Epworth, there existed an auditorium to be used for Methodist camp meetings, missionary and temperance conventions. The camp meetings failed and the lots were sold off by lottery in 1887. In 1893, the site of the Wesley Park Camp auditorium was acquired by the Niagara Falls Collegiate Institute.[48]

Berwick Camp Ground, Nova Scotia

---

[48] http:/www.niagarafrontier.com/earlyhotels.html.

The Methodist camp ground in **Berwick, Nova Scotia** attempted to balance its traditional mission with what its leaders saw as the changing needs of the church and society and continues to operate today. Neil Semple believes that Berwick "represented to many the best elements of the Methodist tradition," as it hosted church gatherings and organizations, such as the Epworth League, the Womens' Missionary Society, and educational events for ministers. Berwick has continued, now belonging to the United Church of Canada, with a diversified program designed to enrich the experience of church members and families.

> The educative value of camp meetings expanded as sermons dealt with history, science, higher criticism, the modern Sunday School, and the practical obligations of the church and its members. Religious, social, and moral instruction and nurturing were important elements of the late-Victorian and Edwardian church, Despite the decline in the conversion function of camp meetings, they developed enterprises that helped create a stable, intelligent, and loyal attachment to Methodism and the kingdom of God.

Berwick Camp Ground, Nova Scotia

Berwick's services in the late 19th and early 20th centuries emphasized evangelism and holiness. By the 1920s sermon topics had diversified, and a more general approach to spiritual growth raised some concern that the original themes and purpose were no longer front and center. "Today [1972] many of us cannot agree theologically with the Methodist style of evangelism, but it did present men with the necessity for making decisions – a task which the United Church finds difficult today." Berwick has undergone a significant shift in its purpose and theology, has continued its close relationship with the church and region, and maintained a sense of rootedness in its past, but as the United Church of Canada continues in a liberal direction, and this camp meeting modifies, softens, or moves away from the singular, transformative thrust of its origins, the camp is seeing more and more contrast with its own roots.

Berwick Camp Ground, Nova Scotia

Much of Canadian Methodism was becoming uncomfortable with what some saw as emotional excesses resulting in temporary commitments and a shallow church culture. Critics caricatured camp meetings of the pioneer era as "extreme enthusiasm" mistaken as "the workings of the Holy Spirit." Even the resurgence of revivalism in the 1870s & 80s could not change the eventual downplaying of the kind of religion typical of camp meetings. Soon, as in some U.S. settings, recreation and cultural enrichment blended with a milder form of preaching and church life to form experiences more to the liking of late-19th century Canadians. What the softened, less demanding and less emotional meetings could not do, or at least could not do as well, was to provide profound, life changing encounters with God in which people were confronted with, and freed from, their sin and empowered to live radically new lives. In many ways they assumed a capacity for growth and goodness under the influence, and in the fellowship, of local churches. After seventy-five years of ministry, A.B. Higgins expressed his appreciation for the camp meetings and grounds in a way that echoes important purposes of camp meetings generally:

We need to take time to refresh our souls, time for God to impart to us His wisdom and strength. We so much need time for that uplift, without which we cannot live the life God intended we should live.

What better place for quiet thought and meditation upon the deep things of life, than under the shadows of the great trees that stand like silent sentinels in the great unwalled Temple of God on the Camp Grounds.[49]

In time, respectability, theological pluralism, and social relevance combined to drive Methodism, in Canada as in the States, away from the earlier focus on conversion and sanctification, or to a redefinition of these that undermined their urgency. Social relevance alone would not have called for a shift in theology or spirituality. Both Wesley and early Methodism engaged society over a host of significant issues and practices. But when harnessed to a desire for social, cultural, and political prominence, and to a theology that redefined the Church's message, the combination left the Church's witness in a weakened condition. While the new relationship between church and society looked promising to some, other saw only "a despiritualized church." Those who insisted on the original message and ministry of the movement would become marginalized. Many would stay clear of the eventual formation of the United Church of Canada. Some would align themselves with the Free Methodists, who would increasingly see themselves as the inheritors of the revival tradition that mainstream Methodism had left behind.[50]

Beulah Camp in New Brunswick has traveled a different road since its late nineteenth century beginning. Beulah was originally organized by Reformed Baptists in the Canadian Maritimes and the State of Maine. Eventually (1996), the camp and its denomination, the Reformed Baptist Alliance of Canada, joined the Wesleyan Church on the basis of common holiness theology and practice. That church had a consistent grounding in the Holiness Movement. Its conference met annually at Beulah Camp. Beulah has seen the usual improvements to its buildings and grounds, including a tabernacle and changes in transportation as these became available. Like other Atlantic camp grounds, Beulah was revolutionized with the availability of steamships. Camp historian Laurence K. Mullen wrote:

---

[49] Neil Semple. *The Lord's Dominion: The History of Canadian Methodism*. Montreal, et al: McGill-Queens University Press, 1996, 217&218; 213; Flemming Holm. *Berwick Camp Meeting: The First Hundred Years, 1872-1972*. Antigonish, NS: Casket, 1972, including quote from A.B. Higgins, 10; 34.

[50] R. Wayne Kleinsteuber. *More than a Memory: the Renewal of Methodism in Canada*. n.c: Light and Life Press Canada, 1984, 57-85, including quote from page 67.

Tabernacle, Beulah Camp, New Brunswick

The story of Beulah Camp – 90 years [as of 1984] of preaching, praying, building, sharing, singing, praising, working, giving – cannot be reduced to five or six type-written pages. Like the history of any sacred shrine, the story cannot be told in wrds [sic], but must be experienced in personal encounter; each person must come and write his own story – and it is in those thousands of personal struggles and triumphant victories that the real history of Beulah Camp is recorded.[51]

Beulah Camp Tabernacle, 21st Century

---

[51] Laurence K. Mullen. *Beulah Camp: A History*. (Unpublished), 1984, 1-7.

Beulah's story is one of faithfulness to its original purpose as a holiness camp ground, in a society where change made that faithfulness both difficult and necessary.

Vesta Mullen wrote an extended remembrance and reflection, including photographs, of life as it has been lived at Beulah. She details changes and continuities in its program, buildings, and leadership. An unusual photo shows the octagonal design of the camp's tabernacle. In a key observation linking Beulah to the larger world of holiness camps across North America, she writes about speakers and programming:

> Over the years, some of the best known preachers in the holiness tradition have ministered at Beulah Camp. ... In addition to those who were invited to preach, a number of outstanding Christian leaders came as visitors. The well-known Methodist evangelist, missionary and temperance worker Amanda Smith was a guest of the Bullocks [leaders at the camp ground] during her stay at the camp in 1902.[52]

While the parallel movement in the United States took a different shape – denominational realignments did not produce anything like the United Church of Canada – its effect on the ministry of camp meetings produced a similar division over their purpose. Moving away from the power and urgency of earlier days also meant a weakening, or perhaps numbing, of the motivation for evangelism of any kind. Leonidas L. Hamline, whose ministry in the mid- 19th century involved writing, editing, preaching, and traveling the "big circuit" as a bishop, used this powerful image to express his passion to see people saved:

> I feel like one who has been wrecked at sea and has got into the long-boat. Persons are sinking all around and he clutches them by the hair. So I see souls are sinking. I feel in a hurry to save them. And it matters not what I eat or what I wear, or who are my companions, for when I have rowed a few miles I shall get home and shall find all my friends there.[53]

Nathan Bangs put it differently as he was introducing himself to a Canadian audience: "I am bound for the heavenly city, and my errand among you is to persuade as many as I can to go with me." What unites these statements is the seriousness of what is at stake.[54]

---

[52] Vesta Mullen. Unpublished Paper of Reflections on Beulah Camp and her experiences there, 20; 42.

[53] F.G. Hibbard. *Biography of Rev. Leonidas S. Hamline (etc.)*. Cincinnati: Hitchcock & Walden; New York: Phillips & Hunt, 1880, 109.

[54] Abel Stevens. *Life and Times of Nathan Bangs, D.D.* New York: Carlton & Porter, 1863, 136.

When we shift the focus to sanctification, the urgency remains. The issue here is whether someone will reach his or her destiny in Christ, God's vision for their life, the grand purpose for which each one has been created. The Bible itself is filled with such visions. Someone is given a name that reflects a destiny as yet unseen, or not fully understood. The name Jesus is meant to convey the fact that "he will save his people from their sins." He will also be called Emmanuel (or Immanuel), "God with us".[55] In the Transfiguration, God reveals His Son in a way that is beyond his disciples' comprehension, but he also shows them something about themselves and their future – the destiny God has for them when they see Jesus' glory in eternity.[56] In the Resurrection, Jesus tries to show them that because he lives, they also will live. And in I John 3: 2, we see ourselves as only grace can make us: "like him" (NIV). The power that can accomplish this belongs only to God.[57] One of the camp meeting songs expressed very well the longing, the hope, and the source of power that alone could work such a transformation:

> O warm my heart with holy fire,
> And kindle there a pure desire:
> Come, sacred Spirit, from above,
> And fill my soul with heavenly love.[58]

If the appeal to cooperate with God's perfecting grace – to become all he has created us to be – were for this life only, that alone would be a compelling mission, but the appeal to holiness in the Wesleyan tradition spans all of eternity. No wonder there was such urgency to seek - following the nation's understandable preoccupation with the Civil War - a new era of spiritual transformation by the power of the Holy Spirit, an explosive new chapter in the Wesleyan quest for holiness, and an explosive new chapter in the resilient life of the camp meeting. "When darkness has covered the earth, and thick darkness the people, God has ever had His agents ready – made ready by a deep, conscious enduement of spiritual power, for the work of calling people back to the life from which they had fallen."[59]

---

[55] Matthew 2:21&23, NIV.

[56] John 17:24.

[57] II Corinthians 3:18; I Thessalonians 5:23-25; II Peter 1:4.

[58] W. McDonald & S Hubbard, eds. *The Wesleyan Sacred Harp (etc.)*. Boston: John P. Jewett; Cleveland: Jewett, Proctor & Worthington; New York: Sheldon, Lamport & Blakeman, 1856, 25.

[59] W. McDonald & John E. Searles. *The Life of Rev. John S. Inskip (etc.)*. Boston: McDonald & Gill, 1885, 9.

This is not to say that a Chautauqua style institution, or a Christian resort that maintains a greater or lesser portion of the spirituality of a camp meeting, is without value or importance. I have gained a great deal, for instance, from time spent at the original Chautauqua in New York State. It does mean, however, that in some significant way, it no longer lives out some of the essential purposes of a camp meeting.

11

Decline, Renewal, and Hope II

"My soul thirsts for God, for the living God. Where can I go and meet with God?"[1]

"For thee, my God, - the living God,
My thirsty soul doth pine;
O where shall I behold thy face,
Thou Majesty divine!"[2]

With all the pressures that have caused camp meetings to compromise, or to become something else, it is noteworthy, to say the least, to find camp meetings continuing their original mission into the present day. This kind of perseverance requires a firm resolve, reaffirmed over and over again, based on the conviction that camp meetings accomplish a necessary and much valued function in the world, whose relevance depends more on an unchanging God than a constantly changing society. To maintain such a ministry over time is not an easy thing, but its reward is better than any benefit resulting from an easier course.

We have seen the risky path of a camp meeting that adds to or modifies its mission or program while attempting to keep its spiritual center. Ocean Grove and Ocean City in New Jersey have done this, though in different ways, winning the gratitude of their attendees and the reward of knowing they have given people spiritual sustenance and a relaxing, energizing break from their normal, often pressurized lifestyles, and knowing as well that they have preserved significant parts of their heritage. Their style and appearance today may be very different from when they began, but they

---

[1] Psalm 42:2, NIV.
[2] "As Pants the Hart," Tate & Brady's New Version, 1696; 1698, in B.W. Gorham. *Choral Echoes (etc.)*. Boston: Henry V. Degen, 1864, #244.

can legitimately rejoice that their foundational identity continues in some form as a witness to the power of God. Where many former campgrounds are no longer recognizable, or recognizable only, or mainly, by their historic buildings and early stories, these campgrounds still hold Christian worship that offers spiritual transformation and fellowship, though the activities that draw participants have multiplied.

Along with the North and South Carolina camp meetings described earlier by Minuette Floyd, I would list four others to represent camp meetings that have decisively rejected pressures to compromise their basic reason for existence, and continue, with only superficial and necessary changes, the program inherited from their origins. While those I include here are not alone in the path they have taken, their steadfastness is unusual and even heroic. They are **Douglas Camp Meeting in Douglas, Massachusetts**; **Indian Springs Holiness Camp Meeting** near **Flovilla, Georgia**; **Camp Sychar** in **Mount Vernon, Ohio**, and **Eaton Rapids Camp Meeting** in **Eaton Rapids, Michigan**. While no one would pretend that nothing has changed at any of these, they have kept their central, foundational purpose intact, resisted temptations to depart from that purpose, and continue to offer living ministry that is solidly within the Wesleyan camp meeting tradition.

We have seen how the camp meetings in Professor Floyd's book have changed in some externals, while remaining true to the heart of their life and ministry. Their backgrounds include relationships with Methodist denominations, either Methodist Episcopal/United Methodist, African Methodist Episcopal, or African Methodist Episcopal Zion. Over the years, these churches and others, often including nearby congregations, have connected with them in various ways. The oldest of these camp meetings is **Mount Carmel, in Lancaster County, South Carolina**, established in 1866. The most recent, **Saint Paul, in Dorchester County, South Carolina**, was founded in 1880. The others in this cluster are **Camp Welfare** (1876), **in Fairfield County, South Carolina**; **McKenzie's Grove** (1875), **in Catawba County, North Carolina**; **Mott's Grove** (1872), **in Catawba County, North Carolina**; **Shady Grove** (1870), **in Dorchester County, South Carolina**, and **Tucker's Grove** (1876), **in Lincoln County, North Carolina**. Not surprisingly, all began operation after the Civil War. While Methodist preachers and lay people have played a central role in their services, others have also been welcome.

There is a strong sense of continuity in these gatherings, with many attending throughout their lives, with beliefs and experiences extending across the generations of participants. Changes in food preparation, in some facilities, and in instrumental music have allowed the core of the experience to remain intact. Even with all the changes happening in the outside world, "camp meetings still offer a secure retreat. They still offer, as the old song says, a rock in a weary land."[3]

Douglas Camp Meeting in Massachusetts traces its spiritual roots back to Cane Ridge and the Communion gatherings in Scotland. In 1875, the first camp meeting in the area was led by two preachers, one Congregational and one Methodist, as part of the national holiness movement. Attendees came from a variety of denominations. In 1876 a location was provided for the new camp ground. In its early years, speakers such as George Hughes, Amanda Berry Smith, and *"Camp Meeting"* John Allen connected these meetings with the national organization. A National Camp Meeting was held at Douglas in 1879. The New England Association for the Promotion of Holiness was formed at this meeting, with William McDonald as president. He would later follow John Inskip as President of the National Association. McDonald coordinated the camp meetings that followed at Douglas. Davies tells us that people attended "not for recreation, but for God and salvation." John Inskip, Daniel Steele, and B.W. Gorham were among the preachers during the 1880s.[4]

Douglas had strong Methodist participation, while making a point of being "undenominational," believing that the Holy Spirit united people of diverse backgrounds. "Indeed, they are so baptized into one Spirit that you cannot tell one from the other." The holiness movement, building on the widespread acceptance of Arminianism in the matter of salvation, provided a somewhat common platform for like-minded people, at the same time when some churches in the Wesleyan movement were losing their consensus on the same issues. "These people believe that the very God of peace can sanctify them wholly, and then preserve them, spirit, soul, and body, blameless unto the coming of our Lord Jesus Christ....[5] They believe that they may be filled with all the fullness of God."[6] A woman attending the camp in 1886 experienced the essence of what had always been the camp meeting tradition. Edward Davies wrote, "She was so wonderfully emptied of self and so gloriously filled with God that heaven came down to earth. The glory of God has filled her soul ever since, even under severe

---

[3] Minuette Floyd. *A Place to Worship: African American Camp Meetings in the Carolinas*. Columbia, South Carolina: University of South Carolina Press, 2018, appendix A; 10.

[4] Edward E.Davies. *Illustrated History of Douglas Camp Meeting*. Boston: McDonald, Gill, 1890, xii-xiv; 1-3; 6; 8&9; 13-17.

[5] I Thess. 5: 23, 24.

[6] Eph. 3: 16-19.

trials." This kind of experience led John A. Wood to say, "the streets of heaven begin below." An anonymous comment linked this camp ground to our ultimate destiny: "Surely Douglas is the next place to heaven itself."

Another factor that helped maintain unity of purpose in the early years was the fact that the property used for this purpose was owned by one person, Deacon George M. Morse. As long as this was the case, investors and developers operating on different principles did not enter the picture. "The people go to worship God, and build each other up in holiness. They make this their great business." Deacon Morse saw it this way: "Sectarianism is vanishing. The people of God are more than ever united."

When so many camp meetings have come and gone, for a variety of reasons, it is no small accomplishment to have the original purpose of Douglas Camp Meeting still gathering people for worship and fellowship in the same holiness tradition, message, and experience.[7]

Indian Spring Holiness Camp Meeting, near **Flovilla, Georgia**, also arose from the Holiness Movement of the late 19th century, including the National Camp Meeting Association for the Promotion of Holiness. The first National Camp Meeting in the South was held in Knoxville, Tennessee in 1874. Kenneth Brown draws the connections from Knoxville, through a series of revivals led by John Inskip and William McDonald across the South, which led to revivals in Georgia, including a National Camp Meeting in Augusta. In its turn, Indian Springs, founded in 1890, has played a significant role in the further expansion of the holiness movement.

The doctrine of Christian perfection or holiness, intrinsic to the Methodist movement, was the primary focus of the new movement, which sought to reaffirm its centrality in the churches and in the lives of their people. Working with leadership from the national movement, leaders from southern churches, including William Dodge and Joseph Key, took the message of holiness to heart and organized its outreach in the region. The rapid spread of the movement in the South was for a time greatly hampered by controversies within the Methodist Episcopal Church, South, including a suspicion that leaders from the North were trying to take over or unduly influence the southern church. In time, the movement more than survived the controversy as camp grounds were established in Georgia and elsewhere in the South. In 1890, the Indian Springs Holiness Camp Ground Association began its work, with William Dodge as its first presi-

---

[7] Edward E. Davies. *Illustrated History of the Douglas Camp-Meeting*. Boston: McDonald, Gill, 1890; 17; 19;23-32; 35; 38; 96; http://douglascampmeeting.com.

dent. Their work helped produce a very successful camp meeting for 1891, featuring a number of well-known southern revival preachers. Subsequent meetings drew large audiences, who responded to powerful evangelists and song-leader Charles D. Tillman, author of many hymns and editor/publisher of revival hymnals. He is best known for "Give Me that Old Time Religion," for which Brown credits him as author, but which Hymary.org lists as "traditional." Several sources indicate that Tillman heard this song at an African-American camp meeting in South Carolina in 1889, then published it in 1891 and popularized it for white worship events.[8]

Like many other camp meetings, Indian Springs built a tabernacle and other facilities to accommodate the crowds who attended. Various attempts to intentionally include African Americans failed, though "Dodge and others maintained contact with black holiness leaders...." Sadly, the times and "social conditions" limited the ability of revival to bridge cultural gaps.

"Throughout the 1920's the annual brochure proclaimed Indian Springs Holiness Camp Meeting as 'The South's Greatest Camp Meeting.'" Year after year these events featured some of the best known preachers in the region and beyond. Among them Bishop Arthur J. Moore (M.E.S.) and Henry Clay Morrison, founder of Asbury Theological Seminary. Morrison "used to say the camp was the closest thing to heaven that he knew." Over many years, the connection with Asbury – both seminary and college - would contribute greatly to the strength of this and similar gatherings. Dennis Kinlaw was converted at Indian Springs as a teenager and later returned many times as a speaker. J.C. McPheeters and John Oswalt served often as evangelists there. Evangelist Harry Denman appears on the list of speakers, as well.

President Joseph P. Luce said in his 1990 President's Report: "The object of this Camp Ground is the spread of the Wesleyan Doctrine of Scriptural Holiness throughout the earth; that Christ's Kingdom may come and His will be done on earth as it is in Heaven." As Kenneth Brown says, "this encampment embraces the evangelical revival tradition in America that reaches back to John Wesley, George Whitefield, Jonathan Edwards, Bishop Francis Asbury, Peter Cartwright and a host of others who fearlessly proclaimed the saving grace of Jesus Christ. This camp meeting stands in the very heart of that history," and "in the very mainstream of the southern holiness revival." The clarity of this commitment is unmistakable. Also important as we consider the ingredients of a lasting and successful camp

---

[8] www.Hymnary.org; www.folkslingers.com; www.bluegrassmessengers.com.

meeting, "Dennis Kinlaw, a product of Indian Springs Camp, has said that the modern holiness movement owes its existence to the independent holiness camp meeting." Already we have seen that while faithfulness to our Wesleyan tradition, along with good working relationships with churches and their leaders, are essential, denominational ownership is unnecessary to a flourishing camp meeting.[9]

Early in the 20th century, W.W. Cary described **Camp Sychar in Mount Vernon, Ohio**, as "one of the greatest camp meetings in America today...." The shared purpose connecting it to other camp grounds included in this present volume is clear from Cary's words of invitation:

> So, reader, turn back to Christ the Saviour. Read the Word and note the emphasis on "Be ye holy as I am holy." Then turn from work and play, from all the regular routine of life; pack up the family and betake yourselves to Camp Sychar, Eaton Rapids, Richland, Indian Springs, or the nearest camp that is now preaching "Holiness unto the Lord."

Camp Sychar also traces its roots to John Wesley, to the early camp meetings following Cane Ridge, and especially to the more recent camp meetings born out of the holiness movement. B.W. Gorham and others from The National Camp Meeting Association for the Promotion of Holiness organized revivals in Ohio, including camp meetings in Alliance and Canton, where the Ohio State Camp Meeting Association began.

The choice of Mount Vernon as its permanent location came only after experimenting with many options across the state. The first camp meeting held at what became Camp Sychar took place in 1887. The following year's meeting prompted this comment concerning the camp's mission: "Truly the Holy Ghost appeared and dedicated the Sychar grounds as holy ground where until Our Lord appears, full salvation should be preached, sinners saved, backsliders reclaimed, believers wholly sanctified, and the people of God be freshly anointed with mighty outpourings of the Spirit of God." That determination would bear fruit on the road this camp has taken, even to the present day.

The camp ground soon faced a different kind of challenge – the lack of enough water. "No water meant a resumption of their wandering again; a defeat to all the bright hopes that already had begun to be harbored." Those who cared for the camp and its ministry took this situation to God in prayer, believing that the same Lord who calmed violent weather on the Sea of Galilee could cause water to flow at Sychar. Soon they were blessed

---

[9] Kenneth O. Brown, *Indian Springs Holiness Camp Meeting (etc.)*. Hazleton, PA: Holiness Archives, 2000, 42--50; 61&62; 67; 77&78; 86; 92-94; 114&115; 152-161.

with a reliable supply, flowing from a well that had earlier produced nothing. The community rejoiced, not only because a critical problem had been solved, but also because to them this much needed water represented the outpouring of the Spirit in lives touched by the camp. Kenneth Brown writes,

> If any one thing could symbolize this camp meeting and its mission to promote the doctrine and experience of Christian holiness, it would be the artesian well that sits in the middle of the campground. Drilled in 1888 in an answer to prayer, named after a Biblical site, this well has the stuff of legends. No wonder an old brochure declared that at Camp Sychar, "Water and Air and Salvation are pure, plentiful and free."

Early speakers at Sychar camp meetings included Henry Clay Morrison, whom we noted at Indian Springs, and who was Asbury Seminary's first president. C.L. Lewis and Joseph Smith were mainstays as well. National Association speakers, such as John Inskip, Wiiliam McDonald, and Amanda Berry Smith also contributed to its life and ethos. Their preaching brought the meaning and promise of justifying and sanctifying grace to those who came seeking a closer walk with their Lord. Dr. Brown notes that "The famous black woman evangelist, Amanda Smith, appeared in 1897, and delighted everyone with her singing and preaching. A former slave, she had been sanctified under the ministry of John S. Inskip and became a holiness evangelist and world traveler."

Amanda Berry Smith

Growing numbers and a spirit of generosity brought about a tabernacle and other buildings, all without moving away from Sychar's original purpose. Even these measures could not keep up with the numbers of people coming to camp meetings there. 1925 saw such high attendance that "... Sunday crowds were larger outside the tabernacle than within."

Unlike camp grounds that sought to combine spiritual and recreational purposes, Sychar held on tenaciously to its initial inspiration. Cary put it well: "From the beginning to the present day the main objective, "Holiness unto the Lord," has been the unswerving policy of Camp Sychar. Salvation of sinners and sanctification of believers above every other purpose is a sufficient program for ten days meeting." While clearly Wesleyan in its theology, like many of the camp meetings in this study, Sychar "has adhered faithfully to an interdenominational position, working with all evangelistic churches, but never seeking to build up exclusive membership in any one denomination." In keeping with this policy, Sychar has not asked people to leave one church in order to join one that is more in tune with the camp's message, but has sent people back to their own churches as witnesses and disciples. The camp has even avoided diversifying its ministry in any way that would obscure the heart of its mission, even if the activity in question is a valuable, Christian effort or unobjectionable recreation. "This policy keeps Sychar steadfast, unswerving, fervent, and God has blessed the camp mightily with the presence of the Holy Spirit." Kenneth Brown presents a slightly different picture, at least in the case of the Epworth League, saying that "Sychar devoted one service per year" to this organization, and in 1911 "invited the Mt. Vernon District Epworth League to hold its annual convention on the grounds...."

Writing in 1933, Cary voiced a staunch commitment he believed had served the camp well for its first (nearly) fifty years. He continued in a similar vein to make sure his point was neither missed nor blunted in any way, and in so doing positioned Camp Sychar in relation to communities that had taken very different paths. His tone shows a kind of fierce determination, arising from the deep appreciation he had for the experience he had known at Sychar:

> There is no more pitiful, and to a discerning mind, more tragic place than the site of a once mighty Holiness camp grounds now turned into a summer resort or Chautauqua grounds. To the spiritually minded such a place has the unwholesome, deadly miasma of a charnel house. Not far from Sychar is such a former camp ground. Once it was resonant with the groans of earnest seekers and the shouts of those entering Canaan land. To this day there are those who formerly went there still attending every summer. Such people are the outstanding champions of every Laodicean [See Revelation

3:14-22, NIV, with its reference to "lukewarm" churches.] move in their home churches, and spiritually the place sends out only gospel-hardened scoffers against righteousness.

Better that an earthquake should swallow up Sychar grounds, obliterating them forever; than that the first compromising step be taken. God give to the present and future boards the same spirit of wisdom and discernment. God said to Moses, 'the place whereon thou standest is holy ground," because He had manifested Himself there. Then surely Sychar is a holy place.[10]

Cary's point suggests that of the hymn, "The Pearl that Worldlings Covet," found in B.W. Gorham's collection, *Choral Echoes*, especially verse 1:

> The pearl that worldlings covet
> Is not the pearl for me;
> Its beauty fades as quickly
> As sunshine on the sea.
> But there's a pearl sought by the wise,
> 'Tis called "the pearl of greatest price;"
> Though few its value see, -
> Oh, that's the pearl for me.[11]

Kenneth O. Brown's history of Camp Sychar brings the record closer to the present (2000). From his vantage point "at the threshold of a new century," he wrote that the camp remained "dedicated to fulfill its mission to spread Scriptural holiness through all these lands." Long before this, the camp had undergone all the usual changes of growth, construction, and externals like dress. It had landed in Mt. Vernon after the Ohio Association had tried several other locations. For decades people had been coming by bus or car instead of horse and wagon. Most tents had been replaced by cottages. Yet when the Association revised its charter in 1987, the camp's purpose remained what it had always been, "the worship of God through the promotion of Scriptural holiness as understood in the Wesleyan-Arminian tradition; and conversion of sinners...." Brown summarizes the permanent mission of the camp in this way:

---

[10] W.W. Cary. *Sychar, An Holiness Camp Meeting*. Wilmore, KY: First Fruits, 2015 [orig. Pentecostal Publishing, 1833], 7; 9; 21; 224; 26-28; 41-43; 48&49; 58-63.

[11] S. Hoyt. "The Pearl that Worldlings Covet," in B.W. Gorham, ed. *Choral Echoes (etc.)*. Boston: Henry V. Degen, 1864, #95, v.1. Gorham was one of the founding national figures whose work in Ohio resulted in the creation of Camp Sychar.

...the leaders of Camp Sychar have taken ... a firm stand regarding the doctrine and experience of holiness as preached by John Wesley. They have understood the call to holiness as a Biblical imperative given to every generation, and they have seen the holiness camp meeting as the best method to carry out that mandate.

Therefore, he concludes, "Camp Sychar will always work hard to fulfill its mission of 'spreading Scriptural holiness." Like other traditional camp grounds, this camp must seek the best way to "hold up the standard of a holy life and adapt that message to these times...." There will always be a need for discerning what elements of the camp are permanent, and what elements can be allowed to change over time. "...there are Biblical principles about the doctrine and experience of the holy life that never change. The challenge is to preach that message and teach those principles to a new generation. And do it in a language they will clearly understand." This has been, or should have been, the main task of every camp meeting in this tradition.[12]

Another impressive example is the holiness camp meeting at **Eaton Rapids, Michigan**. Eaton Rapids has been blessed with an especially complete and masterfully written history. David Baggett, one of its authors, has experienced many of the annual gatherings and has emphasized the camp's faithfulness to its unchanging and permanently relevant purpose.

Growing up at Eaton Rapids, he found each summer's camp meeting to be "an intensive church-on-steroids event" that, by the power of the Spirit, enabled participants to catch a glimpse of "life as it should be." Here were "people of God converging together to worship and find inspiration to walk uprightly and faithfully in this world." Here, as in an earlier age, they found "something of eternal permanence and infinite value," because in this special place, the light of Christ was shining brightly, and heaven itself was not at all far away.

Eaton Rapids Camp Ground began in 1885 as part of the post-Civil War holiness movement that swept the continent. Here people took part not in a place of legalistic restriction, as some have imagined it, but in "life-changing preaching and fellowship" in a place of natural beauty. Unlike the clothing styles that have come and gone, "The needs and hungers that stirred the first attendees in 1885 ... are much the same as the needs and hungers of people today." The purpose and energy that live in this camp, "biblical truth, and the essence of Christian salvation have not changed."

---

[12] Kenneth O. Brown. *A History of Camp Sychar (etc.)*. Hazleton, PA: Holiness Archives, 2000, Preface; 11; 25; 97; 119; 125; 129; 131&132; 143&144.

Many camp meetings - and churches, for that matter – have allowed their foundational values and distinctive identity to change with every fluctuation in the society around them. But Eaton Rapids has not allowed itself to be distracted in that way. "Styles may change; the human condition remains constant." Thus the permanent relevance of a camp ground whose faithfulness to its unchanging God will always have something vital to offer a world that is aimless and confused. "The central idea and unifying thread is this: *Eaton Rapids Camp Meeting has, with remarkable consistency in the course of its history, refused to privilege the pursuit of happiness above or apart from the pursuit of holiness.*"

While some camp meetings have vanished, and others have changed beyond recognition, "Eaton Rapids has endured, faithfully proclaiming the message of justification and sanctification for over 130 years." This is, after all, the message Wesley entrusted to his preachers, without which our Methodist movement really has nothing to live by itself or to offer the world. "The message," as David Baggett says, "is powerful and compelling, wild and beautiful, challenging and stirring, and it's a message needed as much today as it was needed in 1885." Baggett laments that even this camp ground has to deal with distractions that have come with cultural change – "smart phones and internet connections" among them – which make it even more important that the gospel message of freedom and holiness be held forth and lived, unchanged and uncompromised. A ministry like this has to provide alternative priorities that question what the world assumes to be acceptable, necessary, and right, if Christians are going to build their lives around things that matter.[13]

Eaton Rapids Camp Meeting was first and foremost an expression of a longing for the promise of sanctifying grace in the Wesleyan tradition in the late 19th century. Part of the appeal of the camp arose from the nature of urban life in those days. "It was especially attractive to many from metropolitan centers who moved their families here to get away from the perennial turmoil of the city and to give their children the advantage of the great open spaces." It had strong ties to the Methodist Episcopal Church, including a number of bishops and other leaders. The best known of the latter was E. Stanley Jones, missionary to India. Missions would remain a special emphasis there. One speaker, Joseph H Smith, was so well received that he preached at the camp each year for 38 years. Musicians such as George Bennard, composer of "The Old Rugged Cross," and editor of *Divine Praise*, played a vital role in the camp's worship. Henry Clay

---

[13] David & Marybeth Baggett, with Joelee Bateman. *At the Bend of the River Grand (etc.)*. Lexington, KY: Emeth, 2016, xi; xii; xiii; 1-7.

Morrison and J.C. McPheeters; Dennis Kinlaw and John Oswalt; Kenneth Kinghorn and Elsworth Kallas, would take their places in the long and distinguished list, making Asbury College and Seminary key resources for Eaton. Others would come from a variety of institutions and backgrounds, including Leonard Sweet and Senator Mark Hatfield.

The camp meeting for 1891 had as its clear purpose, "the Sanctification of Believers and the Conversion of Sinners." The group operating the camp, known from 1894 on as the Michigan State Holiness Camp Meeting Association, made improvements to facilities as resources allowed. As with other campgrounds, wooden structures, sometimes attractive cottages, and a hotel began to replace the tents so familiar from earlier years and older camp meetings. A Tabernacle would not last forever, and a bookstore proved to be an important resource. But these changes did not signal a change in purpose. The official brochure for 1912 said of the camp's history and mission,

> "The camp meeting has always held true to its purpose, the preaching of 'the fullness of the blessing of the gospel of Christ,' free from fanaticism and side issues. Its meetings have been wonderfully blessed with the presence of the Holy Spirit; and at its altars every year many have been saved and many have found the blessings of heart purity."

The same brochure said, "Although under Methodist auspices, we cordially invite to its services everyone irrespective of church affiliation." Methodism proved to be a great resource and partner, through speakers, missionaries, the Epworth League, etc., but without taking direct control. This would be extremely important when the United Methodist Church was losing its grip on Wesleyan theology and traditional Christian values – something David Baggett calls "cultural capitulation."

The brochure for 1922 restated the camp's theological and spiritual tradition: "This is the camp meeting to attend because it keeps the fires of Pentecostal Evangelism aglow. It is free from fanaticism. Its aim is the highest New Testament Standard of Experience and Holy Living as taught by Wesley." One of the speakers for 1934 gave this tribute: "The fame of Eaton Rapids Camp Meeting is worldwide. To the lovers of full salvation it has been and is one of the great Camps of the Whole Country. Its merit has been established by devout and wise ... control holding tenaciously in its preachment to scriptural holiness."

Even during the economic woes of the Depression, "the camp's steadfast commitment to the holiness message and to fostering a community of believers for edification of the saints both enabled and fortified the ministry on the grounds, no matter what the challenges faced."

In 1950, Christianity and the camp meeting faced a different challenge, one which J.C. McPheeters, who often spoke at Eaton Rapids, compared to the situation 150 years before. In an article for the Pentecostal Herald, he wrote, in part,

> The periods of apostasy and spiritual decline within our nation during the past two decades have been quite similar to the period of lawlessness and immorality that held sway during the period that preceded the revival of 1800. Again the revival fires are burning over the nation in a manner to give encouragement to the people of God. It is the earnest prayer of multitudes hat we may now be in the beginning of another revival period, similar to the great revival of 1800, in which the camp meeting still has a large and important place in this mid-century period. We should plan and expect large things of God during the camp meeting season of 1950. The revival tides are coming in and every camp should help to swell these tides to new heights that have not hitherto been reached.[14]

McPheeters' anchor in historical tradition was matched by his hopeful determination. He was not bound by any discouragement or resigned to a down-sized vision of what could be. The God who has brought glorious revival in an earlier time can surely take us "to new heights that have not hitherto been reached." As John Oswalt stepped into his president's role at the campground, he knew that while "much has changed in the last 120 years ... the needs have not changed at all. In fact," he said, "they are even more pressing today than they were then." Nor had the God who had called camp meetings into being, as a way to offer himself as the one eternal response to those pressing needs; the one who opens the gates of heaven and pours out his Holy Spirit.

Eaton envisions a future built on the same foundation and priorities that have made this camp meeting what it is:

- a life of prayer that resists distraction and values both the freedom and inspiration God provides through this ministry;

- confidence in and excitement about what our unchanging God will accomplish in the days and years ahead, and

---

[14] David & Marybeth Baggett with Joelee Bateman. *At the Bend of the River Grand (etc.)*. Lexington, KY: Emeth, 2016, 54-57; 69; 73; 75&76; 78; 80&81; 88; 99;132-135; 236; 307-331. Darius Salter, Nazarene minister and leader in the holiness movement, says, "For the first four decades of the twentieth century, he [McPheters] was the most popular and commanding preacher on the holiness camp meeting circuit." – Darius L. Salter. *The Demise of the American Holiness Movement (etc.)*. Wilmore, KY: First Fruits, 2020, 194&195.

– the same "Emphasis on Biblical Holiness" that has given life and genuine happiness to all who seek and receive it as God's precious gift.

Camp meetings that hold to this foundation and these priorities can continue to bring the eternal realities of heaven to the persistent needs of earth, even when externals constantly change and insistently demand our attention. The camp meeting is not in itself ultimate, but rather instrumental in the process – an instrument still capable of great things when used in the mission for which it was given.[15]

At a time when so many churches have grown weak and superficial, camp meetings are still pulling people away from lesser preoccupations and empty distractions; pulling toward the life and destiny God offers his people, in Christ, by the power of the Spirit.

"…God wanted to make the unchanging nature of his purpose very clear to the heirs of what was promised…."[16]

"Fill me with Thy hallow'd presence, - Come, oh, come and fill me now."[17]

Some have seen weakening or compromise in the camp meeting movement, and in the Wesleyan theology and spirituality at its heart, as an irreversible trend. Camp meetings that carry on their long tradition are less prominent in the Church, fewer in number, and having to defend their continued usefulness. Many in the churches are no longer aware of the opportunities camp meetings offer. The Chautauqua movement bears a kind of family resemblance to camp meetings, but even at the start acknowledged its different purpose. Some of the largest camp meetings have compromised or given up their founders' purpose by allowing or encouraging such a strong emphasis on recreation as to limit their spiritual program's importance or effectiveness in the lives of participants. Other camp grounds have become church camps, retreat and conference centers, or summer communities with vague ties to their origins. On the other hand, some church camps maintain a strong spiritual program that fulfills several of the original purposes of camp meetings.

---

[15] David & Marybeth Baggett, with Joelee Bateman. *At the Bend of the River Grand (etc.)*. Lexington, KY: Emeth, 2016, 297&298.

[16] Hebrews 6:17, NIV.

[17] Elwood H. Stokes, "Fill Me Now," in J.S. Inskip, ed. *Songs of Triumph (etc.)*. Philadelphia: National Publishing Association for the Promotion of Holiness, 1882, #48.

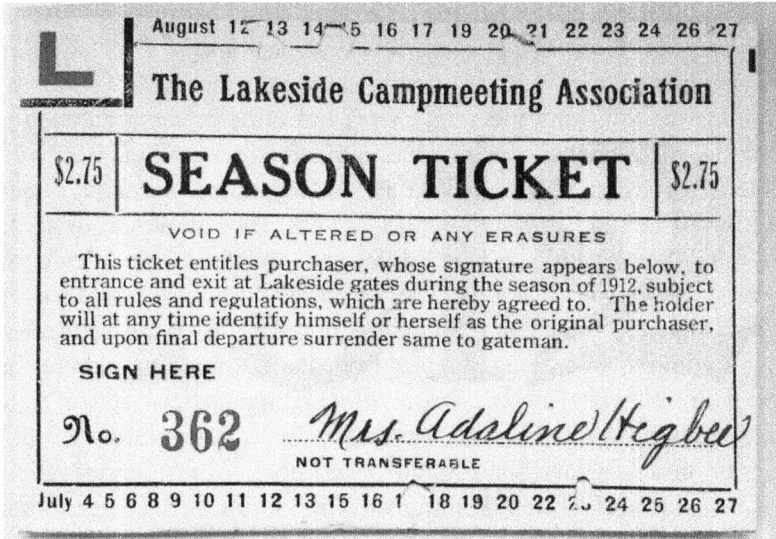

Darius Salter has written a book lamenting *The Demise of the American Holiness Movement*. He paints a picture of camp meetings that have closed or lost their way due to secularization, especially in the last few decades. Technology, school consolidation, the decline of small communities and other factors have dramatically altered the world, and camp meetings have often been unable to successfully transition to the new social realities. "I am working with the thesis that the American Holiness Movement has lost its identity primarily because it has been unable to negotiate modernity." In this he follows Wesleyan scholar Keith Drury's 2005 article, "The Holiness Movement is Dead." Salter is a veteran camp meeting preacher and leader in the larger movement, so he has watched these changes as a knowledgeable insider.[18]

Camp meetings are only part of the Holiness Movement, so Salter details the small numbers of people in holiness churches like his own Church of the Nazarene. He witnessed the end of the Christian Holiness Partnership, originally the dynamic National Camp Meeting Association for the Promotion of Holiness, which once organized and led enormous gatherings, year after year, beginning in 1867. Among the factors he cites in our contemporary situation are the decline of ordinary churches, the rise of the megachurch, and various attempts to revitalize moribund congregations. All of this has been happening in a society that is moving faster and faster and demanding more in every area of life.

---

[18] Darius L. Salter. *The Demise of the American Holiness Movement (etc.)*. Wilmore, KY: First Fruits, 2020, 3.

Camp meetings do not exist in a vacuum, but rather in supportive relationships with churches that connect with their ministry. But, Salter says, "The single most used vehicle for propagating the message of entire sanctification was the camp meeting." Thus a decline in camp meeting participation, for whatever cause, signals a much larger problem. Part of that problem is in what he sees as shallow understanding and weak commitment in most churches. Few attendees in churches of Wesleyan heritage have much familiarity with Charles Wesley's hymns, which often convey the Wesleyan gospel. There is "less emphasis on holiness as it has been traditionally understood and taught." Churches that once were clearly counter-cultural, or at least distinct from the surrounding culture, have blurred those lines. "The peculiarities of worship practices, ethical beliefs, and the esoteria [sic] of doctrine have been fine sand-papered for frictionless entry into the generic and cultural assembly line of American religious options." Add to this radical differences in culture between generations and worship preferences and the picture can look pretty bleak.

Salter contrasts all this with the relative simplicity, clarity, and life-shaping power of long ago camp meetings. He is convinced that the modern churches that compromise their identity and accommodate whatever the culture does or demands will lose their identity in the process. Seeing these things from a Nazarene perspective, he writes:

> We, in the holiness denominations such as the Church of the Nazarene, believe we can continue to maintain a holiness lifestyle while our sacred space and time are eroded by the world's technology, the world's entertainment, and the world's priorities. It cannot be done. In a sense, to be holy in today's world demands a more radical commitment than that of our holiness forefathers.

If the world is having a powerful impact on the churches, the same cannot be said of the reverse, so that the churches have a major challenge on our hands if we are to be true to our calling and effective in our outreach.[19]

Yet after a lengthy, discouraging account of important people and events in the Wesleyan Holiness tradition, Salter ends on a much more positive note. Though he may worry about the future of camp meetings, he strongly affirms his faith in what God is doing and can do, in and beyond his tradition:

> God has not forsaken the Churches who have historically identified themselves with the Wesleyan Holiness Movement. Neither is he partial to

---

[19] Darius L. Salter. *The Demise of the American Holiness Movement (etc.)*. Wilmore, KY: First Fruits, 2020, 3-9; 11.

the Church of the Nazarene, The Wesleyan Church, The Free Methodist Church, The Salvation Army, and the dozens of other denominations, who place themselves under the holiness umbrella. God still shows up wherever his presence is sincerely desired whether the church be Wesleyan Arminian, or five-points Calvinist. To believe that God favors a particular denominational label or brand is fatal. To believe that God is faithful to those who diligently and honestly seek Him with all their heart is the beginning of revival and renewal. There is evidence of this happening throughout Christendom around the world.[20]

---

[20] Darius L. Salter. *The Demise of the American Holiness Movement (etc.)*. Wilmore, KY: First Fruits, 2020, 437.

12

Message

> I have no greater joy than to hear that my children are walking in the truth."[1]

> "The road to heaven by Christ was made,
> With heavenly truth the rails are laid,
> From earth to heaven the line extends
> To life eternal where it ends."[2]

The foundational purpose of camp meetings in the Wesleyan tradition is the doctrine and experience often called the great salvation. Both conversion, made possible by justifying grace, and holiness, made possible by sanctifying grace, are intended in that expression. Conversion, when it is fruitful, leads us into and through a process of transformation which is empowered by the Holy Spirit, freely and actively sought and received.

This essential part of Wesleyan theology and spirituality is both characteristically Wesleyan and intrinsic to Christian orthodoxy. Solidly rooted in the Old and New Testaments, this understanding of Christian life and teaching informs everything that happens on the camp ground. This is the Scriptural Christianity that gave rise to the Methodist movement as our primary purpose. Each speaker conveys this message in his or her own way, and seeks its acceptance and realization in the hearts and minds of the congregation.

The message of holiness is not limited to the Wesleyan or Wesleyan Holiness tradition, though clearly it is our emphasis and reason for be-

---

[1] III John v.4, NIV.

[2] Mrs. Hall Booth, "The Road to Heaven by Christ Was Made," in R.C. Horner & J.V. MacDowell, eds. *Gospel Tent Hymns*. Toronto: William Briggs; Montreal: C.W. Coates; Halifax: S.F. Huestis, 1889, #144.

ing. Its emphasis and some of its vocabulary are distinctive, but far from unique. Wesleyan theology is purposely built on Scripture, along with writings from the early Church, especially those prominent in the East, and on many strands in the Great Tradition of orthodox Christian thinking and practice. It is not sectarian, but seeks common ground across a wide expanse of Christian theology. This is why, at one and the same time, our camp meetings are solidly Wesleyan and genuinely open to others' participation.[3]

The central, Biblical message at the heart of genuinely Wesleyan camp meetings is non-negotiable. Like Jesus Christ, and because he is our Lord and Savior, it is "the same yesterday and today and forever."[4] God's unchanging nature is reflected in our unchanging message.[5] While preachers have always used the full range of spiritual gifts and the uniqueness of their own personalities in presenting the truth, the truth itself is consistent from one generation to another. If it were possible in this passing world for Wesleyan people and their preachers to move from one point in history to another, so they could attend camp meetings in any and every time and place, it should be possible, allowing for differences in language, for each one to recognize and affirm what is being preached. They should be able to recognize brothers and sisters in Christ and in the Connexion. Styles of clothing, colloquial expressions, modes of delivery, etc. could all change, but not that central, foundational message. The Word remains eternally true and relevant, no matter how audiences might change.

In the Letter of Jude, God calls us "to contend for the faith that was once for all entrusted to God's holy people."[6] Anyone who attends a camp meeting should be able to trust that we are doing exactly that. Each sermon

---

[3] For example, see S.T. Kimbrough, Jr. *Orthodox and Wesleyan Spirituality*, Crestwood, NY: St. Vladimir's Seminary Press, 2002; S.T. Kimbrough. *Partakers of the Life Divine (etc.)*. Eugene, OR: Cascade, 2016; Theodore Runyon. *The New Creation: John Wesley's Theology Today*. Nashville: Abingdon, 1998; Michael J. Christensen & Jeffery A. Wittung. *Partakers of the Divine Nature (etc.)*. Grand Rapids, MI: Baker Academic, 2007; Randy L. Maddox. *Responsible Grace (etc.)*. Nashville: Kingswood, 1994; Clarence (Bud) Bence. *John Wesley's Theological Hermeneutic*. Unpublished Dissertation, Emory University, 1981; John R. Tyson. *Charles Wesley on Sanctification*. Grand Rapids, MI: Francis Asbury, 1986; Henry H. Knight. *Anticipating Heaven Below (etc.)*. Eugene, OR: Cascade, 2014; D. Gregory Van Dussen. *Transfiguration and Hope: A Conversation across Time and Space*. Eugene, OR: Wipf & Stock, 2018.

[4] Hebrews 13:8, NIV.

[5] James 1:17&18.

[6] Jude v.3, NIV.

should possess the ring of truth. Everything we seek to accomplish should accurately represent God's eternal reality and purpose. Our fellowship is not just superficial chumminess, the horizontal interaction of human beings. Instead, "our fellowship is with the Father and with his Son, Jesus Christ," for that is the fellowship that makes "joy complete."[7]

Creativity is a divine gift, one we should cherish in ourselves and each other. But we do not create, reshape, redefine, or replace our faith. If ever a camp meeting were to preserve "the form of religion without the power," it would fulfill John Wesley's worst fear for the movement he started and entrusted to us.[8]

In the same way, if we were to somehow maintain the outward appearance of a camp meeting, while diluting or denying its message and substituting one of our own – what Paul in Galatians calls "a different gospel – which is really no gospel at all," we would completely subvert everything else that ersatz camp meeting might do.[9] Without its original, Scriptural, Wesleyan purpose, a camp meeting would be only an empty shell. It might have a Christian and Wesleyan past, or a Christian and Wesleyan appearance, but the living reality would be gone.

For decades following the establishment of the Methodist Episcopal Church, there was little talk of an erosion in theological integrity in the movement, either in the United States or in Canada. The issues that brought about division had to do with slavery and the equality of races, authority and appointment making, and the relationship of Canadian Methodists to British and American denominations. While all these issues were important, and slavery In particular was critical for Christian ethics and consistency with the teaching of Wesley, there was unity in matters of doctrine and the way of salvation. However, by the 1850s Benjamin Titus Roberts and others believed that the M.E. Church was losing its witness on sanctification theology and practice. Free Methodism began in 1860 as a holiness denomination with other important concerns. Individual preachers like Peter Cartwright complained about a perceived drift from Methodism's origins, including issues Roberts raised, but was strongly opposed to any group that broke away from the main body. After the Civil War those who joined in the holiness movement expressed great concern over what they saw as erosion of Wesleyan teaching on Christian perfection and related practices, especially class and camp meetings. The National

---

[7] I John 1:3&4, NIV.

[8] II Timothy 3:5; John Wesley, "Thoughts upon Methodism," in Laura Bartels Felleman. The Form and Power of Religion (etc.). Eugene, OR: Cascade, 2012.

[9] Galatians 1:6&7, NIV.

Camp Meeting Association for the Promotion of Holiness gathered many thousands in national events, attracting people from a variety of Wesleyan and other churches. They produced a vast literature, including hymnals, and drew support from many bishops, presiding elders, academics, and others of influence to their cause. Then from the late 19th century onward, liberal theology and causes gained acceptance in many arenas, including seminary education, and both the holiness cause and camp meetings saw decline. Even so, many camp meetings maintained their original principles and program and today offer teaching and experience consistent with their founding purpose.[10]

George Hughes voiced the concerns propelling the Holiness Movement into a renaissance of camp meetings. He noted a demand in the late 19th century for "A ministry conformed to the spirit of the age," or "a ministry for the times."

> Such phraseology seems to intimate that the ministry of the everlasting gospel is to be different in one age from another, proclaiming a gospel modified to suit the ever-varying tastes of humanity: whereas, the gospel, like its Author, is "the same yesterday, to-day, and forever," universal in its adaptation, and to be ever proclaimed under the same divine unction, if saving in its effects. ... Now it cannot be denied, we think, that there is much *doctrinal indefiniteness* in the modern pulpit. The cardinal truths of Christianity are not set forth so clearly and pungently as is desirable.[11]

From "doctrinal indefiniteness," to redefining holiness; from denial or radical reshaping of basic doctrine, to theological indifference, each step in this downward journey weakens the churches and their witness in venues like camp meetings. There have been times when concerns over methodology in evangelism and spiritual growth were linked to changes in message and purpose. Camp meetings and revival in general had proven resilient in the face of 19th century social change, but as Methodism grew larger and more diversified in its program and theological understandings, these extraordinary means of grace seemed to threaten institutional priorities and control. Some thought it necessary to choose between emotionalism and respectability; camp meetings and local churches. Institutional "Methodism strove to achieve the goals of revival through rational and orderly channels." Some camp meetings themselves responded by moderating or shelving traditional preaching and programs. Gradual abandonment of the

---

[10] James V. Heidinger II. *The Rise of Theological Liberalism and the Decline of American Methodism*. Franklin, TN: Seedbed, 2017.

[11] George Hughes. *Days of Power in the Forest Temple. (etc.)*. Boston: John Bent, 1873, 17.

apparatus of Wesleyan spirituality, from class and band meetings to camp and protracted meetings, increasingly seen as divisive and outmoded, actually changed the character and mission of Methodism. For some, traditional means of grace had to give way to the new emphasis on education. A move from orthodox theology to liberal theologies that attempted to incorporate intellectual trends in a growing educational system, changed the formation and training of pastors. In the process, all too often the medium was changing, but so was the message.

Education could be, and often has been, a great asset in proclaiming the faith. The undoubted advantages of improved education for clergy and others has actually strengthened the ability of camp meeting speakers to penetrate the depths of Scripture and address the needs and concerns of a constantly changing society. Thus many of the speakers at camp meetings have been accomplished academics with advanced degrees. But for some, there would be no limit to changes in the Christian message itself, and the Wesleyan expression of that message in particular. Intellectual growth is not an enemy to the gospel, until Christian academics give priority to secular, rationalist assumptions so that they appear to undermine their own message. What Neil Semple said about Canada applies across the continent: "The influence of liberal theology was felt by Canadian Methodism in areas such as the growing trust in education as a means of grace...."[12] We do well to honor Wesley, Clarke, and others, right down to the present day, who have employed intellectual gifts to better understand and communicate a message that is both eternal and transformative.

Early preachers in our tradition sometimes expressed hopes and fears about the future of their particular church, or of the larger movement. Always the hope was that their spiritual descendants would not lose sight of the purpose and principle teachings of Methodism.

In 1832, Ara Williams wrote *The Inquirer's Guide to Gospel Truth; or Doctrinal Methodism Defended.* In it he says, "The connexion existing between truth and the spiritual well-being of man, as established by the great Head of the Church, renders the situation of a spiritual watchman awfully responsible." In this he is perhaps thinking of the "awfully responsible" position of a teacher of the faith in the Letter of James: "Not many of you should presume to be teachers, my fellow believers, because you know that we who teach will be judged more strictly." There is nothing self-

---

[12] Neil Semple. The Lord's Dominion (etc.). Montreal & Kingston, London & Buffalo: McGill-Queens University Press, 1996, 213; 216; 264.

righteous in these words, since James includes himself among those who must use great care in handling the truth.[13]

Methodist Episcopal Bishop Enoch George, in a letter to Abner Chase, highlighted the importance of maintaining clear, strong teaching in the matter of holiness:

> On this subject of holiness, my dear brother, permit me to plead with you affectionately, and with all the traveling and local preachers, to preach the doctrine and recommend the spirit and practice of holiness by a holy life and pious conversation. And permit me to plead successfully with the exhorters, leaders and members generally, to pursue holiness as the highest and best gift of Heaven, while we are probationers in this world of tribulation. This is no time to lower the gospel standard.... [14].

In closing his book on the ministry of Jacob Albright and other early ministers in the Evangelical Association, Reuben Yeakel stressed the need for his church to maintain the God-given content of its message. Yeakel wanted to avoid the "hollow profession and a worldly form of worship" he saw in some other churches. He also wanted the Wesleyan way of salvation to remain at the center of his church's witness.

> The Evangelical Association is a work of God, and she has a great and highly important mission to fulfill. But she can fulfill this mission only by proclaiming *everywhere* the pure Bible-doctrine which God has given her through the fathers; and does constantly *insist* upon *true* repentance, regeneration through faith, true sanctification of heart and life, and avoids compromise with and conformity to the world, and does *not follow in the footsteps of worldly-minded Churches*....[15]

---

[13] Ara Williams. *The Inquirer's Guide to Gospel Truth; or Doctrinal Methodism Defended (etc.)*. Buffalo: Steele & Faxon, 1832, 3; James 3:1, NIV.

[14] Abner Chase. *Recollections of the Past*. New-York: Published for the Author, Conference Office, 1846, 146&147.

[15] R. Yeakel. *Jacob Albright and His Co-Laborers*. Cleveland: Lauer & Yost, 1883.

Richard Allen

Richard Allen, who became the first Bishop of the African Methodist Episcopal Church, made a wise and gracious distinction that showed his love for the original, essential message of Methodism, the Methodism of John Wesley and also of many American Methodists, including white Methodists he had known, and in spite of the church's failure to live up to its own principles. He could see how the position of the M.E. Church against slavery had deteriorated under pressure over time, which can be seen in successive editions of the M.E. Discipline. He and other African American members of St. George's M.E. Church in Philadelphia were treated with outrageous discrimination and threats by that church's white members, until they had no acceptable alternative but to leave. In response, they established a church that would embody "the good old way, and ... walk therein." Allen and others, including some who had similar experiences in Baltimore, formed the African Methodist Episcopal Church, to rectify the problems they had known, yet remain Methodist. Bishop Allen never lost his original vision of Methodism, though he could only make it live, for himself and his people, in a new Methodist denomination. In time others would feel that they must take similar steps, in order to preserve the core beliefs and values of the movement.[16]

When Henry Boehm looked back at his long ministry, and forward beyond his own time, he said,

> But if there are some things to lament, there is much that calls for gratitude. If we remain true to Methodism, "walking by the same rule and minding the same things" our fathers did, then our future will be grand and glorious as the past, and the result such as to meet the expectations of the most ardent among us.[17]

1866 brought a great celebration of the first century of Methodism in America. Abel Stevens, who was a prolific historian and an insightful observer, wrote a special volume for the occasion. In it he looked to the future and offered this wise and eloquent admonition:

> *Finally, and above all things, Methodism should be reminded of its responsibility to maintain vital, apostolic piety in the land, and to spread it over the world.* This, as we have seen, was its original mission; this its historical stand-point; from this has sprung all its surprising achievements; if this ceases the light will go out in all its sanctuaries. Its spiritual life has, let it be repeated, preserved its doctrinal integrity and its practical vigor through these hundred years. It has never had, at least in America, a serious outbreak of theological heresy. Seldom has it had even an individual judicial case of heterodoxy. Such causes of faction and division have been almost unknown to us. ... Doubtless its peculiar methods have been the proximate cause of its great success, but what would these methods have been without the spiritual energy which has worked them? That energy has been divine, but the energy of the Divine Spirit itself works by the truth; the doctrines of Methodism have therefore been its vital element. Repentance, faith, personal regeneration, the witness of the Spirit, sanctification, these have been the living ideas of Methodist teaching throughout the world. It retains these vital truths to-day unimpaired; let it continue to guard them sacredly, as the very fire on its altars. Let it incessantly expound and enforce them in all its sanctuaries, and these sanctuaries shall continue to be thronged with inquiring, awakened, and living souls.[18]

---

[16] Richard Allen. *The Life Experience and Gospel Labors of the Rt. Rev. Richard Allen (etc.)*. Nashville: Abingdon, 1960, introduction by George A. Singleton; 23-36.

[17] J.B. Wakeley, ed. *Patriarch of One Hundred Years; Being Reminiscences ... of Rev. Henry Boehm*. New York: Nelson & Phillips, 1875, 492.

[18] Abel Stevens. *The Centenary of American Methodism (etc.)*. New York: Carlton & Porter, 1866, 240&241; italics original.

Early Methodist preachers, surprisingly often, in their last moments in this life, asked those around them to tell their colleagues in the conference that the message they had preached all their lives was proving itself in their final test. For the ultimate test of its truth would not be measured by exegetical precision or oratorical acclaim, but by its power in the interface between death and immanent resurrection. The reality they experienced was more than personal opinion, speculative philosophy, or institutional propaganda could ever produce; it was the way into eternal life itself.

As he was dying, Charles Baldwin said, "Tell the preachers of the Ohio Conference that the blessing of sanctification which I have enjoyed for five years, and preached, sustains me now."

Thirty-seven year old Isaac Beall said to a fellow minister from his death bed, "Tell my brethren of the Cincinnati Conference, death has lost its sting and the grave its gloom. ... I have attended my last conference, but I shall meet you all in heaven."

Similarly, George Campbell said, "Tell my brethren in the ministry, to live and die for Christ, and not to fail to meet me in heaven. Language cannot express what I enjoy. Glory to God! Oh, if I could stand and had the voice, I would proclaim to the ends of the earth, 'Come, poor sinners, come to Jesus.'"

William Burr Christie left this word: "Tell my brethren of the conference, if they think my name worthy of being mentioned, that I have not preached an unknown and an unfelt Christ. Tell them that though unworthy and unfaithful, that gospel I preached to others now sustains me."

Nathaniel Cunningham sent this message: "Tell my brethren of the annual conference ... God is love; and I am going to the Methodist preacher's heaven."

Cyrus Foss wanted his colleagues to know "that my belief in the great doctrines of the Methodist Episcopal Church has not suffered the least abatement, but is, if possible, stronger than ever." Later he said to one keeping watch, "This is the happiest day of all my life."

Daniel Griffis, knowing his time in this life was very short, said, "The gospel I have preached sustains me now. Tell my brethren of the conference that the gospel they are called to preach is a wonderful, a powerful gospel."

And Alfred Griffith: "To his conference sent his parting injunction, 'Tell them to preach Christ, the divine Son of God.'"

The purpose of teaching and evangelism, whether at camp meetings or in any other setting, was never merely to set forth correct theology, or to persuade people that the doctrines of Christianity deserved people's intellectual assent, but to let the world know, that embodied in these doctrines was "the Word of life." Preaching Christ was not only to convey accurate information. It was to open people's eyes to "the light of the world," without whom we "walk in darkness." To alter that message is not to improve either the message or the lives of those who hear it; but to "exchange[] the truth about God for a lie...."[19]

Maintaining the message was not about nailing down every last detail of the faith, or reducing our approach to Scripture to a narrow fundamentalism. Rather, it was focused on the truth as it transforms lives and points people to their destiny in Christ.

---

[19] Maxwell Pierson Gaddis. *Last Words and Old Time Memories*. New York & Pittsburgh: Phillips & Hunt; Cincinnati & Chicago: Walden & Stowe, 1880, 12; 29; 45; 51; 59; 97&98; 111; John 8:12, NIV; Romans 1:25. NIV.

13

Power for the Road Ahead

"Grace and peace be yours in abundance through the knowledge of God and of Jesus our Lord. His divine power has given us everything we need for a godly life through our knowledge of him who called us by his own glory and goodness."[1]

"You won't leave like you came in Jesus' name
There's a blessing in this house you can claim"[2]

By taking people out of their normal surroundings and immersing them in high octane spiritual renewal, camp meetings have freed them from encumbrances and empowered them to more faithfully walk the road of life. Old limitations could be swept aside and hope could rise to a new prominence. People could see themselves, other people, and life itself differently, filled with new, grace-empowered possibilities.

Central to the existence of genuinely Wesleyan camp meetings is the theology of conversion and sanctification. Were we to gather, as so often we seem to do, in too many church settings, without a clear, spiritual purpose to unite and sustain us, there would be little benefit. Were we to go one better and gather for vague or scattered reasons, even though they be drawn from Scripture and legitimate Christian beliefs or practices, our continued life as a church and our message to the world would be too diffuse to motivate us or attract others, especially over the long haul and amid countless distractions. What we need to receive from God, through our Wesleyan tradition, and then faithfully pass on to others, needs focus and specificity. Jesse T. Peck called it "the central idea of Christianity," around

---

[1] II Peter 1:2&3, NIV.
[2] Dorothy Norwood, "It's Service Time," in Minuette Floyd. *A Place to Worship (etc.)*. Columbia, SC: University of South Carolina Press, 2018, 65.

which all other ideas, values, and activities take their places. That great central idea is that God is calling us to be more than we are; to become all he created us to be. For that to happen, we need help pulling ourselves away from petty selfishness and myriad distractions so that we can actually walk "the path of life" that leads to eternal joy.[3] We need to be rescued from the emptiness, aimlessness, and destructiveness of this world and set free to live new and abundant lives in Christ. Then, once committed to that path, we need the power of the Spirit to propel us forward to the realization of our God-given purpose. We need an abundance of grace and a reliable band of fellow pilgrims to take us from wherever Christ finds us to the destination that is his vision and gift for us. In other words, we need to be saved from sin and made new creatures in Christ.[4]

Those who gathered, and those who still gather for camp meetings, have found there an outpouring of Christian love, which is both good in itself, and a foretaste of the love we will know in heaven. We can see this in W.F. Farrington's song called "Friendship:"

> Hail! Sweetest, dearest tie that binds
> Our glowing hearts in one;
>
> Hail! sacred hope that tunes our minds
> In harmony divine.
>
> The hope, when days and years are past
> We all shall meet in heaven.
>
> This is the hope, the blissful hope
> Which Jesus' grace has given.[5]

Albert Raboteau shows us how important the friendship and socializing of camp meetings was to enslaved people. At least for some, Christmas celebrations and camp meetings offered much needed relief from the daily routine of slavery, and each had the special blessing of extended time.

> According to Charlie Aarons: "there would be camp meetings held and the slaves from all the surrounding plantations would attend, going ... in these large wagons ... They then would have a jolly time along the way, singing

---

[3] Psalm 16:11, NIV.

[4] Jesse T. Peck. *The Central Idea of Christianity*. Boston: Henry V. Degen, 1856.

[5] W. McDonald & S. Hubbard, eds. *The Wesleyan Sacred Harp (etc.)*. Boston: John P. Jewett; Cleveland: Jewett, Proctor & Worthington; New York: Sheldon, Lamport & Blakeman, 1856, 45.

and calling to one another, and making friends."⁶

When we look at the realities of justifying and sanctifying grace, we are not dealing with peripheral issues, matters we can take or leave while maintaining Christian faith and life intact. Instead, we are seeing the purpose of and within creation, the need and promise of redemption, and the power of the Spirit poured out upon weak and flawed humanity to seek, appropriate, and live by his grace. This is, as Wesley put it, nothing less than "the way to heaven."⁷

Our Wesleyan ancestors found all of this in the means of grace God provided. One of those, always in concert with others, is the extraordinary means of grace called the camp meeting. For many people today, camp meetings may appear antiquated, bizarre, primitive (in its unwarranted, negative association), or even incomprehensible. But when we ask about the specific purposes which the camp meetings served and, in some cases, still serve, it becomes clear that we need, as much as ever before, to accomplish those same purposes in our time and into the future. Rather than invent ways of addressing the basic human, spiritual needs from scratch, it will be wise for us to see whether and how camp meetings – either in their original or adapted forms – might still serve those purposes and address those needs today. We have already seen how various Methodist tradition leaders have tried to preserve or adapt elements of the camp meeting phenomenon to changing times, conditions, and constituencies. We can learn a great deal from their successes, failures, and disappointments. And we can still enjoy and learn from camp meetings and their descendants living out their mandate in our day.

Imagine a gathering of Christians and seekers, along with skeptics, spiritual sightseers, and even some bearing hostility toward the sponsors. In that context, imagine further something so powerful, so unexpected, that people of all sorts were swept off their feet by the experience. The accounts we have from long ago are filled with stories like these. In one of them, the circuit rider James B. Finley was attending a camp meeting among hundreds of indigenous people. Some of them were singing, others praying, pleading for mercy from the Great Spirit. After a time of preaching and exhortation, the preachers brought a large group of tearful people together for prayer, which continued "nearly all night." Those who came with hope and expectation "were overwhelmed with his goodness, and

---

⁶ Albert J. Raboteau. *Slave Religion: The "Invisible Institution" in the Antebellum South.* Oxford, et al: Oxford University Press, 1978, 224.

⁷ John Wesley, Preface to the Sermons, in Albert C. Outler, ed. *The Works of John Wesley.* Nashville: Abingdon, 1984, i: 105.

all united in giving glory to God in the highest." Those who came with a different attitude and expectation "stood amazed and trembled, wept and cried for mercy, while others shouted for joy."[8]

In a very different setting, the Bergen Camp Ground in western New York, "advocates of the doctrine and experience of perfect love" gathered in an atmosphere they felt as "severe persecution" from adversaries in the local conference. Yet even in this situation, we find this surprising result:

> This camp meeting was largely attended, and extensive in its influence. Wonderful were the manifestations of divine power that here took place. Multitudes were converted and sanctified, and many ministers received the baptism of the Holy Ghost, and went to their homes in distant parts of the country to kindle similar fires for God and souls.[9]

In many kinds of weather; in many parts of the continent; under many denominational labels; people from a variety of backgrounds and previously held convictions; for all sorts of good and not so good reasons; among friends and even among enemies, people discovered in camp meetings a power greater than their own, greater than any other, able to build up and strike down, delivering God's redeeming love to all who would receive it.

Minuette Floyd notes that "Many African American campgrounds are more than 145 years old and still going strong today." Likewise there are predominantly white, often holiness camp grounds with strong programs and excellent prospects for future effectiveness.[10]

Along with camp meetings themselves, there are many organizations and activities that carry out, perhaps unaware of their origins, certain key elements of the camp meeting experience. Some of these are adaptations of what once were camp meetings. Other may offer ideas or practices that accomplish, at least in part, something that was once integrated with the other components of a full-blown camp meeting. Some may be explicitly and effectively Christian and even evangelistic in purpose, while others may have gradually walked away from such a purpose. Some may be responding to one of the needs which has been addressed by camp meetings, but without a religious motivation or connection. Still others may still be active, but no longer affiliated with any specific church or denomination.

---

[8] D. W. Clark, ed. *Life Among the Indians ... by Rev. James B. Finley*. Cincinnati: Curts & Jennings; New York: Eaton & Mains, n.d., 310&311.

[9] Joseph Goodwin Terrill, *The Life of Rev. John Wesley Redfield, M.D.* Chicago: Free Methodist Publishing House, 1889, 294&295.

[10] Minuette Floyd. *A Place to Worship: African American Camp Meetings in the Carolinas*. Columbia, SC: University of South Carolina Press, 2018, 22.

All of these provide testimony concerning significant human needs. Any ministry or program that leaves out one or more key components will for that reason fall short of what a camp meeting can provide.[11]

Ferenc M. Szasz, introducing Charles Johnson's study, *The Frontier Camp Meeting*, makes an important observation on the way Methodism "fit" the dynamic new society taking shape in the United States. Although there were differences in both the cultural setting and the organization of Methodism in Canada, much of this statement applies to the entire continent: "...Methodist theology, organization, and institutions meshed perfectly with the religious needs of the new American republic."

Johnson focuses on "the trans-Allegheny West," in places now part of the United States, but Methodism also spread like wildfire "back East," and in Canada, on the frontier and in long-settled communities. Camp meetings became a major part of its flourishing in places like New England and the entire Atlantic coast. They were and are expressions of a universal Gospel.

Even with the many and obvious changes that have come to the Methodist family of churches and their North American context, could it not be that Methodism, in some form, could again "mesh perfectly with the religious needs" of contemporary and future North America? Canadian and U.S. societies are unsure of their foundation and direction, locked in culture wars that show no sign of resolution. The religious scene is in flux and no church or movement is, at this point, offering, in a way that is actually heard, a convincing, unifying vision to fit its confused, conflicted, and often violent context. Although much has changed, and the argument could be (actually has been) made that we are a spent force, victims of our own compromises with culture, I believe there is within our tradition a renewable source of energy coming from God, through our Scriptural and Wesleyan roots. Could we not reclaim what is essential and find there the way of salvation? Could we not demonstrate the necessary resources of freedom, love, and purpose that are part of Christian life and hope? Could there still be enough time, energy, and commitment within our movement to proclaim the truth amid the cacophony of lies that is on offer everywhere we turn? Would there not be others who would join us in such a venture?

Earlier in this book there is a list of "key components and purposes of camp meetings." Now that we have explored the history of these meetings, and all they have contributed over many years, it is time to consider whether their essential message is relevant to our own time, and our hopes

---

[11] Kenneth O. Brown. *Holy Ground, Too; The Camp Meeting Family Tree.* Hazleton, PA: Holiness Archives, 1997.

for the future, in this world and the next. In his day, B.W. Gorham saw camp meetings as "a means of grace, honored of God." Some believed that society had outgrown camp meetings. Gorham argued that their purpose was still relevant and would remain so.

> CAMP MEETING MANUAL,
>
> A PRACTICAL BOOK
>
> FOR
>
> THE CAMP GROUND;
>
> IN TWO PARTS.
>
> BY REV. B. W. GORHAM,
> of the Wyoming Annual Conference.
>
> WITH ILLUSTRATIVE PLATES.
>
> BOSTON:
> PUBLISHED BY H. V. DEGEN,
> NO. 5 CORNHILL.
> 1854.

Camp meetings have proclaimed and facilitated a great hope, based on God's promises, that with his transforming power, people could be infinitely better than we are, and that death could actually be made to yield to eternity. Through them God has provided glimpses of that eternity and power for that transformation.

The key components and purposes of camp meetings explored and encouraged throughout this book are these:

1 - Camp meetings seek most of all, to provide a place and time of worship, in which people are encouraged and empowered to experience the reality and power of God and to grow closer to their fellow worshipers – in fact to all Christians and "everyone else," even those who do not yet claim Christian identity.[12] In worship, we receive a glimpse of heaven as present encouragement and as a vision of our destiny in Christ.

2 – Camp meetings provide a place away from the pressures and distractions of everyday life, work, and responsibilities, so that participants can focus on growing closer to God in a context of Christian community. In order to accomplish this essential purpose, participants, including preachers and other leaders, are encouraged to remain on the ground for as long as possible, preferably for the entire length of the camp meeting. However, a shorter stay can still be spiritually beneficial, and beneficial to the camp community, so long as the participant is fully engaged in the program while at the camp. All of us can take to heart Jesus' words to his friend Martha: "…you are worried and upset about many things, but few things are needed – or indeed only one."[13]

3 – Camp meetings provide a place of worship and community within a natural surrounding that maintains the beauty of God's creation. Campgrounds should be designed so that the natural world is prominent and human creations (streets, walkways, tents, cottages, tabernacles, etc.) are in harmony with the environment.[14]

4 – Camp meetings seek to provide a context and community within which participants encounter God so that they are moved by the Spirit to commit their lives to God, to begin their spiritual journey in Christ, and experience grace-empowered transformation to become like Christ. This journey of faith results in changed attitudes and changed behavior as each person travels through this life and makes the transition to eternal life. "And we all … are being transformed into his image with ever-increasing glory, which comes from the Spirit."[15]

5 – Camp meetings are designed to bring Christians together in one place from a larger area than their own local congregations and communities. This can strengthen the ties of fellowship across churches and communities and limit the isolation sometimes found in local congregations. This can take place mainly within a tradition or ecumenically, but in the

---

[12] I Thessalonians 5:15, NIV.

[13] Luke 10:41&42.

[14] "The earth is the Lord's, and everything in it, the world, and all who live in it…." - Psalm 24:1, NIV.

[15] II Corinthians 3:18, NIV.

movement and examples studied here, generally takes place within the tradition broadly called Wesleyan or Methodist (or Wesleyan Holiness), yet very much open and hospitable to the participation of others. Camp meetings are further designed to bring pastors and leaders together for collaboration, fellowship, and mutual encouragement - beyond what usually happens in local or denominational settings - which mobilizes their shared gifts and downplays competition, misunderstanding, and mistrust. For in Christ, "each member belongs to all the others."[16]

6 – The message of a Wesleyan camp meeting takes its authority from the Bible. Scripture is the foundation for all teaching on a camp ground, and for the way of life of speakers, leaders, and participants. The truth of Scripture must be presented in a clear and compelling way. While styles and externals will inevitably change over time, the truth does not. There must be a consistency between the doctrine of this year's camp meetings and that of our earliest precursor. The form of a camp meeting without the truth of God's Word, is empty. In the Bible, as John Wesley put it, God has given us "the way to heaven."[17]

7 - Camp meetings, like the churches themselves, are best rooted in their tradition, aware of the road traveled and the inheritance of faith handed down across the generations. This kind of rootedness allows for mid-course corrections as a present practice, decision, or course of action is measured against the original purpose of the camp. Tradition can be a deep and rich resource of experience, wisdom, and inspiration, built up over time and available to present day leaders and participants.[18]

8 – Camp meetings are designed to spiritually strengthen each participant, and the churches and ministries in which they live out their sanctification and discipleship. Many organizations and activities drain people's spiritual energies. Camp meetings should offer rest, healing, and revitalization. Here we experience what Jesus promised when he said, "you will find rest for your souls."[19]

9 - Camp meetings inspire us for mission. They move us forward on "the path of life," with "joy in [his] presence," which is not fleeting, shallow, or selfish, but filled with "eternal pleasures." Filled to overflowing

---

[16] Romans 12:5, NIV.

[17] John Wesley, Preface to the Sermons, in Albert C. Outler, ed. *The Works of John Wesley*. Nashville: Abingdon, 1984, i: 105.

[18] "…ask for the ancient paths, ask where the good way is, and walk in it.…" - Jeremiah 6:16, NIV.

[19] Matthew 11:29, NIV.

with the outpouring of God's love, we are inspired to share with others in our needy world.[20]

None of these purposes is now obsolete. Some of them carry an urgency greater than that in past generations, for whom they also were relevant. All of them have an appeal that should gain our recognition and appreciation when we reflect as Wesleyan Christians on our own lives and the needs of our world.

There may be incidental ingredients, cultural peculiarities, or time-bound expressions that can and should be replaced, but encountering the reality of God will always be needed; the message and experience of saving and sanctifying grace will always be needed; getting away from routines and distractions will always be needed; seeking and worshiping God in a natural surrounding will always be needed; transformation of our lives by the power of the Holy Spirit will always be needed; deep and lasting Christian community will always be needed; connecting with resources of our Christian and Wesleyan tradition will always be needed; strength and renewal for churches and their members will always be needed, and inspiration for mission will always be needed.

If we look only, or mainly, to the state of our culture, or the disappointing record of some of our churches, or the limited resources available in our gifted, yet flawed human nature, the task of renewed discipleship through camp meetings will seem unlikely at best. But if we look to the One who fed thousands on a few loaves and fish; the One who calmed storms and initiated an indestructible Church; the One who gave us a mis-

---

[20] Psalm 16:11, NIV.

sion undergirded and empowered by his eternal presence, we have every reason for hope.

Perhaps an autobiographical note is in order here. My membership and ministry is in the United Methodist Church, a body that has long been losing its connection with its founding purpose in the Wesleyan revival. The awareness I have of better days comes largely from our history, before my time. Yet even within our present situation, I find countless faithful people, in my local church and denomination, who rise above discouragement; who encourage my journey and graciously receive encouragement from me. Together with brothers and sisters in the other churches in our Wesleyan tradition – and in other churches who share with us a common Christian identity and purpose, I continually encounter visions of a transfigured present, a promising future, and a heavenly destiny worth every bit of love and energy we can muster for this cause. What we will all need is for the Spirit to reach us in the depths of our being, inspire and unite us in boundless grace, and lead us to do what can only be done in God. That is what happened long ago to people Jesus called. That is what happened when the Wesleys and others gathered people together in outdoor, evangelistic, and sacramental worship. That is what happened at Cane Ridge, and in camp meetings across this continent. That is what will happen whenever we cooperate with the seemingly impossible projects he gives us. God may surprise us with the place of camp meetings in his plan. Wherever he leads, we can rely on "God, who works in [us] to will and to act in order to fulfill his good purpose."[21]

> "How bright is our prospect, O soldiers of Jesus,
> While homeward to zion [sic] we're marching along,
> Each day brings us nearer the end of our journey,
> Each day brings us nearer, the fair land of song."[22]

---

[21] Philippians 2:1, NIV.

[22] Fanny Crosby/John R. Sweeney, in J.S. Inskip, ed. *Songs of Triumph: Adapted to Prayer Meetings, Camp Meetings, and All Other Seasons of Religious Worship*. Philadelphia: National Publishing Association for the Promotion of Holiness, 1882, #26.

Church of God, Anderson, Indiana and Oak Bluffs Methodist, Massachusetts

www.ingramcontent.com/pod-product-compliance
Lightning Source LLC
Chambersburg PA
CBHW062016220426
43662CB00010B/1348